15 Timeless Patterns
for Gorgeous Handcrafted Gar

T0285870

# Crochet
# Sweaters
## with a
# Textured
# Twist

Linda Skuja

PAGE STREET
PUBLISHING CO.

# To fiber artists around the world

PAGE STREET
PUBLISHING CO.

Copyright © 2023 Linda Skuja

First published in 2023 by
Page Street Publishing Co.
27 Congress Street, Suite 1511
Salem, MA 01970
www.pagestreetpublishing.com

Distributed by Macmillan, sales in Canada by The Canadian Manda Group.

27   26   25   24   23        2   3   4   5   6

ISBN-13: 978-1-64567-731-4
ISBN-10: 1-64567-731-1

Library of Congress Control Number: 2022950257

Cover and book design by Rosie Stewart and Linda Skuja for Page Street Publishing Co.
Photography by Inga Bitere

Printed and bound in the United States

# Contents

Introduction                                    5

## Before You Begin                             6
Fit and Ease                                    7
Gauge                                           8
Z-Twist and S-Twist Yarn                        8

## Linear                                      10
Māls Clay Sweater                              13
Piens Milk Sweater                             25
Ēna Shadow Sweater                             35
Sniegs Snow Sweater                            45

## Directional                                 52
Liedags Seashore Sweater                       55
Ainava Landscape Sweater                       75
Zeme Earth Sweater                             89
Jūra Sea Sweater                              103

## Unexpected                                 112
Rasa Dew Sweater                              115
Zvaigznes Stars Wrap Sweater                  129
Saule Sun Sweater                             147

## Thoughtful                                 156
Mēness Moon Sweater                           159
Nora Forest Meadow Sweater                    171
Malduguns Fen Fire Sweater                    185
Nakts Night Tunisian Sweater                  197

Blocking                                      206
Yarn Substitutions                            207
Translating Yardage/Meterage into Skeins      208
Using Different Yarn Weights                  209
Caring for Your Sweaters                      210
Resources                                     212
About the Author                              212
Acknowledgments                               213
Index                                         214

# Introduction

Art is handmade. The past, present and future are all handmade. As inspiring as nature itself is, a vast amount of beauty in this world has been created by humans. Architecture, technology, design, crafts—there's so much that is surprising and worth admiring. Crochet, a craft that dates back for centuries, has a voice that invites so many to explore and embrace. There have been times when crochet has been a witness of its day, or a nostalgic pastime companion. I am not exaggerating when I say that I believe now is the moment when crochet has become one of the many creative beacons that will define the future, and there is still much left to be explored.

For me, designing has always been a form of art, an expression of what I see and feel and a process that can't be avoided. Design and the making of art, I believe, is what creates culture. Over my ten years as an acknowledged crochet designer, I have strived to remove social constructs from my work—an intention that has allowed me to see the true nature of what an innovative and intriguing technique crochet has become today.

Texture is something I've always been interested in, and, little by little, it has expanded throughout my designs and become my signature. Playing with texture has always excited me, and I can't wait to share this incredible facet of crochet with you. With intermediate and advanced crocheters in mind, I've designed this book to make the complicated simple, to provide "a-ha" moments over techniques and constructions used, and to help you find the flow in the process of creation itself. I will show you the many faces of texture, using a variety of exciting sub-techniques, interesting construction styles and intriguing, intentional stitch patterns. With the designs across these pages, you will experience the beauty and fascination that texture can bring to your work.

I hope you will enjoy creating the sweaters from this book as much as I enjoyed designing them.

*Linda Skuja*

# Before You Begin

I've designed this section to help guide you through the basics of crocheting the sweaters in this book. Below you'll find my best knowledge and wisdom so that you can successfully make any of the garments in this book. Before starting on a new pattern, I always suggest going through all of the pages of the pattern. It will help to see the bigger picture—the construction, stitches, materials, etc. Lots of questions that might arise at first make sense when you've read the pattern fully from the start until the very end.

You will find various types of patterns in this book—ones that are worked in rows (back and forth to form a flat piece such as the front or back panel of a sweater) and in rounds (worked around to form a tube with no seams), ones that are made bottom up and ones that are constructed top down. Various yarn weights, stitches and details will keep your process exciting. I hope you'll try all of the various designs and constructions in this book, even the projects that may seem a bit intimidating! Before you know it, you'll have a gorgeous crochet wardrobe on your hands.

# Fit and Ease

It's not a secret—we are all shaped differently, and no standard pattern written for mass audiences will perfectly fit anyone the way a custom-made garment will. Even the smallest modifications to our crochet garments can massively improve their fit, wearability and comfort. That's why the patterns in this book are mostly all designed with the ability to easily make certain modifications in mind.

The easiest modifications to make are to the body and sleeve length of a sweater, especially one that has a straight, relaxed fit. You can add or subtract length as you prefer, but please keep in mind that this will also impact the amount of yarn you will need.

To aid you in seeing the bigger picture, a schematic is always included in every pattern with the measurements that will let you know how big the finished garment will be in key areas (meeting the gauge is a must). If the numbers are confusing to you, I recommend taking a couple of similar tops or sweaters from your closet and measuring them in the same areas as indicated on the schematic. This will help you get a sense of how the pattern compares to something you already own.

Keep in mind that the schematic shows the **finished** measurements of the garment. To choose the proper size, you should look at the recommended ease of the pattern and select a size accordingly. For example, if the pattern says "designed to be worn with 8–10" / 20–25 cm of positive ease," here's what it means.

**Positive ease** refers to how much bigger the garment is than the body—for example, 4" / 10 cm of positive ease for a human who measures 40" / 102 cm around their bust would be a sweater that has a finished measurement of 44" / 112 cm at the bust. **Negative ease** is the opposite, meaning you choose a finished size that is *smaller* than your body—usually used for lighter-weight tops and sweaters.

If your pattern calls for 8–10" / 20–25 cm of positive ease, and your body measures 40" / 102 cm (this measurement must be taken from around the widest part of your torso), you can choose the size in the pattern that fits in this window. If you could fit into two of the sizes listed, it becomes a personal fit decision based on how tight or loose you want your sweater to be. I recommend comparing the fit to items you own to get a sense of what different amounts of ease look and feel like on your body. Remember that the fabric you create will also impact the fit—a soft yarn with good drape will flow over the body, whereas a bulkier and stiffer yarn will tend to "stand up" away from the body and hang a bit more stiffly.

I do *not* recommend choosing a size that is outside of the recommended ease until you have some confidence as a crocheter with making modifications, as sometimes certain design elements won't work well if the pattern does not fit as intended.

# Gauge

I'm sure you hear this all the time: "Please get your gauge right! Make the gauge swatch! Swatch before you start." But what does this actually mean?

When they say "If you don't get the gauge, the gauge will get you," it couldn't be more true. Does gauge matter for all projects? No, if you don't care about the dimensions and density of your finished piece. But if you're making a 3-D object (like a top or sweater) or want to reach certain dimensions and characteristics of a 2-D object—gauge matters! A lot.

**Gauge** is a measurement of how many stitches and rows you should achieve over a certain distance (usually per 4" / 10 cm). The purpose of gauge is to help you make sure that the piece you crochet comes out to be the correct size.

A **gauge swatch** is that little 4 x 4" / 10 x 10–cm square that you make to see if you need to go one hook size (or two, or three) up or down to make the fabric look and feel the same way as the pattern was designed to. Make sure to make the square a little bigger to measure just the regular stitches, because side stitches might not give you precise measurements.

We all crochet differently—some crochet more tightly, some more loosely. That is why it is very important to adjust your hook so you can create a fabric as drapey or tight as the designer has designed. Please pay attention to what stitch the gauge swatch must be made in (dc, hdc, sc, etc.), and if the swatch should be measured blocked or unblocked (you will find this info at the beginning of every pattern).

# Z-Twist and S-Twist Yarn

When it comes to choosing the yarn for your project there are some important things to keep in mind. One of them is the yarn twist. There are multiple ways to prepare and spin fleece and fiber into yarn. When it comes to the finished product—which is yarn that we can buy—we can distinguish three major groups: S-twist, Z-twist and untwisted /unspun. You can tell which is which by looking at a strand of yarn. See how the ply or plies all lean in one direction, either like the center stroke of an *S* ( \ ) or a *Z* ( / ). It doesn't matter how you are viewing the strand, or which end is up or down. Most of the yarns are S-twist and are produced with knitting in mind, no matter how the individual fibers, strand and plies are spun.

Please remember: If you crochet with your right hand, Z-twists will favor your process, but if you're left-handed, S-twists will be your friends.

I'm going to continue to explain this with right-handed crocheters in mind. If you crochet with your right hand, the process of crocheting makes a Z-twist: Each time you yarn over and draw a loop through, you are giving the yarn a little counter-clockwise twist. You will feel this especially when working with tall stitches like trebles, double trebles and taller. When you crochet with S-twist yarn, you are untwisting as you go. If you crochet and un-crochet the strand multiple times, then a loosely S-twisted yarn will most likely become separated and the yarn will become really splitty. The opposite happens in knitting—S-twist favors the knitting process, knitting reinforces S-twist and keeps the plies coherent and the strand stable.

Yarn manufacturers create the final skein (ball, cone) without additional twist. It is done by rotating the spindle that holds the skein, so the yarn is wound straight onto the core, not twisted around the core. You do this as well when you wind a hank onto a ball-winder. You are not putting any additional twist into the strand, from the perspective of the yarn itself. But from the perspective of the user, there is some twist happening: When you use the skein, you either begin with the end on the outside of the skein, or you search inside the skein for the center pull yarn end. The skein stays put, the yarn winds around the skein as it comes off and you are adding twist. If you're looking at the skein from one end and continue to wind the skein it would be in a clockwise direction, then pulling the feed directly from the outside from this end will add S-twist.

If you pull from the center end, you will add Z-twist. And vice versa: If looking at the skein from one end, the yarn is winding counter-clockwise. Pulling from outside of that skein would add Z-twist, and pulling from the center end would add S-twist.

Most of the time and for most users this information on yarn twists won't be very essential and they will never have a problem. But if you're noticing that your yarn is splitting, getting loose and it only gets worse as you go, you should probably pay attention to your yarn twist and the way you're pulling your yarn from the skein. The yarn twist will also have an impact on the slant.

Now that you are armed with all of my best knowledge for beautiful crochet garments, I hope you'll enjoy diving into all of the patterns on offer!

# Linear

In this chapter, the classic post stitches we know and love get a refreshing twist. In the crochet world, post stitches have always played a pivotal role in delivering new and exciting innovations, like creating post-stitch "drawings," optical illusions and all kinds of crisscross lines and patterns. Post stitches play an essential role when it comes to creating textured stitches. Set in a straight line, they create a visual succession and a sense of arrangement across a crochet fabric.

With linearity as its hallmark, this chapter tells a story of fabrics divided by lines that come together in harmonious and balanced compositions. Whether it's Māls (page 13) or Piens (page 25) that draw attention to finer and more fragile lines, or Sniegs (page 45) with its bold and confident pattern, or the way that Ēna (page 35) is reminiscent of a cozy, hand-crafted hug, all of these sweaters are a true celebration of post stitching.

# Māls Clay Sweater

Throughout history and around the world, people have developed the art of forming clay to make ceramic objects, or pottery. Just as clay becomes art in a potter's hands, the Māls Sweater gives you the feeling of sculpting and molding the textured stitches into a fiber masterpiece. The vertical bars and post stitch diagonals form an intricate yoke that balances with repetitive post stitch lines on the body.

# Māls Clay Sweater Construction Notes

*The Māls Sweater is a round yoke and straight boxy style sweater with fitted sleeves. It is worked top down in joined rounds (unless otherwise noted) to the bust line, then is split for the body and sleeves. The sweater is worked in one piece and is seamless. It comes in nine sizes and includes instructions for adjusting the length of the body and sleeves.*

## Sizes

1 (2, 3, 4, 5) (6, 7, 8, 9)

**Finished bust:** 30 (34, 38, 42, 46) (50, 54, 58, 62)" / 76 (86, 97, 107, 117) (127, 137, 147, 157) cm

## Gauge

18 sts x 11 rows = 4" / 10 cm in dc after blocking

## Yarn

Fingering weight, Quince & Co. Tern (75% Wool, 25% Silk), 221 yds (202 m) per 50-g skein, or use any fingering weight wool-silk blend to achieve a similar effect

## Yardage/Meterage

1505 (1635, 1925, 2080, 2325) (2545, 2810, 3030, 3250) yds / 1375 (1495, 1760, 1900, 2125) (2325, 2570, 2770, 2970) m

## Shown in

Colorway Terra Cotta

## Hooks

7 / 4.5 mm for the main sections of the Yoke, Body and Sleeves, or size needed to obtain gauge

G/6 / 4 mm for ribbing, or one size smaller than size needed to obtain gauge

## Notions

Tapestry needle, 4 stitch markers

## Skills

Experience with making crocheted top-down sweaters

## Abbreviations (US terms)

BL = back loop
BPdc = back post double crochet
BPdtr = back post double treble
BPsc = back post single crochet
BPtr = back post treble
Ch = chain
Dc = double crochet
Dtr = double treble
Dc2tog = double crochet 2 together
FPtr = front post treble
Hdc = half double crochet
Rnd(s) = round(s)
RS = right side
Sc = single crochet
Sc2tog = single crochet 2 together
Sl st = slip stitch
St(s) = stitch(es)
Tr = treble
WS = wrong side

| Size | A—finished bust | B—yoke depth | C—body length | D—full length | E—upper arm | F—sleeve length |
|---|---|---|---|---|---|---|
| 1 | 30" / 76 cm | 7.75" / 19.5 cm | 13.75" / 35 cm | 21.5" / 54.5 cm | 11.5" / 29 cm | 17.75" / 45 cm |
| 2 | 34" / 86 cm | 8.25" / 21 cm | 13.75" / 35 cm | 22" / 56 cm | 12" / 30.5 cm | 17.75" / 45 cm |
| 3 | 38" / 97 cm | 8.75" / 22 cm | 15" / 38 cm | 23.75" / 60 cm | 12.5" / 32 cm | 17.75" / 45 cm |
| 4 | 42" / 107 cm | 9.25" / 23.5 cm | 15" / 38 cm | 24.25" / 61.5 cm | 13.75" / 35 cm | 16.5" / 42 cm |
| 5 | 46" / 117 cm | 9.75" / 25 cm | 16.25" / 41 cm | 26" / 66 cm | 15" / 38 cm | 16.5" / 42 cm |
| 6 | 50" / 127 cm | 10.25" / 26 cm | 16.25" / 41 cm | 26.5" / 67 cm | 17" / 43 cm | 16.5" / 42 cm |
| 7 | 54" / 137 cm | 10.75" / 27 cm | 17.25" / 44 cm | 28" / 71 cm | 18.5" / 47 cm | 15.25" / 39 cm |
| 8 | 58" / 147 cm | 11.25" / 28.5 cm | 17.25" / 44 cm | 28.5" / 72.5 cm | 19.5" / 49.5 cm | 15.25" / 39 cm |
| 9 | 62" / 157 cm | 11.75" / 30 cm | 18.5" / 47 cm | 30.25" / 77 cm | 20" / 51 cm | 15.25" / 39 cm |

*The sweater is designed to be worn with no ease. Size 2 is modeled on 32" / 82-cm bust model.*

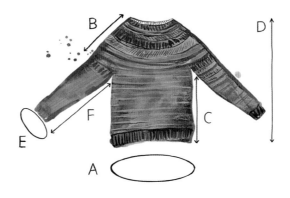

# Māls Clay Sweater Pattern

**Throughout:** Ch 1 at the beginning of row counts as turning chain and is not counted as a stitch.

## Yoke Ribbing

Using your smaller hook and leaving an approximately 10" / 25 cm-long yarn end for sewing the ribbing ends together, ch 9.

**Row 1:** Hdc in 3rd ch from hook (beginning ch-2 counts as first hdc), hdc in each ch across, turn. 8 sts total

**Rows 2–75 (–75, –75, –78, –78) (–78, –81, –81, –81):** Ch 2 (here and throughout this counts as first hdc), hdc in BL across, turn. 8 sts

**Last row of the ribbing:** Don't turn. Rotate the ribbing clockwise by 90 degrees.

## Yoke

Have RS facing and change to your larger hook.

**For rnd 1 you'll be working across the side of the yoke ribbing:** Work 2 sc in every row of hdcs to make 150 (150, 150, 156, 156) (156, 162, 162, 162) sc total.

**Rnd 1:** Ch 1, sc around (as described above), join with sl st to the first sc to form a round (here and throughout this is referred to as "join"). 150 (150, 150, 156, 156) (156, 162, 162, 162) sts

Sew the beginning and end of the ribbing. (You can also do this at the finishing stage, if you'd prefer.)

**Rnd 2:** Ch 1, sc around, join. 150 (150, 150, 156, 156) (156, 162, 162, 162) sts

**Rnd 3:** Ch 2 (counts as first dc), BPdc around, join.

**Rnd 4:** Ch 3 (counts as first tr), BPtr around, join.

**Rnd 5:** Ch 4 (counts as first dtr), BPdtr around, join.

**Rnd 6:** Ch 1 (turning ch), sc in first st, BPsc around, join.

**Rnd 7:** [Dc in next st, 2 dcs in next st, dc in next st] around, (place a marker in/at the last dc you just made), join. 200 (200, 200, 208, 208) (208, 216, 216, 216) sts

**Rnd 8:** Ch 2, FPtr around the marked st (removing the marker as you do so).

[Skip next st, dc in next dc, FPtr around just skipped st] 99 (99, 99, 103, 103) (103, 107, 107, 107) times, (place a marker in/at the last st you just made), join. 200 (200, 200, 208, 208) (208, 216, 216, 216) sts

**Rnd 9:** Ch 2, FPtr around the marked post st (remove marker).

[Skip next st, dc in next dc, FPtr around just skipped post st] 99 (99, 99, 103, 103) (103, 107, 107, 107) times, join. 200 (200, 200, 208, 208) (208, 216, 216, 216) sts

**Rnd 10:** Ch 1, sc in first st, sc around, join.

**Rnd 11:** Ch 1, 2 (2, 2, 2, 2) (2, 0, 0, 0) sc in first st, BPsc around, 0 (0, 0, 1, 1) (1, 0, 0, 0) more sc in last st, join. 201 (201, 201, 210, 210) (210, 216, 216, 216) sts

**Rnd 12:** Skip first st, [ch 7, dc in third ch from hook, dc in each of next 4 chs, skip next 2 sts on working rnd, sc in next st (one 5-dc bar made)] rep around omitting sc on last bar, sl st in first 5 chs of first bar. 67 (67, 67, 70, 70) (70, 72, 72, 72) bars

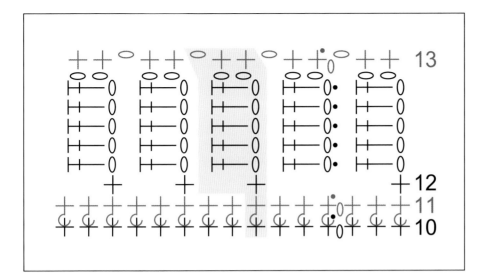

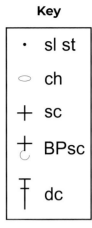

**Key**

| | |
|---|---|
| · | sl st |
| ⌒ | ch |
| + | sc |
| ⟊ | BPsc |
| T | dc |

*Reduced sample of stitch diagram rnds 10–13.*

*Stitch repeat shown in grey.*

*On rnd 11, some sizes begin and end with extra sc in the first and last stitch; check the written instructions for your size.*

**Rnd 13:** Ch 1, [2 sc in ch-2 sp at end of next 5-dc bar, ch 1 (1, 2, 2, 2) (2, 2, 2, 2)] around, join. 201 (201, 268, 280, 280) (280, 288, 288, 288) sts

**Rnd 14 (sizes 1 and 2 only):** Ch 1, 2 sc in 1st st. [Sc in next 4 sts, 2 sc in next st] 40 times, join.

**Rnd 14 (sizes 3–9):** Ch 1, sc around, join. 242 (242, 268, 280, 280) (280, 288, 288, 288) sts

**Rnd 15:** Ch 1, BPsc around, join.

**Rnd 16:** Ch 2, dc in next st (place marker), dc around, join.

**Rnd 17:** Turn to WS. Ch 2, BPtr around the marked st (remove marker). [Skip next st, dc in next dc, BPtr around just skipped st] 120 (120, 133, 139, 139) (139, 143, 143, 143) times, (mark last st just made), join. 242 (242, 268, 280, 280) (280, 288, 288, 288) sts

**Rnd 18:** Do not turn, continue with WS facing. Ch 2, BPtr around the marked post st (remove marker). [Skip next st, dc in next dc, BPtr around just skipped post st] 120 (120, 133, 139, 139) (139, 143, 143, 143) times, join and turn to RS. 242 (242, 268, 280, 280) (280, 288, 288, 288) sts

**Rnd 19:** Ch 1, sc around, join.

**Rnd 20:** Ch 1, BPsc around, join.

**Rnd 21:** Ch 1, sc around, join.

**Rnd 22:** Ch 4, BPdtr around, join. 242 (242, 268, 280, 280) (280, 288, 288, 288) sts total

**Size 1 only:** Mark first st of the rnd and continue to Short Rows Shaping (page 20).

**Rnd 23 (sizes 2–9):** Ch 3, BPtr around, join.

**Rnd 24 (size 2 only):** Ch 1, [sc in next 16 sts, 2 sc in next st] 14 times. Sc in next 4 sts, join. Mark first st of the rnd and continue to Short Rows Shaping.

**Rnd 24 (sizes 3–9):** Ch 1, sc around, join. x (256, 268, 280, 280) (280, 288, 288, 288) sts

**Rnd 25 (sizes 3–9):** Ch 2, BPdc around, join.

**Rnd 26 (sizes 3–9):** Ch 1, 2 sc in first st, sc in each st to last, 2 sc in last st, join. x (x, 270, 282, 282) (282, 290, 290, 290) sts

**Size 3 only:** Mark first st of the rnd and continue to Short Rows Shaping.

**Rnd 27 (sizes 4–9):** Ch 4, BPdtr around, join.

**Rnd 28 (sizes 4–9):** Ch 1, [sc in next 27 sts, 2 sc in next st] x (x, x, 10, 10) (10, 10, 10, 10) times.

Sc in next x (x, x, 2, 2) (2, 10, 10, 10) sts, join. x (x, x, 292, 292) (292, 300, 300, 300) sts

**Size 4 only:** Mark first st of the rnd and continue to Short Rows Shaping.

**Rnd 29 (sizes 5–9):** Ch 3, BPtr around, join.

**Rnd 30 (sizes 5–9):** Ch 1, [sc in next 13 sts, 2 sc in next st] x (x, x, x, 20) (20, 21, 21, 21) times. Sc in next x (x, x, x, 12) (12, 6, 6, 6) sts, join. x (x, x, x, 312) (312, 321, 321, 321) sts

**Size 5 only:** Mark first st of the rnd and continue to Short Rows Shaping.

**Rnd 31 (sizes 6–9):** Ch 3, BPdtr around, join.

**Rnd 32 (sizes 6–9):** Ch 1, [sc in next 9 sts, 2 sc in next st] x (x, x, x, x) (30, 31, 31, 31) times. Sc in next x (x, x, x, x) (12, 11, 11, 11) sts, join. x (x, x, x, x) (342, 352, 352, 352) sts

**Size 6 only:** Mark first st of the rnd and continue to Short Rows Shaping.

**Rnd 33 (sizes 7–9):** Ch 3, BPtr around, join.

**Rnd 34 (sizes 7–9):** Ch 1, [sc in next 24 sts, 2 sc in next st] x (x, x, x, x) (x, 14, 14, 14) times. Sc in next x (x, x, x, x) (x, 2, 2, 2) sts, join. x (x, x, x, x) (x, 366, 366, 366) sts

**Size 7 only:** Mark first st of the rnd and continue to Short Rows Shaping.

**Rnd 35 (sizes 8–9):** Ch 2, BPdc around, join.

**Rnd 36 (sizes 8–9):** Ch 1, [sc in next 17 sts, 2 sc in next st] x (x, x, x, x) (x, x, 20, 20) times. Sc in next x (x, x, x, x) (x, x, 6, 6) sts, join. x (x, x, x, x) (x, x, 386, 386) sts

**Size 8 only:** Mark first st of the rnd and continue to Short Rows Shaping.

**Rnd 37 (size 9 only):** Ch 2, BPdc around, join.

**Rnd 38 (size 9 only):** Ch 1, [sc in next 23 sts, 2 sc in next st] 16 times. Sc in next 2 sts, join. x (x, x, x, x) (x, x, x, 402) sts

**Size 9 only:** Mark first st of the rnd and continue to Short Rows Shaping.

## Short Rows Shaping

This next section raises the back of your sweater for a better fit. You will work back and forth in rows, working 10 fewer sts in each row. Use stitch markers in the first st of each row if you are unsure what to count.

**All sizes:** At this point you should have 22 (24, 26, 28, 30) (32, 34, 36, 38) yoke rounds and a stitch count of 242 (256, 270, 292, 312) (342, 366, 386, 402).

**Row 1:** BPsc around next 121 (128, 135, 146, 156) (171, 183, 193, 201) sts, turn.

**Row 2:** Skip first st, sc until 9 sts left unworked, turn. 111 (118, 125, 136, 146) (161, 173, 183, 191) sts

**Row 3:** Skip first st, sc until 9 sts left unworked, turn. 101 (108, 115, 126, 136) (151, 163, 173, 181) sts

**Row 4:** Skip first st, sc until 9 sts left unworked, turn. 91 (98, 105, 116, 126) (141, 153, 163, 171) sts

**Row 5:** Skip first st, sc until 9 sts left unworked, turn. 81 (88, 95, 106, 116) (131, 143, 153, 161) sts

**Row 6:** Skip first st, sc until 9 sts left unworked, fasten off. 71 (78, 85, 96, 106) (121, 133, 143, 151) sts

Attach yarn to the marked stitch (at the beginning of rnd) and sc in next 121 (128, 135, 146, 156) (171, 183, 193, 201) sts, BPsc around next 121 (128, 135, 146, 156) (171, 183, 193, 201) sts, join and fasten off. Block the yoke before continuing on to the Body.

## Separating Body and Sleeves

Skip next 26 (27, 27, 29, 30) (34, 36, 38, 38) sts, sc in next st (mark), sc in next 68 (74, 81, 88, 95) (103, 110, 117, 124) sts, ch 0 (2, 4, 6, 8) (10, 12, 14, 16), skip next 52 (53, 53, 57, 60) (67, 72, 75, 76) sts, sc in next 69 (75, 82, 89, 96) (104, 111, 118, 125) sts, ch 0 (2, 4, 6, 8) (10, 12, 14, 16), skip remaining sts and join to marked st.

## Body

Have RS facing and continue to work with your larger hook.

**Rnd 1:** Ch 1, sc around (work 1 sc into each ch of ch-sps), join. 138 (154, 172, 190, 208) (228, 246, 264, 282) sts

**Rnd 2:** Ch 1, BPsc around, join.

**Rnds 3–5:** Ch 2, dc around, join.

**Rnd 6:** Ch 3, BPtr around, join.

**Rnds 7–8:** Ch 2, dc around, join.

[Repeat rnds 6–8] another 11 (11, 12, 12, 13) (13, 14, 14, 15) times, or until the desired length is reached minus 2" / 5 cm for the ribbing, then fasten off.

### Body Ribbing

Using your smaller hook, ch 13.

**Row 1:** Hdc in 3rd ch from hook, hdc in each ch across, turn. 12 sts

**Rows 2–92 (–103, –115, –127, –139) (–152, –164, –176, –188):** Ch 2, hdc in BL across, turn. 12 sts

Rotate the ribbing clockwise. Work across the side of the ribbing. Work 3 sc in every 2 rows of hdcs.

**Sizes 2, 3, 4, 5 only:** Work 1 sc in last row.

End with 138 (154, 172, 190, 208) (228, 246, 264, 282) sts.

## Sleeve

### Make 2

With main gauge hook (larger hook), attach new yarn (with RS facing) with a sl st at the approximate center of the underarm. You will have 52 (55, 57, 63, 68) (77, 84, 89, 92) sts to begin with.

**Rnd 1 (sizes 1, 2):** Work sc across until 2 sts left, sc2tog over next 2 sts, join.

**Rnd 1 (sizes 3, 4, 7):** Work sc across, join.

**Rnd 1 (sizes 5, 6, 8, 9):** Sc across, work 1 more sc in last st, join. 51 (54, 57, 63, 69) (78, 84, 90, 93) sts

**Rnd 2:** Ch 1, BPsc around, join.

**Rnd 3:** [Ch 7, dc in 3rd ch from hook, dc in each of ch 4, skip next 2 sts (on the working rnd), sc in next st] rep 16 (17, 18, 20, 22) (25, 27, 29, 30) times. Ch 7, dc in 3rd ch from hook, dc in each of ch 4, skip next 2 sts (on the working rnd). 17 (18, 19, 21, 23) (26, 28, 30, 31) bars. Sl st to first ch and in each of ch 5 up the first bar.

**Rnd 4:** Ch 1, (2 sc around ch-2 sp, ch 1) repeat around, join.

**Rnd 5:** Ch 1, sc around, join.

**Rnd 6:** Ch 1, BPsc around, join.

**Rnds 7–9:** Ch 2, dc around, join. ✎

**Rnd 10:** Ch 3, BPtr around, join.

**Rnds 11–12:** Ch 2, dc2tog over next 2 sts, dc around, join. (1 st dec each round)

Repeat rnds 10-12 another 11 (11, 11, 10, 10) (10, 9, 9, 8) times, ending with 27 (30, 33, 41, 47) (56, 64, 70, 75) sts, or until the desired length is reached minus 2" / 5 cm for the ribbing.

**Next rnd:** Ch 1, BPsc around, join and fasten off.

## Cuff

Using your smaller hook, ch 12.

**Row 1:** Hdc in 3rd ch from hook, hdc across, join. 11 sts

**Rows 2–20 (–20, –22, –24, –24) (–26, –28, –30, –30):** Ch 2, hdc across, join.

Fasten off and sew the cuff on.

## Finishing

Turn the sweater WS out. Sew the side of the yoke ribbing. Sew the Body and Sleeve ribbing on, if you have not already done so.

Dry block, holding the iron approximately 1" / 2.5 cm above the sweater and steam all over.

Leave to dry completely (or block according to fiber type).

# Piens Milk Sweater

Piens combines aesthetics, simplicity and functionality, and infuses it with thoughtful craftsmanship and impeccable style. The down-flowing post stitch lines make this piece a complete classic, adding a touch of interest with the puff stitch panicles. The result is this ethereal design with a contemporary edge. Just as milk is the genesis of a new life, the classic Piens sweater is as timeless and essential, and never goes out of style.

# Piens Milk Sweater Construction Notes

*The Piens is an oversized short-sleeved sweater that is worked top down in joined rounds. The sweater is split for the body and sleeves at the bust line. The sleeve ribbing sections are worked last.*

## Sizes

1 (2, 3, 4)

**To fit bust up to:** 34–38 (42–46, 50–54, 58–62)" / 86–97 (107–117, 127–137, 147–157) cm

**Finished bust:** 48.75 (54.25, 60.5, 66.25)" / 124 (138, 154, 168) cm

## Gauge

17 sts x 13 rows = 4" / 10 cm in dc after blocking

## Yarn

Sport weight, Alize Cotton Baby Soft (50% cotton, 50% acrylic), 295 yds / 270 m per 100-g skein

## Yardage/Meterage

1415 (1650, 1920, 2200) yds / 1295 (1510, 1755, 2010) m

**Shown in**

Color 62

## Hook

G/6 / 4 mm, or size needed to obtain gauge

## Notions

Tapestry needle

## Skills

Experience with making crocheted sweaters

### Abbreviations (US terms)

Betw = between

Ch = chain

Dc = double crochet

Dc2tog = two double crochet worked together

Dc3tog = three double crochet worked together

FPdc = front post double crochet

Fsc = foundation single crochet

Puff st = puff stitch

Rep = repeat

Rnd(s) = round(s)

RS = right side

Sl st = slip stitch

St(s) = stitch(es)

WS = wrong side

## Special stitches

**Puff st:** Yo, insert hook in the indicated st, yo, pull loop through st and make loop same height as previous sts in working row, [yo, insert hook in same st, yo, pull loop through st and make loop same height as working row] 3 times, pull through 8 loops on hook (2 loops left on hook), yo, pull through both loops.

**V-puff:** (Puff st, ch 1, puff st) worked in the same stitch.

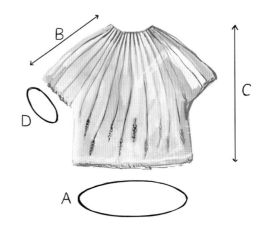

| Size | A—finished bust | B—yoke depth | C—full length | D—upper arm |
|------|-----------------|--------------|---------------|-------------|
| 1 | 48.5" / 123.5 cm | 14.5" / 37 cm | 21.5" / 54.5 cm | 16.5" / 42 cm |
| 2 | 54.25" / 137.5 cm | 16.25" / 41.5 cm | 23.25" / 59 cm | 18.75" / 47.5 cm |
| 3 | 60.75" / 154 cm | 18" / 46 cm | 25" / 63.5 cm | 20.75" / 52.5 cm |
| 4 | 66.25" / 168 cm | 20" / 51 cm | 26.75" / 68 cm | 22.75" / 58 cm |

*Hem and Sleeve Ribbing measures 0.5" / 1 cm. The sweater is designed to be worn with 14.75–10.75 (12.25–8.25, 10.5–6.5, 8.25–4.25)" / 38–27 (31–21, 27–17, 21–11) cm positive ease. Size 1 is modeled on 30" / 77-cm bust model.*

# Piens Milk Sweater Pattern

**Throughout:** Ch 3 counts as 1 st = dc / FPdc.

## Yoke

**All sizes:** With WS facing, fsc 88, turn.

**Rnd 1:** Ch 3, dc across, join with sl st in top of ch-3 to begin working in the round. 88 sts

**Rnd 2:** Ch 3, [FPdc around next dc, dc in next dc] 43 times. FPdc around last dc, join.

**Rnd 3:** Ch 3, [FPdc around next post st, dc in next st] 43 times. FPdc around last post st, join.

**Rnd 4:** Ch 3, 1 more dc in first st. [FPdc around next post st, 2 dc in next dc] 43 times. FPdc around last post st, join. 132 sts

**Rnds 5–8:** Ch 3, dc in next dc. [FPdc around next post st, dc in next 2 dc] 43 times. FPdc around last post st, join.

**Rnd 9:** Ch 3, 2 dc in next dc. [FPdc around next post st, dc in next dc, 2 dc in next dc] 43 times. FPdc around last post st, join. 176 sts

**Rnds 10–14:** Ch 3, dc in next 2 dc. [FPdc around next post st, dc in next 3 dc] 43 times. FPdc around last post st, join.

**Rnd 15:** Ch 3, 2 dc in next dc, dc in next dc. [FPdc around next post st, dc in next dc, 2 dc in next dc, dc in next dc] 43 times. Fpdc around last post st, join. 220 sts

**Rnds 16–21:** Ch 3, dc in next 3 dc. [FPdc around next post st, dc in next 4 dc] 43 times. FPdc around last post st, join.

**Rnd 22:** Ch 3, dc in next 2 dc, 2 dc in next dc. [FPdc around next post st, dc in next 3 dc, 2 dc in next dc] 43 times. FPdc around last post st, join. 264 sts

**Rnds 23–29:** Ch 3, dc in next 4 dc. [FPdc around next post st, dc in next 5 dc] 43 times. FPdc around last post st, join.

**Rnd 30:** Ch 3, dc in next 3 dc, 2 dc in next dc. [FPdc around next post st, dc in next 4 dc, 2 dc in next dc] 43 times. FPdc around last post st, join. 308 sts

**Rnds 31–38:** Ch 3, dc in next 5 dc. [FPdc around next post st, dc in next 6 dc] 43 times. FPdc around last post st, join.

**Rnd 39:** Ch 3, dc in next 4 dc, 2 dc in next dc. [FPdc around next post st, dc in next 5 dc, 2 dc in next dc] 43 times. FPdc around last post st, join. 352 sts

**Rnds 40–48:** Ch 3, dc in next 6 dc. [FPdc around next post st, dc in next 7 dc] 43 times. FPdc around last post st, join.

**Size 1:** Continue to Separating Body and Sleeves.

**Sizes 2–4:** Continue to work from rnd 49.

**Rnd 49:** Ch 3, dc in next 5 dc, 2 dc in next dc. [FPdc around next post st, dc in next 6 dc, 2 dc in next dc] 43 times. FPdc around last post st, join. 396 sts

**Rnds 50–54:** Ch 3, dc in next 7 dc. [FPdc around next post st, dc in next 8 dc] 43 times. FPdc around last post st, join.

**Size 2:** Continue to Separating Body and Sleeves.

**Sizes 3–4:** Continue to work from rnd 55.

**Rnd 55:** Ch 3, dc in next 6 dc, 2 dc in next dc. [FPdc around next post st, dc in next 7 dc, 2 dc in next dc] 43 times. FPdc around last post st, join. 440 sts

**Rnds 56–60:** Ch 3, dc in next 8 dc. [FPdc around next post st, dc in next 9 dc] 43 times. FPdc around last post st, join.

**Size 3:** Continue to Separating Body and Sleeves.

**Size 4:** Continue to work from rnd 61.

**Rnd 61:** Ch 3, dc in next 7 dc, 2 dc in next dc. [FPdc around next post st, dc in next 8 dc, 2 dc in next dc] 43 times. FPdc around last post st, join. 484 sts

**Rnds 62–66:** Ch 3, dc in next 9 dc. [FPdc around next post st, dc in next 10 dc] 43 times. FPdc around last post st, join.

**Size 4:** Continue to Separating Body and Sleeves.

## Separating Body and Sleeves

Continue to work with RS facing.

Ch 3, dc in next 3 (3, 4, 4) dc, skip next 71 (81, 89, 99) sts, dc in next 4 (4, 5, 5) dc. [FPdc around next post st, dc in next 6 (7, 8, 9) dc, skip next st, V-puff in next post st, skip next st, dc in next 6 (7, 8, 9) dc] 6 times. FPdc around next post st, dc in next 4 (4, 5, 5) dc, skip next 71 (81, 89, 99) sts, dc in next 4 (4, 5, 5) dc. Rep betw [ ] 6 times. FPdc around last post st, join. 210 (234, 262, 286) sts; 174 (198, 226, 250) dc/FPdc, 12 V-puff sts

## Body

Continue to work with RS facing.

**Rnd 1:** Ch 3, dc in next 2 (2, 3, 3) dc, dc2tog over next 2 dc, dc in next 3 (3, 4, 4) dc.

[FPdc around next post st, dc in next 6 (7, 8, 9) dc, V-puff in next ch-1 sp, dc in next 6 (7, 8, 9) dc] 6 times. FPdc around next post st, dc in next 3 (3, 4, 4) dc, dc2tog over next 2 dc, dc in next 3 (3, 4, 4) dc. Rep betw [ ] 6 times. FPdc around last post st, join. 208 (232, 260, 284) sts; 172 (196, 224, 248) dc/FPdc, 12 V-puffs

**Rnd 2:** Ch 3, dc in next 0 (0, 1, 1) dc, dc2tog over next 2 dc, dc in next dc, dc2tog over next 2 dc, dc in next 1 (1, 2, 2) dc. [FPdc around next post st, dc in next 6 (7, 8, 9) dc, V-puff in next ch-1 sp, dc in next 6 (7, 8, 9) dc] 6 times. FPdc around next post st, dc in next 1 (1, 2, 2) dc, dc2tog over next 2 dc, dc in next dc, dc2tog over next 2 dc, dc in next 1 (1, 2, 2) dc. Rep betw [ ] 6 times. FPdc around last post st, join. 204 (228, 256, 280) sts; 168 (192, 220, 244) dc/FPdc, 12 V-puffs

**Rnd 3:** Ch 3, dc in next 4 (4, 6, 6) dc. [FPdc around next post st, dc in next 6 (7, 8, 9) dc, V-puff in next ch-1 sp, dc in next 6 (7, 8, 9) dc] 6 times. FPdc around next post st, dc in next 5 (5, 7, 7) dc. Rep betw [ ] 6 times. FPdc around last post st, join.

**Rnd 4:** Ch 2, dc in next dc (counts as dc2tog), dc in next 1 (1, 3, 3) dc, dc2tog over next 2 dc. [FPdc around next post st, dc in next 6 (7, 8, 9) dc, V-puff in next ch-1 sp, dc in next 6 (7, 8, 9) dc] 6 times. FPdc around next post st, dc2tog over next 2 dc, dc in next 1 (1, 3, 3) dc, dc2tog over next 2 dc. Rep betw [ ] 6 times. FPdc around last post st, join in first dc. 200 (224, 252, 276) sts; 164 (188, 216, 240) dc/FPdc, 12 V-puffs

**Rnd 5:** Ch 3, dc in next 2 (2, 4, 4) dc. [FPdc around next post st, dc in next 6 (7, 8, 9) dc, dc in next puff st, puff st in next ch-1 sp, dc in next puff st, dc in next 6 (7, 8, 9) sts] 6 times. FPdc around next post st, dc in next 3 (3, 5, 5) sts. Rep betw [ ] 6 times. FPdc around last post st, join. 200 (224, 252, 276) sts; 188 (212, 240, 264) dc/FPdc, 12 puff sts

**Rnd 6:** Ch 2, dc2tog over next 2 sts (counts as dc3tog = 1 st), dc in next 0 (0, 2, 2) dc. [FPdc around next post st, dc in next 7 (8, 9, 10) dc, puff st in next st, dc in next 7 (8, 9, 10) dc] 6 times. FPdc around next post st, dc3tog over next 3 dc, dc in next 0 (0, 2, 2) dc. Rep betw [ ] 6 times. FPdc around last post st, join in dc2tog. 196 (220, 248, 272) sts; 184 (208, 236, 260) dc/FPdc, 12 puff sts

Turn to WS, sl st in first 2 sts, turn back to RS.

**Rnd 7:** Ch 3, dc3tog over next 3 sts (= post st, dc, post st).

**Sizes 3 and 4 only:** Dc2tog over next 2 dc.

**All sizes:** [Dc in next 7 (8, 9, 10) dc, puff st in next st, dc in next 7 (8, 9, 10) dc, FPdc around next post st] 5 times. Dc in next 7 (8, 9, 10) dc, puff st in next st, dc in next 7 (8, 9, 10) dc. Dc3tog over next 3 sts (= post st, dc, post st).

**Sizes 3 and 4 only:** Dc2tog over next 2 sts.

**All sizes:** Rep betw [ ] 5 times. Dc in next 7 (8, 9, 10) dc, puff st in next st, dc in next 6 (7, 8, 9) dc, join. 192 (216, 242, 266) sts; 180 (204, 230, 254) dc/FPdc, 12 puff sts

**Rnd 8:** Ch 3, dc (dc, dc2tog, dc2tog) in/over next 1 (1, 2, 2) st(s). [Dc in next 7 (8, 9, 10) dc, puff st in next st, dc in next 7 (8, 9, 10) dc, FPdc around next post st] 5 times. Dc in next 7 (8, 9, 10) dc, puff st in next st, dc in next 7 (8, 9, 10) dc. Dc (dc, dc2tog, dc2tog) in/over next 1 (1, 2, 2) st(s).

Rep betw [ ] 5 times. Dc in next 7 (8, 9, 10) dc, puff st in next st, dc in next 6 (7, 8, 9) dc, join. 192 (216, 240, 264) sts; 180 (204, 228, 252) dc/ FPdc, 12 puff sts

Sl st in next 3 sts.

**Rnd 9:** Ch 3, dc in next 12 (14, 16, 18) sts. [Skip next st, V-puff in next post st, skip next st, dc in next 13 (15, 17, 19) sts] 11 times. Skip next st, V-puff in next st, join.

**Rnds 10–13:** Ch 3, dc in next 12 (14, 16, 18) dc. [V-puff in next ch-1 sp, dc in next 13 (15, 17, 19) dc] 11 times. V-puff in next ch-1 sp, join.

**Rnd 14:** Ch 3, dc in next 12 (14, 16, 18) dc, dc in next puff st. [Puff st in next ch-1 sp, dc in next puff st, dc in next 13 (15, 17, 19) dc, dc in next puff st] 11 times. Puff st in next ch-1 sp, dc in next puff st, join.

**Rnds 15–17:** Ch 3, dc in next 13 (15, 17, 19) dc. [Puff st in next st, dc in next 15 (17, 19, 21) dc] 11 times. Puff st in next st, dc in last dc, join.

**Rnds 18–20:** Ch 3, dc around, join.

**Rnd 21:** Ch 3, [FPdc around next dc, BPdc around next dc] around to last st, FPdc around last st, join.

**Rnd 22:** Sl st around, fasten off.

## Sleeve Ribbing

### Make 2

With RS facing, attach yarn with sl st in the approximate center of underarm.

**Rnd 1:** Ch 3, [FPdc around next st, BPdc around next st] around, join.

**Rnd 2:** Sl st around, fasten off.

## Finishing

Weave in yarn ends and block according to fiber type.

# Ēna Shadow Sweater

In this sweater, relief raglan lines are reimagined into linked, continuous extensions that evoke balance and interconnectedness with hugging post stitch under-shadows. Designed for everyday wear, Ēna showcases a fragile play of shadows adding interest to an otherwise casual piece.

# Ēna Shadow Sweater Construction Notes

*Ēna is a raglan sweater worked top down in joined rounds. The sweater is split for the body and sleeves at the bust line. The sleeves are worked last over skipped stitches from end of yoke.*

## Sizes

1 (2, 3, 4, 5) (6, 7, 8, 9)

**To fit bust:** 30 (34, 38, 42, 46) (50, 54, 58, 62)" / 76 (86, 97, 107, 117) (127, 137, 147, 157) cm

**Finished bust:** 38.75 (42.25, 45, 47.75, 50.5) (53, 55.75, 58.5, 61.75)" / 98.5 (107, 114.5, 121.5, 128.5) (134.5, 141.5, 148.5, 157) cm

## Gauge

14 sts x 9 rows = 4" / 10 cm in dc after blocking with larger hook

## Yarn

Sport weight, Hobbii Vintage Hank (70% wool, 30% bamboo), 262 yds / 240 m per 100-g skein, or use any sport weight wool-bamboo blend to achieve a similar effect

## Yardage/Meterage

975 (1050, 1155, 1235, 1310) (1365, 1445, 1535, 1640) yds / 890 (960, 1055, 1130, 1200) (1250, 1320, 1405, 1500) m

### Shown in
Color Grey (17957)

## Hooks

I/9 / 5.5 mm for the main sections of the Body, Sleeves and Yoke, or size needed to obtain gauge

H/8 / 5 mm for ribbing

## Notions

6 stitch markers

Tapestry needle

## Skills

Experience with making crocheted sweaters

### Abbreviations (US terms)

Ch = chain

Dc = double crochet

Dc2tog = double crochet 2 together

FPdc = front post double crochet

FPtr = front post treble

Fsc = foundation single crochet

LL = long loop

Rnd(s) = round(s)

RS = right side

Sl st = slip stitch

St(s) = stitch(es)

### Special stitches

**Long loop (LL):** Pull up a long loop (same height as sts in working row) at beginning of rnd (does not count as a st throughout).

| Size | A—finished bust | B—yoke depth | C—full length | D—sleeve length | E—upper arm |
|------|-----------------|--------------|---------------|-----------------|-------------|
| 1 | 38.75" / 98.5 cm | 10.25" / 26 cm | 18" / 46 cm | 18.25" / 46.5 cm | 13.5" / 34.5 cm |
| 2 | 42.25" / 107 cm | 10.75" / 27 cm | 18.75" / 47.5 cm | 18" / 45.5 cm | 15.25" / 38.5 cm |
| 3 | 45" / 114.5 cm | 11.25" / 28.5 cm | 19" / 48.5 cm | 17.5" / 44.5 cm | 16.5" / 42 cm |
| 4 | 47.75" / 121.5 cm | 11.5" / 29.5 cm | 19.5" / 49.5 cm | 17.25" / 43.5 cm | 18" / 45.5 cm |
| 5 | 50.5" / 128.5 cm | 12" / 30.5 cm | 20" / 50.5 cm | 16.5" / 42 cm | 19.5" / 49.5 cm |
| 6 | 53" / 134.5 cm | 12.5" / 31.5 cm | 20.25" / 51.5 cm | 16.25" / 41 cm | 20.5" / 52 cm |
| 7 | 55.75" / 141.5 cm | 13" / 33 cm | 20.75" / 53 cm | 15.75" / 40 cm | 21.75" / 55.5 cm |
| 8 | 58.5" / 148.5 cm | 13.5" / 34 cm | 21.25" / 54 cm | 15.25" / 39 cm | 23.5" / 59.5 cm |
| 9 | 61.75" / 157 cm | 13.75" / 35 cm | 21.75" / 55 cm | 15" / 38 cm | 25" / 63.5 cm |

*Hem and sleeve ribbing measures 1.75" / 4.5 cm. Neck ribbing measures 1" / 2.5 cm. The sweater is designed to be worn with 8.75 (8.5, 6.75, 5.5, 4.5) (3, 1.75, 0.75, 0)" / 22.5 (21, 17.5, 14.5, 11.5) (7.5, 4.5, 1.5, 0) cm positive ease. Size 2 is modeled on 35" / 89-cm bust model.*

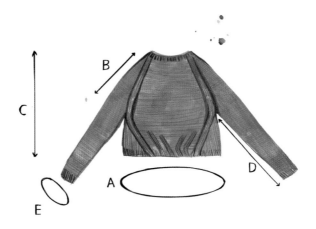

# Ēna Shadow Sweater Pattern

Make a ch 2 as your first dc of the round or use LL to start the rnd (doesn't count as a stitch) and begin with a dc as written.

The sleeve and body length are adjustable.

Note that there are both I Ptr and FPdc worked in some rounds; take care to work the correct stitch.

## Yoke

With smaller hook, fsc 66 (66, 70, 72, 76) (80, 84, 88, 92).

**Rnd 1:** Dc across, join with sl st to begin working in the round.

**Rnd 2:** Dc in first st. [FPdc around next st, dc in next st] around to last st, FPdc around last st, join.

Change to larger hook.

**Rnd 3:** [Dc in next 7 (7, 7, 11, 11) (11, 15, 15, 15) sts, 2 dc in next st] 8 (8, 8, 6, 6) (6, 5, 5, 5) times. Dc in next 2 (2, 6, 0, 4) (8, 4, 8, 12) sts, join. 74 (74, 78, 78, 82) (86, 89, 93, 97) sts

**Rnd 4:** 2 dc in first st, dc in next 19 (19, 19, 19, 19) (21, 20, 22, 22) sts, 2 dc in next st, FPdc around next 4 sts, 2 dc in next st, dc in next 6 (6, 8, 8, 10) (10, 12, 12, 14) sts, 2 dc in next st, FPdc around next 4 sts, 2 dc in next st, dc in next 19 (19, 19, 19, 19) (21, 21, 23, 23) sts, 2 dc in next st, FPdc around next 4 sts, 2 dc in next st, dc in next 6 (6, 8, 8, 10) (10, 12, 12, 14) sts, 2 dc in next st, FPdc around next 4 sts, join. 82 (82, 86, 86, 90) (94, 97, 101, 105) sts

**Rnd 5:** 2 dc in first st, dc in next 21 (21, 21, 21, 21) (23, 22, 24, 24) sts, 2 dc in next st, FPdc around next 4 sts, 2 dc in next st, dc in next 8 (8, 10, 10, 12) (12, 14, 14, 16) sts, 2 dc in next st, FPdc around next 4 sts, 2 dc in next st, dc in next 21 (21, 21, 21, 21) (23, 23, 25, 25) sts, 2 dc in next st, FPdc around next 4 sts, 2 dc in next st, dc in next 8 (8, 10, 10, 12) (12, 14, 14, 16) sts, 2 dc in next st, FPdc around next 4 sts, join. 90 (90, 94, 94, 98) (102, 105, 109, 113) sts

**Rnd 6:** 2 dc in first st, dc in next 23 (23, 23, 23, 23) (25, 24, 26, 26) sts, 2 dc in next st, FPdc around next 4 sts, 2 dc in next st, dc in next 10 (10, 12, 12, 14) (14, 16, 16, 18) sts, 2 dc in next st, FPdc around next 4 sts, 2 dc in next st, dc in next 23 (23, 23, 23, 23) (25, 25, 27, 27) sts, 2 dc in next st, FPdc around next 4 sts, 2 dc in next st, dc in next 10 (10, 12, 12, 14) (14, 16, 16, 18) sts, 2 dc in next st, FPdc around next 4 sts, join. 98 (98, 102, 102, 106) (110, 113, 117, 121) sts

**Rnd 7:** 2 dc in first st, [dc across to dc before next FPdc, 2 dc in next st, FPdc around next 4 FPdc*, 2 dc in next st] 4 times, ending last rep at *, join. 106 (106, 110, 110, 114) (118, 121, 125, 129) sts

Repeat rnd 7 until there are 23 (24, 25, 26, 27) (28, 29, 30, 31) rnds after the fsc rnd, with 234 (242, 254, 262, 274) (286, 297, 309, 321) sts in the last rnd.

Don't fasten off, continue to Separating Body and Sleeves.

## Separating Body and Sleeves

Dc in next 61 (63, 65, 67, 69) (71, 73, 75, 77) sts, FPdc around next 4 sts, ch 0 (4, 7, 10, 13) (15, 18, 21, 25), skip next 48 (50, 52, 54, 56) (58, 60, 62, 64) sts, FPdc around next 4 sts, dc in next 61 (63, 65, 67, 69) (71, 73, 75, 77) sts, FPdc around next 4 sts, ch 0 (4, 7, 10, 13) (15, 18, 21, 25), skip next 48 (50, 52, 54, 56) (58, 60, 62, 64) sts, FPdc around next 4 sts, join. 138 (150, 160, 170, 180) (188, 198, 208, 220) sts

# Body

Continue to work with larger hook.

**Rnd 1:** [Dc in next 61 (63, 65, 67, 69) (71, 73, 75, 77) sts, FPdc around next 4 sts, dc in next 0 (4, 7, 10, 13) (15, 18, 21, 25) sts, FPdc around next 4 sts] twice, join. 138 (150, 160, 170, 180) (188, 198, 208, 220) sts

To make the Body of the sweater longer: repeat rnd 1 as many times as you wish.

**Rnd 2:** [Dc2tog over next 2 sts, dc in next 57 (59, 61, 63, 65) (67, 69, 71, 73) sts, dc2tog over next 2 sts, FPtr around next 3 (4, 4, 4, 4) (4, 4, 4, 4) sts, 2 dc in next st, FPdc around next 0 (2, 5, 8, 11) (13, 16, 19, 23) sts, 2 dc in next st, FPtr around next 3 (4, 4, 4, 4) (4, 4, 4, 4) sts] twice, join.

**Rnd 3:** [Dc2tog over next 2 sts, dc in next 55 (57, 59, 61, 63) (65, 67, 69, 71) sts, dc2tog over next 2 sts, FPtr around next 4 sts, 2 dc in next st, FPdc around next 0 (4, 7, 10, 13) (15, 18, 21, 25) sts, 2 dc in next st, FPtr around next 4 sts] twice, join.

**Rnd 4:** [Dc2tog over next 2 sts, dc in next 53 (55, 57, 59, 61) (63, 65, 67, 69) sts, dc2tog over next 2 sts, FPtr around next 4 sts, 2 dc in next st, FPdc around next 2 (6, 9, 12, 15) (17, 20, 23, 27) sts, 2 dc in next st, FPtr around next 4 sts] twice, join.

**Rnd 5:** [Dc2tog over next 2 sts, dc in next st, 2 dc in next st, FPtr around next 4 sts, skip next st, dc in next 37 (39, 41, 43, 45) (47, 49, 51, 53) sts, skip next st, FPtr around next 4 sts, 2 dc in next st, dc in next st, dc2tog over next 2 sts, FPtr around next 4 sts, 2 dc in next st, FPdc around next 4 (8, 11, 14, 17) (19, 22, 25, 29) sts, 2 dc in next st, FPtr around next 4 sts] twice, join.

**Rnd 6:** [Dc2tog over next 2 sts, dc in next st, 2 dc in next st, FPtr around next 4 sts, skip next st, dc in next 35 (37, 39, 41, 43) (45, 47, 49, 51) sts, skip next st, FPtr around next 4 sts, 2 dc in next st, dc in next st, dc2tog over next 2 sts, FPtr around next 4 sts, 2 dc in next st, FPdc around next 6 (10, 13, 16, 19) (21, 24, 27, 31) sts, 2 dc in next st, FPtr around next 4 sts] twice, join.

**Rnd 7:** [Dc2tog over next 2 sts, dc in next st, 2 dc in next st, FPtr around next 4 sts, skip next st, dc in next 33 (35, 37, 39, 41) (43, 45, 47, 49) sts, skip next st, FPtr around next 4 sts, 2 dc in next st, dc in next st, dc2tog over next 2 sts, FPtr around next 4 sts, 2 dc in next st, FPdc around next 8 (12, 15, 18, 21) (23, 26, 29, 33) sts, 2 dc in next st, FPtr around next 4 sts] twice, join.

**Rnd 8:** [Dc2tog over next 2 sts, dc in next st, 2 dc in next st, FPtr around next 4 sts, skip next st, dc in next 2 sts, 2 dc in next st, FPtr around next 4 sts, skip next st, dc in next 15 (17, 19, 21, 23) (25, 27, 29, 31) sts, skip next st, FPtr around next 4 sts, 2 dc in next st, dc in next 2 sts, skip next st, FPtr around next 4 sts, 2 dc in next st, dc in next st, dc2tog over next 2 sts, FPtr around next 4 sts, 2 dc in next st, FPdc around next 10 (14, 17, 20, 23) (25, 28, 31, 35) sts, 2 dc in next st, FPtr around next 4 sts] twice, join.

**Rnd 9:** [Dc2tog over next 2 sts, dc in next st, 2 dc in next st, FPtr around next 4 sts, skip next st, dc in next 2 sts, 2 dc in next st, FPtr around next 4 sts, skip next st, dc in next 13 (15, 17, 19, 21) (23, 25, 27, 29) sts, skip next st, FPtr around next 4 sts, 2 dc in next st, dc in next 2 sts, skip next st, FPtr around next 4 sts, 2 dc in next st, dc in next st, dc2tog over next 2 sts, FPtr around next 4 sts, 2 dc in next st, FPdc around next 12 (16, 19, 22, 25) (27, 30, 33, 37) sts, 2 dc in next st, FPtr around next 4 sts] twice, join.

**Rnd 10:** [Dc2tog over next 2 sts, dc in next st, 2 dc in next st, FPtr around next 4 sts, skip next st, dc in next 2 sts, 2 dc in next st, FPtr around next 4 sts, skip next st, dc in next 11 (13, 15, 17, 19) (21, 23, 25, 27) sts, skip next st, FPtr around next 4 sts, 2 dc in next st, dc in next 2 sts, skip next st, FPtr around next 4 sts, 2 dc in next st, dc

in next st, dc2tog over next 2 sts, FPtr around next 4 sts, 2 dc in next st, FPdc around next 14 (18, 21, 24, 27) (29, 32, 35, 39) sts, 2 dc in next st, FPtr around next 4 sts] twice, join.

**Rnd 11:** [Dc2tog over next 2 sts, dc in next st, 2 dc in next st, FPtr around next 4 sts, skip next st, dc in next 2 sts, 2 dc in next st, FPtr around next 4 sts, skip next st, dc in next 9 (11, 13, 15, 17) (19, 21, 23, 25) sts, skip next st, FPtr around next 4 sts, 2 dc in next st, dc in next 2 sts, skip next st, FPtr around next 4 sts, 2 dc in next st, dc in next st, dc2tog over next 2 sts, FPtr around next 4 sts, 2 dc in next st, FPdc around next 16 (20, 23, 26, 29) (31, 34, 37, 41) sts, 2 dc in next st, FPtr around next 4 sts] twice, join.

**Rnd 12:** [Dc2tog over next 2 sts, dc in next st, 2 dc in next st, FPtr around next 4 sts, skip next st, dc in next 2 sts, 2 dc in next st, FPtr around next 4 sts, skip next st, dc in next 7 (9, 11, 13, 15) (17, 19, 21, 23) sts, skip next st, FPtr around next 4 sts, 2 dc in next st, dc in next 2 sts, skip next st, FPtr around next 4 sts, 2 dc in next st, dc in next st, dc2tog over next 2 sts, FPtr around next 4 sts, 2 dc in next st, FPdc around next 18 (22, 25, 28, 31) (33, 36, 39, 43) sts, 2 dc in next st, FPtr around next 4 sts] twice, join.

**Rnd 13:** [Dc2tog over next 2 sts, dc in next st, 2 dc in next st, FPtr around next 4 sts, skip next st, dc in next 2 sts, 2 dc in next st, FPtr around next 4 sts, skip next st, dc in next 5 (7, 9, 11, 13) (15, 17, 19, 21) sts, skip next st, FPtr around next 4 sts, 2 dc in next st, dc in next 2 sts, skip next st, FPtr around next 4 sts, 2 dc in next st, dc in next st, dc2tog over next 2 sts, FPtr around next 4 sts, 2 dc in next st, FPdc around next 20 (24, 27, 30, 33) (35, 38, 41, 45) sts, 2 dc in next st, FPtr around next 4 sts] twice, join.

**Rnd 14:** [Dc2tog over next 2 sts, dc in next st, 2 dc in next st, FPtr around next 4 sts, skip next st, dc in next 2 sts, 2 dc in next st, FPtr around next 4 sts, skip next st, dc in next 3 (5, 7, 9, 11) (13, 15, 17, 19) sts, skip next st, FPtr around next 4 sts, 2 dc in next st, dc in next 2 sts, skip next st, FPtr around next 4 sts, 2 dc in next st, dc in next st, dc2tog over next 2 sts, FPtr around next 4 sts, 2 dc in next st, FPdc around next 22 (26, 29, 32, 35) (37, 40, 43, 47) sts, 2 dc in next st, FPtr around next 4 sts] twice, join.

Change to smaller hook.

**Rnd 15:** Sl st in next st. LL, [FPtr around next 33 (35, 37, 39, 41) (43, 45, 47, 49) sts, skip next st, FPtr around next 4 sts, 2 dc in next st, FPtr around next 24 (28, 31, 34, 37) (39, 42, 45, 49) sts, 2 dc in next st, FPtr around next 4 sts, skip next st] twice, join.

**Rnd 16:** Sl st in next st. LL, [FPtr around next 31 (33, 35, 37, 39) (41, 43, 45, 47) sts, skip next st, FPtr around next 4 sts, 2 dc in next st, FPtr around next 26 (30, 33, 36, 39) (41, 44, 47, 51) sts, 2 dc in next st, FPtr around next 4 sts, skip next st] twice, join.

**Rnd 17:** Sl st in next st. LL, [FPtr around next 29 (31, 33, 35, 37) (39, 41, 43, 45) sts, skip next st, FPtr around next 4 sts, 2 dc in next st, FPtr around next 28 (32, 35, 38, 41) (43, 46, 49, 53) sts, 2 dc in next st, FPtr around next 4 sts, skip next st] twice, join.

**Rnd 18:** Sl st in next st. LL, [FPtr around next 27 (29, 31, 33, 35) (37, 39, 41, 43) sts, skip next st, FPtr around next 4 sts, 2 dc in next st, FPtr around next 30 (34, 37, 40, 43) (45, 48, 51, 55) sts, 2 dc in next st, FPtr around next 4 sts, skip next st] twice, join.

**Last rnd (optional):** Sl st around, fasten off.

## Sleeve

### Make 2

With larger hook and RS facing, attach new yarn with a sl st at approximate center of underarm.

**Rnd 1:** LL, dc in each st and ch around, join. 48 (54, 59, 64, 69) (73, 78, 83, 89) sts

**Rnd 2 (decrease rnd):** LL, dc in first st, dc2tog over next 2 sts, dc around until only 3 sts remain unworked, dc2tog over next 2 sts, dc in last st, join. 46 (52, 57, 62, 67) (71, 76, 81, 87) sts

**Sizes 1–5:** [Rep rnd 1 twice, rep rnd 2 once] 10 (11, 11, 11, 10) (x, x, x, x) times, then rep rnd 1 another 6 (2, 1, 0, 2) (x, x, x, x) time(s) for a total of 38 (37, 36, 35, 34) (x, x, x, x) rnds and 26 (30, 35, 40, 47) (x, x, x, x) sts.

**Sizes 6–9:** [Rep rnd 1 once, rep rnd 2 once] x (x, x, x, x) (15, 5, 5, 5) times, then rep rnd 2 another x (x, x, x, x) (0, 13, 16, 16) times, then rep rnd 1 another x (x, x, x, x) (1, 7, 3, 2) time(s) for a total of x (x, x, x, x) (33, 32, 31, 30) rnds and x (x, x, x, x) (41, 40, 41, 45) sts.

## Cuff

Change to smaller hook.

**Rnds 1–4:** LL, FPtr around, join.

**Last rnd (optional):** Sl st around, fasten off.

## Finishing

Sew the neck split. Weave in all ends. Block according to fiber type.

# Sniegs Snow Sweater

Just as satisfying as it is to walk through a fresh powdery snowfall, leaving your trace behind, it is also extremely enjoyable to make a quick cozy sweater in just one day or so. This squishy goodness of a sweater will work up exceptionally fast. The textured post stitches keep things interesting and in no time you'll end up with a cozy pile of warm, fuzzy snow in which to wrap yourself. This sweater is perfect to wear while snuggled in front of the TV or a fireplace—whichever is your vibe.

# Sniegs Snow Sweater Construction Notes

*Sniegs is an oversized batwing sweater worked bottom up starting with a sideways ribbing. The front and back are each worked separately, and the shoulder seams are crocheted (or sewn) together. Then both cuffs and neck ribbing are worked and sewn on. The neckline ribbing is made separately and sewn on afterwards.*

## Sizes

1 (2, 3, 4, 5) (6, 7, 8, 9)

**To fit waist:** 24 (28, 32, 36, 40) (44, 48, 52, 56)" / 61 (71, 81, 91, 102) (112, 122, 132, 142) cm

**To fit bust:** 30 (34, 38, 42, 46) (50, 54, 58, 62)" / 76 (86, 97, 107, 117) (127, 137, 147, 157) cm

## Gauge

10 sts x 6 rows = 4" / 10 cm in dc after blocking

## Yarn

Bulky weight, Hobbii Snowstorm (100% wool), 54 yds / 50 m per 50-g skein, or use any bulky weight roving wool yarn to achieve a similar effect

## Yardage/Meterage

610 (655, 730, 775, 860) (910, 990, 1040, 1095) yds / 560 (600, 670, 710, 785) (830, 905, 950, 1000) m

### Shown in

Color Ivory (01)

## Hook

L/11 / 8 mm for the main sections of the Body and ribbing, or size needed to obtain gauge

## Notions

Tapestry needle for sewing seams and ribbing on

## Skills

Experience with making crocheted sweaters

### Abbreviations (US terms)

BL = back loop

BPdc = back post double crochet

Ch = chain

Dc = double crochet

Dc2tog = double crochet 2 together

FPdc = front post double crochet

FPsc = front post single crochet

Hdc = half double crochet

Rnd(s) = round(s)

RS = right side

Sc = single crochet

Sc-hdc-tog = single crochet and half double crochet together

Sl st = slip stitch

St(s) = stitch(es)

WS = wrong side

Yo = yarn over

### Special stitches

**Sc-hdc-tog:** Insert hook in indicated st, yo, draw yarn through stitch, yo, insert hook in next indicated st, yo, draw yarn through st, yo, draw yarn through all 4 loops on hook.

| Size | A—waist | B—width without cuffs | C—width with cuffs | D—body length | E—armholes | F—neck width (without ribbing) |
|---|---|---|---|---|---|---|
| 1 | 24" / 61 cm | 25.75" / 65.5 cm | 32.75" / 83.5 cm | 19" / 48 cm | 11.75" / 30 cm | 7.5" / 19 cm |
| 2 | 28" / 71 cm | 27.5" / 70 cm | 34.75" / 88 cm | 19" / 48 cm | 11.75" / 30 cm | 7.75" / 20 cm |
| 3 | 32" / 81 cm | 29.25" / 74.5 cm | 36.5" / 92.5 cm | 19.5" / 49.5 cm | 13" / 33 cm | 8.25" / 21 cm |
| 4 | 36" / 91 cm | 31" / 79 cm | 38.25" / 97 cm | 19.5" / 49.5 cm | 13" / 33 cm | 7.75" / 20 cm |
| 5 | 40" / 102 cm | 32.75" / 83.5 cm | 40" / 101.5 cm | 20" / 51 cm | 14.25" / 36 cm | 8.25" / 21 cm |
| 6 | 44" / 112 cm | 34.75" / 88 cm | 41.75" / 106 cm | 20" / 51 cm | 14.25" / 36 cm | 8.75" / 22 cm |
| 7 | 48" / 122 cm | 36.5" / 92.5 cm | 43.5" / 110.5 cm | 20.75" / 52.5 cm | 15.25" / 39 cm | 9" / 23 cm |
| 8 | 52" / 132 cm | 38.25" / 97 cm | 45.25" / 115 cm | 20.75" / 52.5 cm | 15.25" / 39 cm | 8.75" / 22 cm |
| 9 | 56" / 142 cm | 40" / 101.5 cm | 47" / 119.5 cm | 20.75" / 52.5 cm | 15.25" / 39 cm | 9" / 23 cm |

*Body and Sleeve ribbing measures 3.5" / 9 cm. Neck ribbing measures 1.5" / 4 cm. The sweater is designed with no ease at the waist. Size 2 is modeled on 30" / 77-cm bust model.*

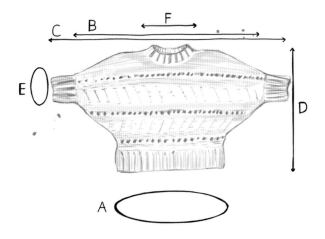

# Sniegs Snow Sweater Pattern

**Throughout:** Ch 1 at the beginning of row counts as turning chain and is not counted as a stitch.

Ch 2: Counts as first hdc (= 1 st).

Ch 3: Counts as first dc (= 1 st).

Ch 4: Counts as first dc + 1 ch (= 2 sts).

## Front

### Front Ribbing

With L/11 / 8 mm hook, ch 11 (last 2 ch counts as first hdc on next row).

**Row 1:** Hdc in third ch from hook, hdc in each ch across, turn. 10 sts

**Rows 2–25 (–28, –32, –35, –38) (–42, –45, –48, –52):** Ch 2 (counts as first hdc), hdc in BL across, turn. 10 sts

**Last row of the ribbing:** Don't turn. Rotate the ribbing clockwise by 90 degrees.

## Body

For row 1 you'll be working across the side of the ribbing:

**Sizes x (2, 3, x, 5) (6, x, 8, 9) only:** Work 3 sc in every 2 rows of hdc then add additional sts in final row end as noted in row 1.

**Sizes 1 (x, x, 4, x) (x, 7, x, x) only:** Work 3 sc in every 2 rows of hdc omitting last row end, work added sts in final row end as noted in row 1.

**Row 1:** With RS facing and using your L/11 / 8 mm hook, ch 1, sc across (as described above), 2 (1, 0, 2, 1) (0, 2, 1, 0) more sc in last row of hdc, turn. 38 (43, 48, 53, 58) (63, 68, 73, 78) sts

**Row 2:** Ch 1, 2 sc in first st, sc across to last st, 2 sc in last st, turn. 40 (45, 50, 55, 60) (65, 70, 75, 80) sts

**Row 3:** (Ch 3, dc) in first st, dc across to last st, 2 dc in last st, turn. 42 (47, 52, 57, 62) (67, 72, 77, 82) sts

**Row 4:** Ch 1, FPsc across, turn.

**Row 5:** (Ch 4, dc) in first st. [Ch 1, skip next st, dc in next st] to last 2 sts, ch 1, skip next st, (dc, ch 1, dc) in last st, turn. 46 (51, 56, 61, 66) (71, 76, 81, 86) sts

**Row 6:** Ch 1, 2 sc in first st, sc across to last st, 2 sc in last st, turn. 48 (53, 58, 63, 68) (73, 78, 83, 88) sts

**Row 7:** (Ch 3, dc) in first st, BPdc to last st, 2 dc in last st, turn. 50 (55, 60, 65, 70) (75, 80, 85, 90) sts

**Row 8:** (Ch 2, hdc) in first st, hdc in next 2 sts. [Ch 1, BPdc around next st, skip next st, hdc in next 3 sts] 9 (10, 11, 12, 13) (14, 15, 16, 17) times. Hdc in next st, 2 hdc in last st, turn. 52 (57, 62, 67, 72) (77, 82, 87, 92) sts

**Row 9:** (Ch 2, hdc) in first st, hdc in next 4 sts. [Skip next st, FPdc around next post st, ch 1, hdc in next ch-1 sp, hdc in next 2 sts] 9 (10, 11, 12, 13) (14, 15, 16, 17) times. Hdc in next st, 2 hdc in last st, turn. 54 (59, 64, 69, 74) (79, 84, 89, 94) sts

**Row 10:** (Ch 2, hdc) in first st, hdc in next 5 sts, hdc in next ch-1 sp. [Ch 1, BPdc around next post st, skip next st, hdc in next 3 sts] 9 (10, 11, 12, 13) (14, 15, 16, 17) times. Hdc in next st, 2 hdc in last st, turn. 56 (61, 66, 71, 76) (81, 86, 91, 96) sts

**Row 11:** (Ch 2, hdc) in first st, hdc in next 4 sts. [Skip next st, FPdc around next post st, ch 1, hdc in next ch-1 sp, hdc in next 2 sts] 9 (10, 11, 12, 13) (14, 15, 16, 17) times. Hdc in next 5 sts, 2 hdc in last st, turn. 58 (63, 68, 73, 78) (83, 88, 93, 98) sts

**Row 12:** Ch 1, 2 sc in first st, sc across to last st, 2 sc in last st, turn. 60 (65, 70, 75, 80) (85, 90, 95, 100) sts

**Row 13:** (Ch 3, dc) in first st, BPdc across to last st, 2 dc in last st, turn. 62 (67, 72, 77, 82) (87, 92, 97, 102) sts

**Row 14:** (Ch 4, dc) in first st. [Ch 1, skip next st, dc in next st] to last 2 sts, ch 1, skip next st, (dc, ch 1, dc) in last st, turn. 66 (71, 76, 81, 86) (91, 96, 101, 106) sts

**Row 15:** (Ch 3, dc) in first st, dc across to last st, 2 dc in last st, turn. 68 (73, 78, 83, 88) (93, 98, 103, 108) sts

**Row 16:** Ch 1, 2 sc in first st, FPsc to last st, 2 sc in last st, turn. 70 (75, 80, 85, 90) (95, 100, 105, 110) sts

**Row 17:** Ch 3, dc across, turn.

**Row 18:** Ch 2. [Hdc in next 3 sts, skip next st, BPdc around next st, ch 1] 13 (14, 15, 16, 17) (18, 19, 20, 21) times. Hdc in next 4 sts, turn.

**Row 19:** Ch 2, hdc in next 4 sts. [Ch 1, FPdc around next post st, skip next st, hdc in next 3 sts] 13 (14, 15, 16, 17) (18, 19, 20, 21) times, turn.

**Row 20:** Ch 2, hdc in next st. [Skip next st, BPdc around next post st, ch 1, hdc in next 3 sts] 13 (14, 15, 16, 17) (18, 19, 20, 21) times. Skip next st, BPdc around next post st, ch 1, hdc in next st, turn.

**Row 21:** Ch 2, hdc in next st. [Ch 1, FPdc around next post st, skip next st, hdc in next 3 sts] 13 (14, 15, 16, 17) (18, 19, 20, 21) times. Ch 1, FPdc around next post st, skip next st, hdc in next st, turn.

**Row 22:** Ch 1, sc across, turn.

**Row 23:** Ch 3, BPdc across, turn.

**Row 24:** Ch 4, skip next st, dc in next st. [Ch 1, skip next st, dc in next st] across to last 1 (2, 1, 2, 1) (2, 1, 2, 1) sts.

**Sizes 1, 3, 5, 7, 9:** Make 1 dc in last st, turn.

**Sizes 2, 4, 6, 8:** Ch 1, skip next st, dc in last st, turn.

**Row 25:** Ch 3, dc across, turn.

**Row 26:** Ch 1, FPsc across, turn.

**Row 27:** Ch 3, dc across, turn.

**Row 2:** Ch 2, dc in next st (counts as dc2tog over first 2 sts), dc in next 6 (8, 10, 13, 15) (17, 19, 22, 24) sts, hdc in next 5 sts, sc in next 5 sts, turn. 17 (19, 21, 24, 26) (28, 30, 33, 35) sts

**Row 3:** Ch 1 (mark), skip first st, sc in next 8 sts, hdc in next 5 sts, dc in next 1 (3, 5, 8, 10) (12, 14, 17, 19) sts, dc2tog over next 2 sts, turn. (In this row ch 1 counts as a stitch) 16 (18, 20, 23, 25) (27, 29, 32, 34) sts

**Row 4:** Ch 2, dc in next st (counts as dc2tog over first 2 sts), dc in next 5 sts, hdc in next 5 sts, sc in next 3 (5, 7, 10, 12) (14, 16, 19, 21) sts, sc-hdc-tog over next 2 marked sts (remove markers), 2 sc in next st, sc in next 3 sts, sl st in next 5 sts, fasten off. 25 (27, 29, 32, 34) (36, 38, 41, 43) sts

Continue to work Front Shoulder 2.

## Front Shoulder 2

Attach yarn with sl st to the other end of your last row of front part and repeat instructions for Shoulder 1.

# Back

Repeat the instructions for Front, stopping right before Shoulder parts.

## Upper Back

**Next row 1:** Ch 1, sc in next 10 sts (mark last sc = M1), hdc in next 5 sts (mark first of the hdcs = M2), dc in next 40 (45, 50, 55, 60) (65, 70, 75, 80) sts, hdc in next 5 sts (mark last hdc = M3), sc in next 10 sts (mark first sc = M4), turn and fasten off. 70 (75, 80, 85, 90) (95, 100, 105, 110) sts

**Sizes 1, 2:** Continue to Shoulder 1.

**Sizes 3, 4:** Repeat row 27 one more time and continue to Shoulder 1.

**Sizes 5, 6:** Repeat row 27 two more times and continue to Shoulder 1.

**Sizes 7, 8, 9:** Repeat row 27 three more times and continue to Front Shoulder 1.

## Front Shoulder 1

**Row 1:** Ch 1, sc in next 10 sts (mark last sc just made), hdc in next 5 sts, dc in next 12 (14, 16, 19, 21) (23, 25, 28, 30) sts, dc2tog over next 2 sts, turn. 28 (30, 32, 35, 37) (39, 41, 44, 46) sts

**Next row 2:** Attach yarn with sl st to M3. Sc in first 5 sts (move M3 to first sc of this row—this is where you'll start your Back Shoulder 1), hdc in next 5 sts, dc in next 30 (35, 40, 45, 50) (55, 60, 65, 70) sts, hdc in next 5 sts, sc in next 5 sts (mark last st by moving M2 up—this is where you'll start your Back Shoulder 2), fasten off. 50 (55, 60, 65, 70) (75, 80, 85, 90) sts

## Back Shoulder 1

Attach yarn with sl st to M3 to start working toward the neck (remove the marker following the instructons for Front Shoulder 1 row 3). Rep rows 3 and 4 of Front Shoulder 1—don't fasten off after row 4, continue to crochet the shoulder of Front and Back parts together.

Take the Front and put both—Front and Back—parts together RS facing each other. Crochet the shoulder seam together using sl sts: Ch 1 (turning ch), insert hook through both loops of first st of Back and through both loops of Front, yo and pull yarn through all loops on hook, continue to work like this across all sts of the shoulder, fasten off. (Or you can sew the shoulder seam if you prefer.)

## Back Shoulder 2

Attach yarn with sl st to M2. Repeat rows 3 and 4 of Front Shoulder 1—don't fasten off after row 4, continue to crochet the shoulder of Front and Back parts together.

With WS facing, sew both side seams.

## Cuff

### Make 2

With L/11 / 8 mm hook, ch 11 (last 2 ch counts as first hdc on next row).

**Row 1:** Hdc in third ch from hook, hdc in each ch across, turn. 10 sts

**Rows 2–19 (–19, –22, –22, –25) (–25, –28, –28, –28):** Ch 2 (counts as first hdc), hdc in BL across, turn. 10 sts

Stretch the Cuff and sew it on to the armhole, then sew the beginning and end of the Cuff together.

## Neck Ribbing

With L/11 / 8 mm hook, ch 6 (last 2 ch counts as first hdc on next row).

**Row 1:** Hdc in third ch from hook, hdc in each ch across, turn. 5 sts

**Rows 2–33 (–34, –35, –34, –35) (–36, –37, –36, –37):** Ch 2 (counts as first hdc), hdc in BL across, turn. 5 sts

Stretch the Neck Ribbing and sew it all over the neckline starting from the shoulder seam, then sew the beginning and end of the Neck Ribbing together.

## Finishing

Turn the sweater to the WS and weave in all ends. Block the sweater according to fiber type and turn the sweater back to RS.

# Directional

Short rows have been widely known as a technique to give shape: to the heel of a sock, to bust darts, to raise the back part of a sweater, to give a better fit. But more rarely they have been used as a design technique of their own.

Exploring crochet short rows for a decade has allowed me to develop and call it one of my signature techniques. When I first tried it, I knew I was hooked—and it is now my favorite approach to make all of my asymmetrical designs truly come alive. Short rows have claimed the leading role in so many of my designs ever since.

Crochet short rows can seem a bit intimidating at first, due to their atypical creation and shaping, but they will allow you to think outside of the techniques that you're used to. Once you get the hang of them, you'll thank yourself for taking on this challenge as the outstanding results that short rows provide transcend the traditional back-and-forth of crochet. What's most important—you'll be the proud owner of a piece like no other.

Whether it's the Liedags (page 55), Ainava (page 75), Jūra (page 103) or Zeme Sweater (page 89) you're making, they will each take you on a short rows adventure surrounding you with streamlines, waves, fields and grasslands, or you might just discover a scenery of your own. What do you see in this striking technique?

# Liedags Seashore Sweater

When was the last time you took your shoes off and felt the ripple marks while walking down the seashore? To be sure—the Liedags sweater will take you on a walk like no other. The short rows "shells" mimic the ripples on the beach, while the sideways construction together with back loop stitches is like nothing you've seen before. May this crochet journey be full of stunning surprises and exciting short rows paths!

# Liedags Seashore Construction Notes

*Liedags is worked sideways in columns. The back and front are crocheted separately, the sleeves are made separately and then sewn on. The crew neck is then crocheted right onto the neckline.*

## Sizes

1 (2, 3, 4, 5) (6, 7, 8, 9)

**Finished bust:** 38 (42, 46, 50, 54) (58, 62, 66, 70)" / 97 (107, 117, 127, 137) (147, 157, 168, 178) cm

**To fit bust:** 30 (34, 38, 42, 46) (50, 54, 58, 62)" / 76 (86, 97, 107, 117) (127, 137, 147, 157) cm

## Gauge

13 sts x 17 rows = 4" / 10 cm in sc after blocking

## Yarn

Worsted weight, Hobbii Divina (65% Alpaca, 25% Polyamide, 10% Merino Wool), 164 yds / 150 m per 50-g skein, or use any light untwisted worsted weight wool blend to achieve a similar effect

## Yardage/Meterage

1115 (1198, 1280, 1444, 1608) (1690, 1886, 1936, 2083) yds / 1020 (1095, 1170, 1320, 1470) (1545, 1725, 1770, 1905) m

**Shown in**
Colorway Taupe (8)

## Hooks

K/10½ / 6.5 mm for the main sections of Body and Sleeves, or size needed to obtain gauge

H/8 / 5 mm for the neckline ribbing, or two sizes smaller than size needed to obtain gauge

## Notions

Tapestry needle

6 stitch markers

## Skills

Experience with making crocheted sweaters

Experience with crochet short rows

### Abbreviations (US terms)

BL = back loop

Ch = chain

Prev = previous

RS = right side

Sc = single crochet

Sc2tog = single crochet 2 stitches together

Sl st = slip stitch

St(s) = stitch (stitches)

WS = wrong side

| Size | A—finished bust | B—finished half-bust | C—length | D—sleeve length | E—upper arm |
|------|-----------------|----------------------|----------|-----------------|-------------|
| 1 | 38" / 97 cm | 19" / 48 cm | 20.5" / 52 cm | 18" / 45.5 cm | 10.25" / 26 cm |
| 2 | 42" / 107 cm | 21" / 53.5 cm | 20.5" / 52 cm | 17.5" / 44.5 cm | 11" / 28 cm |
| 3 | 46" / 117 cm | 23" / 58.5 cm | 20.5" / 52 cm | 17.25" / 43.5 cm | 12" / 30.5 cm |
| 4 | 50" / 127 cm | 25" / 63.5 cm | 22.25" / 56.5 cm | 16.75" / 42.5 cm | 13" / 33 cm |
| 5 | 54" / 137 cm | 27" / 68.5 cm | 22.25" / 56.5 cm | 16.5" / 42 cm | 13.75" / 35 cm |
| 6 | 58" / 147 cm | 29" / 73.5 cm | 22.25" / 56.5 cm | 16.25" / 41 cm | 15" / 38 cm |
| 7 | 62" / 157 cm | 31" / 78.5 cm | 24" / 61 cm | 15.75" / 40 cm | 16" / 40.5 cm |
| 8 | 66" / 168 cm | 33" / 84 cm | 24" / 61 cm | 15.25" / 39 cm | 18" / 45.5 cm |
| 9 | 70" / 178 cm | 35" / 89 cm | 24" / 61 cm | 15" / 38.5 cm | 19" / 48 cm |

*Neck width measures 7.5" / 19 cm. The sweater is designed to be worn with 8" / 20 cm of positive ease. Size 2 is modeled on 32" / 82-cm bust model.*

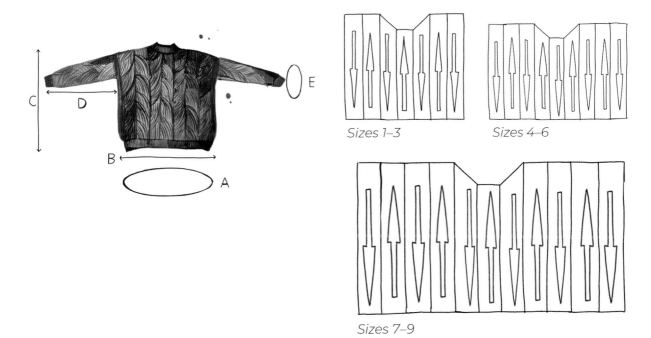

Sizes 1–3

Sizes 4–6

Sizes 7–9

# Liedags Seashore Sweater Pattern

**Throughout all parts of the sweater:** Make all sts in BL (if not stated differently).

## Front/Back

Make 1 Front and 1 Back following the instructions below.

Using your larger hook, ch 75 (75, 75, 81, 81) (81, 87, 87, 87), (last ch counts as turning ch of next row).

**Row 1:** Sc in 2nd ch from hook, sc in next 64 (64, 64, 70, 70) (70, 76, 76, 76) ch, sl st in next 9 sts, turn. 74 (74, 74, 80, 80) (80, 86, 86, 86) sts

**From now on:** Make all stitches in BL.

**Row 2:** Ch 1 (turning ch, is not counted as a st), sl st in first 9 sts, BLsc in next 65 (65, 65, 71, 71) (71, 77, 77, 77) sts, turn.

**Size 1:** Continue to Column 1.

**Row 3:** Ch 1, BLsc in first 65 (65, 65, 71, 71) (71, 77, 77, 77) sts, sl st in next 9 sts, turn. 74 (74, 74, 80, 80) (80, 86, 86, 86) sts

**Row 4:** Ch 1, sl st in first 9 sts, BLsc in next 65 (65, 65, 71, 71) (71, 77, 77, 77) sts, turn.

**Size 2:** Repeat Rows 3 and 4 twice (4 more rows total).

**Sizes 3, 5, 8:** Repeat Rows 3 and 4 four times (8 more rows total).

**Sizes 4, 7:** Repeat Rows 3 and 4 one time (2 more rows total).

**Size 6, 9:** Repeat Rows 3 and 4 six times (12 more rows total).

Continue to Column 1.

Next you'll begin working in columns that consist of various short-row shells.

## Starting Columns

### Column 1

(Consists of Beginning Shell, Full Shells and End Shell with Ribbing)

Continue working all sc sts as BLsc.

### Beginning Shell

**Row 1:** Ch 1 (here and throughout—turning ch, is not counted as a st), sc in first 2 sts, sl st in next 2 sts, turn. 4 sts

**Row 2:** Ch 1 (mark ch 1), skip first sl st, sc in next 2 sts, 2 sc in next st, turn. 4 sts

**Row 3:** Ch 1, sc in first 4 sts and in marked st (remove marker), sl st in next 2 sts, turn. 7 sts

**Row 4:** Ch 1 (mark), skip first sl st, sc in next 5 sts, 2 sc in next st, turn. 7 sts

**Row 5:** Ch 1, sc in first 7 sts and in marked st (remove marker), sl st in next 2 sts, turn. 10 sts

**Row 6:** Ch 1 (mark), skip first sl st, sc in next 8 sts, 2 sc in next st, turn. 10 sts

**Row 7:** Ch 1, sc in first 10 sts and in marked st (remove marker), sl st in next 2 sts, turn. 13 sts

**Row 8:** Ch 1 (mark), skip first sl st, sc in next 11 sts, 2 sc in next st, turn. 13 sts

**Row 9:** Ch 1, sc in first 13 sts and in marked st (remove marker), sl st in next 2 sts, turn. 16 sts

**Row 10:** Ch 1 (mark), skip first sl st, sc in next 14 sts, 2 sc in next st, turn. 16 sts

**Row 11:** Ch 1, sc in first 16 sts and in marked st (remove marker), do not turn. 17 sts

Beginning Shell complete.

Continue to work Full Shells.

# Full Shell Chart

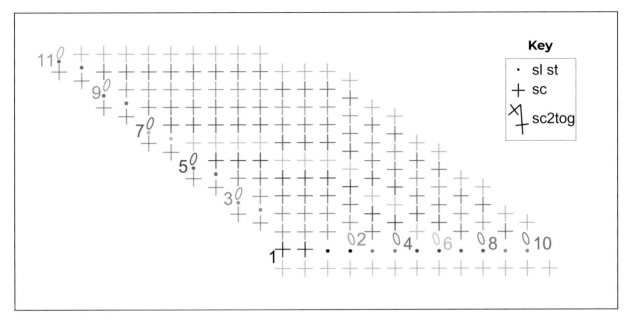

*Gray sts are previous shell (on left) and previous column (below).*

To make it easier to navigate the upcoming sections of this pattern, each shell or shell-part is color-coded with its own unique color (**grey**, **blue**, **purple** and **peach**). When you are instructed to repeat a specific shell or shell section, please look for instructions in the corresponding color.

## Full Shell

**Row 1:** Sc in next 2 sts, sl st in next 2 sts, turn. 4 sts

**Row 2:** Ch 1 (mark), skip first sl st, sc in next 3 sts, sl st in next 2 sts of prev shell, turn. 5 sts

**Row 3:** Ch 1 (mark), skip first sl st, sc in next 4 sts and in marked st (remove marker), sl st in next 2 sts, turn. 7 sts

**Row 4:** Ch 1 (mark), skip first sl st, sc in next 6 sts and in marked st (remove marker), sl st in next 2 sts of prev shell, turn. 9 sts

**Row 5:** Ch 1 (mark), skip first sl st, sc in next 8 sts and in marked st (remove marker), sl st in next 2 sts, turn. 11 sts

**Row 6:** Ch 1 (mark), skip first sl st, sc in next 10 sts and in marked st (remove marker), sl st in next 2 sts of prev shell, turn. 13 sts

**Row 7:** Ch 1 (mark), skip first sl st, sc in next 12 sts and in marked st (remove marker), sl st in next 2 sts, turn. 15 sts

**Row 8:** Ch 1 (mark), skip first sl st, sc in next 14 sts and in marked st (remove marker), sl st in next 2 sts of prev shell, turn. 17 sts

**Row 9:** Ch 1 (mark), skip first sl st, sc in next 16 sts and in marked st (remove marker), sl st in next 2 sts, turn. 19 sts

**Row 10:** Ch 1 (mark), skip first sl st, sc in next 18 sts and in marked st (remove marker), sl st in next 2 sts of prev shell, turn. 21 sts

**Row 11:** Ch 1 (mark), skip first sl st, sc in next 20 sts and in marked st (remove marker), do not turn. 21 sts

**Full Shell complete.**

Make 4 (4, 4, 4, 4) (4, 5, 5, 5) Full Shells total in Column 1.

Continue to work End Shell with Ribbing.

End Shell with Ribbing

**Row 1:** Sc in next 2 sts, sl st in next 2 sts, turn. 4 sts

**Row 2:** Ch 1 (mark), skip first sl st, sc in next 3 sts, sl st in next 2 sts of prev shell, turn. 5 sts

**Row 3:** Ch 1 (mark), skip first sl st, sc in next 4 sts and in marked st (remove marker), sc in next 1 (1, 1, 7, 7) (7, 1, 1, 1) st(s), sl st in next 9 sts, turn. 15 (15, 15, 21, 21) (21, 15, 15, 15) sts

**Row 4:** Ch 1, sl st in first 9 sts, skip next st, sc in next 5 (5, 5, 11, 11) (11, 5, 5, 5) sts and in marked st (remove marker), sl st in next 2 sts of prev shell, turn. 17 (17, 17, 23, 23) (23, 17, 17, 17) sts

**Row 5:** Ch 1 (mark), skip first sl st, sc in next 7 (7, 7, 13, 13) (13, 7, 7, 7) sts, sl st in next 9 sts, turn. 16 (16, 16, 22, 22) (22, 16, 16, 16) sts

**Row 6:** Ch 1, sl st in first 9 sts, skip next st, sc in next 6 (6, 6, 12, 12) (12, 6, 6, 6) sts and in marked st (remove marker), sl st in next 2 sts of prev shell, turn. 18 (18, 18, 24, 24) (24, 18, 18, 18) sts

**Row 7:** Ch 1 (mark), skip first sl st, sc in next 8 (8, 8, 14, 14) (14, 8, 8, 8) sts, sl st in next 9 sts, turn. 17 (17, 17, 23, 23) (23, 17, 17, 17) sts

**Row 8:** Ch 1, sl st in first 9 sts, skip next st, sc in next 7 (7, 7, 13, 13) (13, 7, 7, 7) sts and in marked st (remove marker), sl st in next 2 sts of prev shell, turn. 19 (19, 19, 25, 25) (25, 19, 19, 19) sts

**Row 9:** Ch 1 (mark), skip first sl st, sc in next 9 (9, 9, 15, 15) (15, 9, 9, 9) sts, sl st in next 9 sts, turn. 18 (18, 18, 24, 24) (24, 18, 18, 18) sts

**Row 10:** Ch 1, sl st in first 9 sts, skip next st, sc in next 8 (8, 8, 14, 14) (14, 8, 8, 8) sts and in marked st (remove marker), sl st in next 2 sts of prev shell, turn. 20 (20, 20, 26, 26) (26, 20, 20, 20) sts

**Row 11:** Ch 1 (mark), skip first sl st, sc in next 10 (10, 10, 16, 16) (16, 10, 10, 10) sts, sl st in next 9 sts, turn. 19 (19, 19, 25, 25) (25, 19, 19, 19) sts

**End Shell with Ribbing complete.**

**Next row:** Ch 1, sl st in first 9 sts, skip next st, sc in next 9 (9, 9, 15, 15) (15, 9, 9, 9) sts and in marked st (remove marker). [Sc in next 11 sts and in marked st (remove marker)] 4 (4, 4, 4, 4) (4, 5, 5, 5) times. Sc in next 7 sts, turn. 74 (74, 74, 80, 80) (80, 86, 86, 86) sts

**Next row:** Ch 1, sc in first 65 (65, 65, 71, 71) (71, 77, 77, 77) sts, sl st in next 9 sts, turn.

Column 1 completed.

Continue to work Column 2.

## Column 2

(Consists of 1 Beginning Shell with Ribbing, Full Shells and 1 End Shell)

### Beginning Shell with Ribbing

**Row 1:** Ch 1, sl st in next 9 sts, sc in next 2 (2, 2, 8, 8) (8, 2, 2, 2) sts, sl st in next 2 sts, turn. 13 (13, 13, 19, 19) (19, 13, 13, 13) sts

**Row 2:** Ch 1 (mark), skip first sl st, sc in next 2 (2, 2, 8, 8) (8, 2, 2, 2) sts, 2 sc in next st, sl st in next 9 sts, turn. 13 (13, 13, 19, 19) (19, 13, 13, 13) sts

**Row 3:** Ch 1, sl st in first 9 sts, sc in next 4 (4, 4, 10, 10) (10, 4, 4, 4) sts and in marked st (remove marker), sl st in next 2 sts, turn. 16 (16, 16, 22, 22) (22, 16, 16, 16) sts

**Row 4:** Ch 1 (mark), skip first sl st, sc in next 5 (5, 5, 11, 11) (11, 5, 5, 5) sts, 2 sc in next st, sl st in next 9 sts, turn. 16 (16, 16, 22, 22) (22, 16, 16, 16) sts

**Row 5:** Ch 1, sl st in first 9 sts, sc in next 7 (7, 7, 13, 13) (13, 7, 7, 7) sts and in marked st (remove marker), sl st in next 2 sts, turn. 19 (19, 19, 25, 25) (25, 19, 19, 19) sts

**Row 6:** Ch 1 (mark), skip first sl st, sc in next 8 (8, 8, 14, 14) (14, 8, 8, 8) sts, 2 sc in next st, sl st in next 9 sts, turn. 19 (19, 19, 25, 25) (25, 19, 19, 19) sts

**Row 7:** Ch 1, sl st in first 9 sts, sc in next 10 (10, 10, 16, 16) (16, 10, 10, 10) sts and in marked st (remove marker), sl st in next 2 sts, turn. 22 (22, 22, 28, 28) (28, 22, 22, 22) sts

**Row 8:** Ch 1 (mark), skip first sl st, sc in next 11 (11, 11, 17, 17) (17, 11, 11, 11) sts, 2 sc in next st, sl st in next 9 sts, turn. 22 (22, 22, 28, 28) (28, 22, 22, 22) sts

**Row 9:** Ch 1, sl st in first 9 sts, sc in next 13 (13, 13, 19, 19) (19, 13, 13, 13) sts and in marked st (remove marker), sl st in next 2 sts, turn. 25 (25, 25, 31, 31) (31, 25, 25, 25) sts

**Row 10:** Ch 1 (mark), skip first sl st, sc in next 14 (14, 14, 20, 20) (20, 14, 14, 14) sts, 2 sc in next st, sl st in next 9 sts, turn. 25 (25, 25, 31, 31) (31, 25, 25, 25) sts

**Row 11:** Ch 1, sl st in first 9 sts, sc in next 16 (16, 16, 22, 22) (22, 16, 16, 16) sts and in marked st (remove marker), do not turn. 26 (26, 26, 32, 32) (32, 26, 26, 26) sts

**Beginning Shell with Ribbing complete.**

Make 4 (4, 4, 4, 4) (4, 5, 5, 5) Full Shells (see Column 1 [page 60]) total in Column 2.

### End Shell

**Row 1:** Sc in next 2 sts, sl st in next 2 sts, turn. 4 sts

**Row 2:** Ch 1 (mark), skip first sl st, sc in next 3 sts, sl st in next 2 sts of prev shell, turn. 5 sts

**Row 3:** Ch 1 (mark), skip first sl st, sc in next 4 sts and in marked st (remove marker), sl st in next st, turn. 6 sts

**Row 4:** Ch 1, skip sl st, sc in next 5 sts and in marked st (remove marker), sl st in next 2 sts of prev shell, turn. 8 sts

**Row 5:** Ch 1 (mark), skip first sl st, sc in next 7 sts, turn. 7 sts

**Row 6:** Ch 1, skip first st, sc in next 6 sts and in marked st (remove marker), sl st in next 2 sts of prev shell, turn. 9 sts

**Row 7:** Ch 1 (mark), skip first sl st, sc in next 8 sts, turn. 8 sts

**Row 8:** Ch 1, skip first st, sc in next 7 sts and in marked st (remove marker), sl st in next 2 sts of prev shell, turn. 10 sts

**Row 9:** Ch 1 (mark), skip first sl st, sc in next 9 sts, turn. 9 sts

**Row 10:** Ch 1, skip first st, sc in next 8 sts and in marked st (remove marker), sl st in next 2 sts of prev shell, turn. 11 sts

**Row 11:** Ch 1 (mark), skip first sl st, sc in next 10 sts, turn. 10 sts

**End Shell complete.**

**Next row:** Ch 1, skip first st, sc in next 9 sts and in marked st (remove marker). [Sc in next 11 sts and in marked st (remove marker)] 4 (4, 4, 4, 4) (4, 5, 5, 5) times. Sc in next 7 (7, 7, 13, 13) (13, 7, 7, 7) sts, sl st in next 9 sts, turn. 74 (74, 74, 80, 80) (80, 86, 86, 86) sts

**Next row:** Ch 1, sl st in first 9 sts, sc in next 65 (65, 65, 71, 71) (71, 77, 77, 77) sts, turn.

**Sizes 1–3:** Continue to Neckline Columns.

## Column 3

**Sizes 4–9 only:** Repeat instructions for Column 1.

**Sizes 4–6:** Continue to Neckline Columns.

**Sizes 7–9:** Continue to Column 4.

## Column 4

**Sizes 7–9 only:** Repeat instructions for Column 2.

Continue to Neckline Columns.

# Neckline Columns

**All sizes:** Make 3 columns to form the Neckline following instructions for your size.

**Sizes 1–3 and 7–9 only:** (sizes 4–6 Neckline Columns are on pages 68–69)

## Neckline Column 1 (Sizes 1–3 and 7–9)

### Beginning Shell with Neck Shaping

**Row 1:** Ch 1, sc in first 2 sts, sl st in next 2 sts, turn. 4 sts

**Row 2:** Ch 1 (mark), skip first sl st, sc in next 3 sts, turn. 3 sts

**Row 3:** Ch 1, skip first st, sc in next 2 sts and in marked st (remove marker), sl st in next 2 sts, turn. 5 sts

**Row 4:** Ch 1 (mark), skip first sl st, sc in next 4 sts, turn. 4 sts

**Row 5:** Ch 1, skip first st, sc in next 3 sts and in marked st (remove marker), sl st in next 2 sts, turn. 6 sts

**Row 6:** Ch 1 (mark), skip first sl st, sc in next 5 sts, turn. 5 sts

**Row 7:** Ch 1, skip first st, sc in next 4 sts and in marked st (remove marker), sl st in next 2 sts, turn. 7 sts

**Row 8:** Ch 1 (mark), skip first sl st, sc in next 6 sts, turn. 6 sts

**Row 9:** Ch 1, skip first st, sc in next 5 sts and in marked st (remove marker), sl st in next 2 sts, turn. 8 sts

**Row 10:** Ch 1 (mark), skip first sl st, sc in next 7 sts, turn. 7 sts

**Row 11:** Ch 1, skip first st, sc in next 6 sts and in marked st (remove marker), do not turn. 7 sts

Beginning Shell with Neck Shaping complete.

## Beginning Shell with Neck Shaping Chart

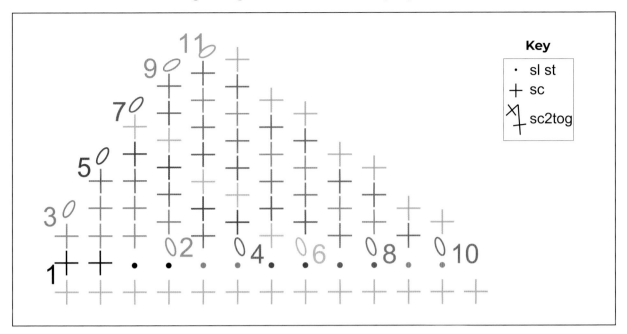

**Key**

| | |
|---|---|
| · | sl st |
| + | sc |
| ⅄ | sc2tog |

### Next Shell

**Rows 1–9:** Rep **Full Shell** Rows 1–9 (see Starting Column 1 [page 60]). 19 sts

**Row 10:** Ch 1 (mark), skip first sl st, sc in next 18 sts, do not work into marked st (remove marker), turn. 18 sts

**Row 11:** Ch 1, sc in first 18 sts and in marked st (remove marker). 19 sts

Next Shell completed.

**Next 3 (3, 3, x, x) (x, 4, 4, 4) Full Shells:**
Repeat instructions for Starting Column 1 Full Shell.

You should now have a Beginning Shell with Neck Shaping and another 4 (4, 4, x, x) (x, 5, 5, 5) Full Shells.

Make 1 **End Shell with Ribbing** (see Column 1 [page 62]).

**Next row:** Ch 1, sl st in first 9 sts, skip next st, sc in next 9 (9, 9, x, x) (x, 9, 9, 9) sts and in marked st (remove marker). [Sc in next 11 sts and in marked st (remove marker)] 3 (3, 3, x, x) (x, 4, 4, 4) times. Sc in next 8 sts, turn. 63 (63, 63, x, x) (x, 75, 75, 75) sts

**Next row:** Ch 1, sc in next 54 (54, 54, x, x) (x, 66, 66, 66) sts, sl st in next 9 sts, turn.

### Neckline Column 2 (Sizes 1–3 and 7–9)

Make 1 **Beginning Shell with Ribbing** (see Starting Column 2 [page 63]).

Make 3 (3, 3, x, x)(x, 4, 4, 4) **Full Shells** (see Starting Column 1 [page 61]).

### Neckline End Shell

**Row 1:** Ch 1, sc in first 2 sts, sl st in next 2 sts, turn. 4 sts

**Row 2:** Ch 1 (mark), skip first sl st, sc in next 3 sts, sl st in next 2 sts of prev shell, turn. 5 sts

**Row 7:** Ch 1 (mark), skip first sl st, sc in next 8 sts, turn. 8 sts

**Row 8:** Ch 1, skip first st, sc in next 7 sts and in marked st (remove marker), sl st in next 2 sts of prev shell, turn. 10 sts

**Row 9:** Ch 1 (mark), skip first sl st, sc in next 9 sts, turn. 9 sts

**Row 10:** Ch 1, skip first st, sc in next 8 sts and in marked st (remove marker), sl st in next 2 sts of prev shell, turn. 11 sts

**Row 11:** Ch 1 (mark), skip first sl st, sc in next 10 sts, turn. 10 sts

Neckline End Shell complete.

**Next row:** Ch 1, sc in first 10 sts and in marked st (remove marker). [Sc in next 11 sts and in marked st (remove marker)] 3 (3, 3, x, x) (x, 4, 4, 4) times. Sc in next 7 (7, 7, x, x) (x, 7, 7, 7) sts, sl st in next 9 sts, turn. 63 (63, 63, x, x) (x, 75, 75, 75) sts

**Next row:** Ch 1, sl st in first 9 sts, sc in next 54 (54, 54, x, x) (x, 66, 66, 66) sts, turn.

## Neckline Column 3 (Sizes 1–3 and 7–9)

### Neckline Beginning Shell

Ch 13 (last ch counts as turning ch on next row), turn. 13 sts

**Row 1:** Sc in 2nd ch from hook and in next 8 ch, 2 sc in next ch, sc in next 2 ch, sl st in next st (on Neckline Column 2), turn. 14 sts

**Row 2:** Ch 1 (mark), skip sl st, sc in next 2 sts, 2 sc in each of next 2 sts, sc in next 6 sts, sl st in next 2 sts, turn. 14 sts

**Row 3:** Ch 1 (mark), skip first sl st, sl st in next 3 sts, sc in next 10 sts, skip marked st (remove marker), sl st in next st (on Neckline Column 2), turn.

**Row 3:** Ch 1 (mark), skip first sl st, sc in next 4 sts and in marked st (remove marker), sl st in next st, turn. 6 sts

**Row 4:** Ch 1, skip sl st, sc in next 5 sts and in marked st (remove marker), sl st in next 2 sts of prev shell, turn. 8 sts

**Row 5:** Ch 1 (mark), skip first sl st, sc in next 7 sts, turn. 7 sts

**Row 6:** Ch 1, skip first st, sc in next 6 sts and in marked st (remove marker), sl st in next 2 sts of prev shell, turn. 9 sts

## Neckline Beginning Shell Chart

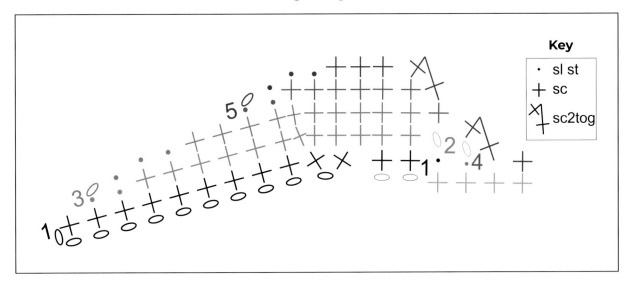

**Key**
- · sl st
- + sc
- ⋏ sc2tog

**Row 4:** Ch 1 (mark), skip sl st, sc in next 7 sts, sl st in next 2 sts, mark next st, turn. 9 sts

**Row 5:** Ch 1 (mark), skip first sl st, sl st in next 3 sts, sc in next 3 sts, sc2tog over next 2 sts, sc2tog over marked st and next st (on Neckline Column 2), remove marker, sc in next st. 9 sts

Neckline Beginning Shell completed.

### Next Shell

**Rows 1–9:** Rep Full Shell Rows 1–9 (see Starting Column 1 [page 60]). 19 sts

**Row 10:** Ch 1 (mark), skip first sl st, sc in next 18 sts and in marked st (remove marker), sl st in next st, sl st in next 2 marked sts (remove markers), turn. 22 sts

**Row 11:** Ch 1 (mark), skip first sl st, sc in next 21 sts and in marked st (remove marker). 22 sts

Next Shell completed.

Make 3 (3, 3, x, x) (x, 4, 4, 4) **Full Shells** total (see Column 1 [page 61]).

### Neckline End Shell with Ribbing

**Rows 1–2:** As for **End Shell with Ribbing** (see Column 1 [page 62]).

**Row 3:** Ch 1 (mark), skip first sl st, sc in next 4 sts and in marked st (remove marker), sl st in next 9 sts, turn. 14 (14, 14, x, x) (x, 14, 14, 14) sts

**Row 4:** Ch 1, sl st in first 9 sts, sc in next 5 (5, 5, x, x) (x, 5, 5, 5) sts and in marked st (remove marker), sl st in next 2 sts of prev shell, turn. 17 (17, 17, x, x) (x, 17, 17, 17) sts

**Rows 5–11:** As for **End Shell with Ribbing** (see Column 1 [page 62]).

**Next row:** Ch 1, sl st in first 9 sts, skip next st, sc in next 9 (9, 9, x, x) (x, 9, 9, 9) sts and in marked st (remove marker). [Sc in next 11 sts and in marked st (remove marker)] 3 (3, 3, x, x) (x, 4, 4, 4) times. Sc in next 12 sts and in marked st (remove marker), Sc in next 3 sts and in next marked st (remove marker), 2 sts in next st, turn. 74 (74, 74, x, x) (x, 86, 86, 86) sts

**Next row:** Ch 1, sc in next 65 (65, 65, x, x) (x, 77, 77, 77) sts, sl st in next 9 sts, turn.

**Sizes 1–3 and 7–9:** Neckline complete.

Continue to Finishing Rows.

## Neckline Column 1 (Sizes 4–6)

Start with **Beginning Shell with Ribbing** (see Column 2 [page 63]).

Make x (x, x, 3, 3) (3, x, x, x) **Full Shells** (see Column 1 [page 61]).

### Neckline End Shell

**Row 1:** Sc in first 7 sts, sl st in next 2 sts, turn. 9 sts

**Row 2:** Ch 1 (mark), skip first sl st, sc in next 8 sts, sl st in next 2 sts of prev shell, turn. 10 sts

**Row 3:** Ch 1 (mark), skip first sl st, sc in next 9 sts and in marked st (remove marker), sl st in next 2 sts, turn. 12 sts

**Row 4:** Ch 1 (mark), skip first sl st, sc in next 11 sts and in marked st (remove marker), sl st in next 2 sts of prev shell, turn. 14 sts

**Row 5:** Ch 1 (mark), skip first sl st, sc in next 13 sts and in marked st (remove marker), sl st in next 2 sts, turn. 16 sts

**Row 6:** Ch 1 (mark), skip first sl st, sc in next 15 sts and in marked st (remove marker), sl st in next 2 sts of prev shell, turn. 18 sts

**Row 7:** Ch 1 (mark), skip first sl st, sc in next 17 sts and in marked st (remove marker), sl st in next 2 sts, turn. 20 sts

**Row 8:** Ch 1 (mark), skip first sl st, sc in next 19 sts and in marked st (remove marker), sl st in next 2 sts of prev shell, turn. 22 sts

**Row 9:** Ch 1 (mark), skip first sl st, sc in next 21 sts and in marked st (remove marker), sl st in next 2 sts, turn. 24 sts

**Row 10:** Ch 1 (mark), skip first sl st, sc in next 23 sts and in marked st (remove marker), do not turn. 24 sts

Continue Row 10—sc in next 13 sts and in marked st (remove marker). [Sc in next 11 sts and in marked st (remove marker)] 2 times, sc in next 13 sts, sl st in next 9 sts, turn. 84 sts

**Next row:** Ch 1, sl st in first 9 sts, sc in next 63 sts, leave remaining sts unworked and turn. 72 sts

**Sizes 4–6:** Neckline Column 1 complete.

## Neckline Column 2 (Sizes 4–6)

### Neckline Beginning Shell

**Row 1:** Ch 1, 2 sc in first st, sc in next 5 sts, sl st in next 2 sts, turn. 9 sts

**Row 2:** Ch 1 (mark), skip first sl st, sc in next 8 sts, turn. 8 sts

**Row 3:** Ch 1, 2 sc in first st, sc in next 7 sts and in marked st (remove marker), sl st in next 2 sts, turn. 12 sts

**Row 4:** Ch 1 (mark), skip first sl st, sc in next 11 sts, turn. 11 sts

**Row 5:** Ch 1, 2 sc in first st, sc in next 10 sts and in marked st (remove marker), sl st in next 2 sts, turn. 15 sts

**Row 6:** Ch 1 (mark), skip first sl st, sc in next 14 sts, turn. 14 sts

**Row 7:** Ch 1, 2 sc in first st, sc in next 13 sts and in marked st (remove marker), sl st in next 2 sts, turn. 18 sts

**Row 8:** Ch 1 (mark), skip first sl st, sc in next 17 sts, turn. 17 sts

**Row 9:** Ch 1, 2 sc in first st, sc in next 16 sts and in marked st (remove marker), sl st in next 2 sts, turn. 21 sts

**Row 10:** Ch 1 (mark), skip first sl st, sc in next 20 sts, turn. 20 sts

**Row 11:** Ch 1, 2 sc in first st, sc in next 19 sts and in marked st (remove marker). 22 sts

Make 3 **Full Shells** (see Column 1 [page 61]).

Make 1 **End Shell with Ribbing** (see Column 1 [page 62]).

**Next row:** Ch 1, sl st in first 9 sts, skip next st, sc in next 15 sts and in marked st (remove marker). [Sc in next 11 sts and in marked st (remove marker)] 3 times. Sc in next 12 sts, turn. 73 sts

**Next row:** Ch 1, sc in next 64 sts, sl st in next 9 sts, turn.

Sizes 4–6: Neckline Column 2 completed.

## Neckline Column 3 (Sizes 4–6)

Make 1 **Beginning Shell with Ribbing** (see Column 2 [page 63]).

Make 3 **Full Shells** (see Column 1 [page 61]).

### End Shell

**Row 1:** Sc in first 9 sts, 2 sc in next st, turn. 11 sts

**Row 2:** Ch 1, 2 sc in first st, sc in next 10 sts, sl st in next 2 sts of prev shell, turn. 14 sts

**Row 3:** Ch 1 (mark), skip first sl st, sc in next 12 sts, 2 sc in next st, turn. 14 sts

**Row 4:** Ch 1, 2 sc in first st, sc in next 13 sts and in marked st (remove marker), sl st in next 2 sts of prev shell, turn. 18 sts

**Row 5:** Ch 1 (mark), skip first sl st, sc in next 16 sts, 2 sc in next st, turn. 18 sts

**Row 6:** Ch 1, 2 sc in first st, sc in next 17 sts and in marked st (remove marker), sl st in next 2 sts of prev shell, turn. 22 sts

**Row 7:** Ch 1 (mark), skip first sl st, sc in next 20 sts, 2 sc in next st, turn. 22 sts

**Row 8:** Ch 1, 2 sc in first st, sc in next 21 sts and in marked st (remove marker), sl st in next 2 sts of prev shell, turn. 26 sts

**Row 9:** Ch 1 (mark), skip first sl st, sc in next 24 sts, 2 sc in next st, turn. 26 sts

**Row 10:** Ch 1, sc in next 26 sts and in marked st (remove marker), sl st in next 2 sts of prev shell, turn. 29 sts

**Row 11:** Ch 1 (mark), skip first sl st, sc in next 28 sts, turn. 28 sts

**Next row:** Ch 1, [sc in next 5 sts, sc2tog over next 2 sts] 4 times, sc in marked st (remove marker). [Sc in next 5 sts, sc2tog over next 2 sts, sc in next 4 sts and in marked st (remove marker)] 3 times. Sc in next 13 sts, sl st in next 9 sts, turn. 80 sts

**Next row:** Ch 1, sl st in first 9 sts, sc in next 71 sts, turn.

Sizes 4–6: Neckline Column 3 completed.

Sizes 4–6: Continue to Finishing Rows.

## Finishing Rows

Sizes 1–3: Make one Column 2, then make one Column 1.

Sizes 4–6: Make one Column 1, then make one Column 2, then one Column 1.

Sizes 7–9: Make [one Column 2, then make one Column 1] twice.

**Next row 1:** Ch 1, sc in next 65 (65, 65, 71, 71) (71, 77, 77, 77) sts, sl st in next 9 sts, turn. 74 (74, 74, 80, 80) (80, 86, 86, 86) sts

**Next row 2:** Ch 1, sl st in next 9 sts, sc in next 65 (65, 65, 71, 71) (71, 77, 77, 77) sts, turn.

Size 1: Fasten off.

**Size 2:** Repeat [Next row 1 and Next row 2] two times (4 more rows total), fasten off.

**Sizes 3, 5, 8:** Repeat [Next row 1 and Next row 2] four times (8 more rows total), fasten off.

**Sizes 4, 7:** Repeat [Next row 1 and Next row 2] one time (2 more rows total), fasten off.

**Sizes 6, 9:** Repeat [Next row 1 and Next row 2] six times (12 more rows total), fasten off.

## Sleeve

Make 2

**How to determine your individual sleeve length:** Measure from the center back of your neck, along your shoulder and down your arm to the wrist (or desired sleeve length) and record this length. Measure from the center back to the end of the shoulder of the sweater before working the sleeve, subtract this length from your neck-wrist measurement to find the difference, find which size corresponds to that measure-ment. As sleeve length is always a very individual measurement, it might differ from the size you were making for the body.

Using your larger hook, ch 61 (60, 59, 58, 57) (56, 55, 54, 53).

**Row 1:** Sc in 2nd ch from hook (first ch counts as turning ch of next row, is not counted as a stitch), sc in next 50 (49, 48, 47, 46) (45, 44, 43, 42) ch, sl st in next 9 ch, turn. 60 (59, 58, 57, 56) (55, 54, 53, 52) sts

**Row 2:** Ch 1, sl st in first 9 sts, sc in next 51 (50, 49, 48, 47) (46, 45, 44, 43) sts, turn.

**Size 1:** Continue to Sleeve Column 1.

**Row 3 (sizes 2–9 only):** Ch 1, sc in first x (50, 49, 48, 47) (46, 45, 44, 43) sts, sl st in next 9 sts, turn.

**Row 4 (sizes 2–9 only):** Ch 1, sl st in first 9 sts, sc in next x (50, 49, 48, 47) (46, 45, 44, 43) sts, turn.

**Sizes 2 and 5:** Fasten off and continue to Sleeve Column 1.

**Sizes 3–4 and 6–9:** Repeat rows 3 and 4 another x (x, 1, 2, x) (1, 2, 4, 5) time(s).

You should now have x (4, 6, 8, 4) (6, 8, 12, 14) rows total.

Continue to Sleeve Column 1.

## Sleeve Column 1

Sleeve Beginning Shell

**Row 1:** Ch 1 (here and throughout—turning ch is not counted as a stitch), sc in first 2 sts, sl st in next 2 sts, turn. 4 sts

**Row 2:** Ch 1 (mark), skip first sl st, sc in next 2 sts, 2 sc in next st, turn. 4 sts

**Row 3:** Ch 1, sc in first 4 sts and in marked st (remove marker), sl st in next 2 sts, turn. 7 sts

**Row 4:** Ch 1 (mark), skip first sl st, sc in next 5 sts, 2 sc in next st, turn. 7 sts

**Row 5:** Ch 1, sc in first 7 sts and in marked st (remove marker), sl st in next 2 sts, turn. 10 sts

**Row 6:** Ch 1 (mark), skip first sl st, sc in next 8 sts, 2 sc in next st, turn. 10 sts

**Row 7:** Ch 1, sc in first 10 sts and in marked st (remove marker), sl st in next 2 sts, turn. 13 sts

**Row 8:** Ch 1 (mark), skip first sl st, sc in next 11 sts, 2 sc in next st, turn. 13 sts

**Row 9:** Ch 1, sc in first 13 sts and in marked st (remove marker), sl st in next 2 sts, turn. 16 sts

**Row 10:** Ch 1 (mark), skip first sl st, sc in next 14 sts, 2 sc in next st, turn. 16 sts

**Row 11:** Ch 1, sc in first 16 sts and in marked st (remove marker). 17 sts

Sleeve Beginning Shell completed.

Make 2 **Full Shells** (see Column 1 of Body [page 61]).

### Sleeve End Shell with Ribbing

**Row 1:** Sc in next 2 sts, sl st in next 2 sts, turn. 4 sts

**Row 2:** Ch 1 (mark), skip first sl st, sc in next 3 sts, sl st in next 2 sts of prev shell, turn. 5 sts

**Row 3:** Ch 1 (mark), skip first sl st, sc in next 4 sts and in marked st (remove marker), sc in next 11 (10, 9, 8, 7) (6, 5, 4, 3) sts, sl st in next 9 sts, turn. 25 (24, 23, 22, 21) (20, 19, 18, 17) sts

**Row 4:** Ch 1, sl st in first 9 sts, skip next st, sc in next 15 (14, 13, 12, 11) (10, 9, 8, 7) sts and in marked st (remove marker), sl st in next 2 sts of prev shell, turn. 27 (26, 25, 24, 23) (22, 21, 20, 19) sts

**Row 5:** Ch 1 (mark), skip first sl st, sc in next 17 (16, 15, 14, 13) (12, 11, 10, 9) sts, sl st in next 9 sts, turn. 26 (25, 24, 23, 22) (21, 20, 19, 18) sts

**Row 6:** Ch 1, sl st in next 9 sts, skip next st, sc in next 16 (15, 14, 13, 12) (11, 10, 9, 8) sts and in marked st (remove marker), sl st in next 2 sts of prev shell, turn. 28 (27, 26, 25, 24) (23, 22, 21, 20) sts

**Row 7:** Ch 1 (mark), skip first sl st, sc in next 18 (17, 16, 15, 14) (13, 12, 11, 10) sts, sl st in next 9 sts, turn. 27 (26, 25, 24, 23) (22, 21, 20, 19) sts

**Row 8:** Ch 1, sl st in first 9 sts, skip next st, sc in next 17 (16, 15, 14, 13) (12, 11, 10, 9) sts and in marked st (remove marker), sl st in next 2 sts of prev shell, turn. 29 (28, 27, 26, 25) (24, 23, 22, 21) sts

**Row 9:** Ch 1 (mark), skip first sl st, sc in next 19 (18, 17, 16, 15) (14, 13, 12, 11) sts, sl st in next 9 sts, turn. 28 (27, 26, 25, 24) (23, 22, 21, 20) sts

**Row 10:** Ch 1, sl st in first 9 sts, skip next st, sc in next 18 (17, 16, 15, 14) (13, 12, 11, 10) sts and in marked st (remove marker), sl st in next 2 sts of prev shell, turn. 30 (29, 28, 27, 26) (25, 24, 23, 22) sts

**Row 11:** Ch 1 (mark), skip first sl st, sc in next 20 (19, 18, 17, 16) (15, 14, 13, 12) sts, sl st in next 9 sts, turn. 29 (28, 27, 26, 25) (24, 23, 22, 21) sts

Sleeve End Shell with ribbing completed.

**Next row:** Ch 1, sl st in first 9 sts, skip next st, sc in next 19 (18, 17, 16, 15) (14, 13, 12, 11) sts and in next marked st (remove marker). [Sc in next 11 sts and in next marked st (remove marker)] twice. Sc in next 7 sts, turn. 60 (59, 58, 57, 56) (55, 54, 53, 52) sts

**Next row:** Ch 1, sc in next 51 (50, 49, 48, 47) (46, 45, 44, 43) sts, sl st in next 9 sts, turn.

Sleeve Column 1 completed.

Continue to Sleeve Column 2.

## Sleeve Column 2

### Sleeve Beginning Shell with Ribbing

**Row 1:** Ch 1, sl st in first 9 sts, sc in next 12 (11, 10, 9, 8) (7, 6, 5, 4) sts, sl st in next 2 sts, turn. 23 (22, 21, 20, 19) (18, 17, 16, 15) sts

**Row 2:** Ch 1 (mark), skip first sl st, sc in next 12 (11, 10, 9, 8) (7, 6, 5, 4) sts, 2 sc in next st, sl st in next 9 sts, turn. 23 (22, 21, 20, 19) (18, 17, 16, 15) sts

**Row 3:** Ch 1, sl st in first 9 sts, sc in next 14 (13, 12, 11, 10) (9, 8, 7, 6) sts and in marked st (remove marker), sl st in next 2 sts, turn. 26 (25, 24, 23, 22) (21, 20, 19, 18) sts

**Row 4:** Ch 1 (mark), skip first sl st, sc in next 15 (14, 13, 12, 11) (10, 9, 8, 7) sts, 2 sc in next st, sl st in next 9 sts, turn. 26 (25, 24, 23, 22) (21, 20, 19, 18) sts

**Row 5:** Ch 1, sl st in first 9 sts, sc in next 17 (16, 15, 14, 13) (12, 11, 10, 9) sts and in marked st (remove marker), sl st in next 2 sts, turn. 29 (28, 27, 26, 25) (24, 23, 22, 21) sts

**Row 6:** Ch 1 (mark), skip first sl st, sc in next 18 (17, 16, 15, 14) (13, 12, 11, 10) sts, 2 sc in next st, sl st in next 9 sts, turn. 29 (28, 27, 26, 25) (24, 23, 22, 21) sts

**Row 7:** Ch 1, sl st in first 9 sts, sc in next 20 (19, 18, 17, 16) (15, 14, 13, 12) sts and in marked st (remove marker), sl st in next 2 sts, turn. 32 (31, 30, 29, 28) (27, 26, 25, 24) sts

**Row 8:** Ch 1 (mark), skip first sl st, sc in next 21 (20, 19, 18, 17) (16, 15, 14, 13) sts, 2 sc in next st, sl st in next 9 sts, turn. 32 (31, 30, 29, 28) (27, 26, 25, 24) sts

**Row 9:** Ch 1, sl st in first 9 sts, sc in next 23 (22, 21, 20, 19) (18, 17, 16, 15) sts and in marked st (remove marker), sl st in next 2 sts, turn. 35 (34, 33, 32, 31) (30, 29, 28, 27) sts

**Row 10:** Ch 1 (mark), skip first sl st, sc in next 24 (23, 22, 21, 20) (19, 18, 17, 16) sts, 2 sc in next st, sl st in next 9 sts, turn. 35 (34, 33, 32, 31) (30, 29, 28, 27) sts

**Row 11:** Ch 1, sl st in first 9 sts, sc in next 26 (25, 24, 23, 22) (21, 20, 19, 18) sts and in marked st (remove marker). 36 (35, 34, 33, 32) (31, 30, 29, 28) sts

Sleeve Beginning Shell with Ribbing completed.

Make 2 **Full Shells** (see Column 1 [page 61]).

Make 1 **End Shell** (See Column 2 [page 63]).

**Next row:** Ch 1, skip first st, sc in next 9 sts and in marked st (remove marker). [Sc in next 11 sts and in marked st (remove marker)] twice. Sc in next 17 (16, 15, 14, 13) (12, 11, 10, 9) sts, sl st in next 9 sts, turn. 60 (59, 58, 57, 56) (55, 54, 53, 52) sts

**Next row:** Ch 1, sl st in first 9 sts, sc in next 51 (50, 49, 48, 47) (46, 45, 44, 43) sts.

**All sizes:** Make 1 more Sleeve Column 1.

**Sizes 1–4:** Continue to Sleeve Finishing Rows.

**Sizes 5–9:** Make 1 more Sleeve Column 2.

## Sleeve Finishing Rows

**Sizes 1–4:** Work Row 1 first, then Row 2.

**Sizes 5–9:** Work Row 2 first, then Row 1.

**Row 1:** Ch 1, sl st in first 9 sts, sc in next 51 (50, 49, 48, 47) (46, 45, 44, 43) sts, turn. 60 (59, 58, 57, 56) (55, 54, 53, 52) sts

**Row 2:** Ch 1, sc in first 51 (50, 49, 48, 47) (46, 45, 44, 43) sts, sl st in next 9 sts, turn.

**Sizes 1–4:** Repeat rows 1 and 2 another 1 (2, 3, 4, x) (x, x, x, x) time(s). [4 (6, 8, 10, x) (x, x, x, x) finishing rows total], fasten off.

**Sizes 5–9:** Repeat rows 2 and 1 another x (x, x, x, 2) (3, 4, 5, 6) times. [x (x, x, x, 6) (8, 10, 12, 14) finishing rows total], fasten off.

## Finishing

Block all parts of the sweater according to fiber type.

Sew both shoulder seams.

## Crew Neck

A crew neck is worked straight onto the neckline.

Have RS facing and, using your smaller hook, attach yarn with sl st to the neckline at either shoulder seam.

**Base round:** Sc around the neckline spreading stitches evenly to get approximately 80 (80, 80, 84, 84) (84, 88, 88, 88) sts total.

(On this round—make regular sc, not in the BL.) Join with sl st to the first st to form a round.

Ch 12 (last ch counts as turning ch of next row), turn. (Begin to work sts in BL again.)

**Row 1:** Work down the chain and attach to the base rnd—sl st in 2nd ch from hook, sl st in next 10 ch, sl st to the next 2 sts of base rnd (work through both loops of base rnd for a more stable attachment). 13 sts

**Row 2:** Work up the chain—skip first st, sl st in next 12 sts, turn. 12 sts

**Row 3:** Ch 1, sl st in next 11 sts, skip next st, sl st in next 2 sts of base rnd (use markers if needed to mark your last worked stitch of base rnd), turn. 13 sts

Repeat rows 2 and 3 around the neckline. Join the last and first rows with sl sts or leave a longer tail and sew the split using whip stitch. Fasten off.

Pin the center of the Sleeve to the outer side of the shoulder seam. Sew the sleeve to Front and Back. Note that in order to look symmetrical, put one sleeve with the RS facing and the other with the WS facing. (There are no particular RS or WS of the sleeves—you can choose which one is which). Sew the sleeve seams and side seams of the sweater, fasten off and weave in all yarn ends.

# Ainava Landscape Sweater

The texture of Ainava is inspired by the ups and downs of a serrated landscape that plays with subtle highlights, shadows and the perception of volume itself. Post stitches of varying heights pile up in lines to create a scenery-like, pleated fabric, like plowed fields sliding by, watched from the passenger seat of a car driving through the countryside in late fall.

# Ainava Landscape Sweater Construction Notes

*Ainava is a bottom-up oversized batwing sweater designed with a mixture of crochet short rows and post stitches. It is started with sideways ribbing, then worked with crochet short rows in triangle-like parts—meaning rows are not crocheted until the end of the row on one side, then the next "triangle" part is worked over the first one. The shoulder parts are worked to overlay each other in the center front and center back. The front and back are each worked separately with shoulders that overlap at the front and back. The shoulder seams are crocheted (or sewn) together. The ribbed sleeves are made separately and sewn on afterwards.*

## Sizes

1 (2, 3, 4, 5) (6, 7, 8, 9)

**To fit bust:** 30 (34, 38, 42, 46) (50, 54, 58, 62)" / 76 (86, 97, 107, 117) (127, 137, 147, 157) cm

**Finished bust:** 48 (52, 56, 59.75, 63.75) (67.75, 71.75, 75.5, 79.5)" / 122 (132, 142, 152, 162) (172, 182, 192, 202) cm

## Gauge

22 sts x 13 rows = 4" / 10 cm in dc after blocking

## Yarn

Fingering weight, Schoppel Admiral Hanf (67% wool, 23% Nylon, 10% Hemp), 459 yds / 420 m per 100-g skein

## Yardage/Meterage

1835 (1995, 2140, 2365, 2505) (2660, 2890, 3055, 3170) yds / 1680 (1825, 1955, 2165, 2290) (2435, 2645, 2795, 2900) m

## Shown in

Colorways 2379 Silky Black and 2377 Elephant Hide

**A Note on Color:** The sample is made in two very similar colorways to add interest, but the amount of yarn is shown for the total yardage/meterage. I suggest using two similar colorways and mixing them up freely as you work the pattern. For example: one color for each short rows triangle, then mix it up for the shoulders and sleeves.

## Hook

G/6 / 4 mm for the main sections of the Body and Sleeves, or size needed to obtain gauge

F/5 / 3.75 mm for Ribbing, or one size smaller than your main gauge hook

## Notions

Tapestry needle for sewing seams

16 stitch markers

## Skills

Experience with making crocheted sweaters

Experience with working post stitches and crochet short rows

## Abbreviations (US terms)

BL = back loop

BPdc = back post double crochet

BPdtr = back post double treble

BPdtr2tog = back post double treble 2 together

BPdtr3tog = back post double treble 3 together

BPhdc = back post half double crochet

BPsc = back post single crochet

BPtr = back post treble

Ch = chain

Dc = double crochet

Dtr = double treble

FPdc = front post double crochet

FPdtr = front post double treble

FPdtr2tog = front post double treble 2 together

FPdtr3tog = front post double treble 3 together

FPhdc = front post half double crochet

FPsc = front post single crochet

FPtr = front post treble

Hdc = half double crochet

Rem = remaining

RS = right side

Sc = single crochet

Sc-hdc-tog = single crochet and half double crochet together (see Special Stitch).

Sl st(s) = slip stitch(es)

St(s) = stitch(es)

Tr = treble

WS = wrong side

Yo = yarn over

## Special stitch

**Sc-hdc-tog:** insert hook in indicated st, yo, draw yarn through st, yo, insert hook in next indicated st, yo, draw yarn through st, yo, draw yarn through all 4 loops on hook.

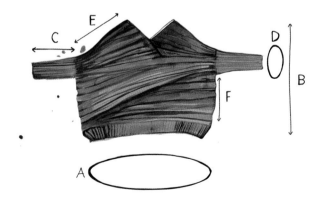

| Size | A—finished bust | B—length | C—sleeve length | D—upper arm | E—shoulder width | F—height of one short rows section |
|---|---|---|---|---|---|---|
| 1 | 48" / 122 cm | 18.5" / 47 cm | 9" / 23 cm | 9" / 23 cm | 8.5" / 21.5 cm | 9" / 23 cm |
| 2 | 52" / 132 cm | 19" / 48 cm | 9" / 23 cm | 9.5" / 24 cm | 8.75" / 22.5 cm | 9" / 23 cm |
| 3 | 56" / 142 cm | 19" / 48 cm | 9" / 23 cm | 9.75" / 25 cm | 10" / 25.5 cm | 9" / 23 cm |
| 4 | 59.75" / 152 cm | 20.5" / 52 cm | 9" / 23 cm | 10.25" / 26 cm | 10.5" / 27 cm | 9" / 23 cm |
| 5 | 63.75" / 162 cm | 20.5" / 52 cm | 9" / 23 cm | 10.5" / 27 cm | 11.5" / 29.5 cm | 9" / 23 cm |
| 6 | 67.75" / 172 cm | 20.5" / 52 cm | 9" / 23 cm | 11" / 28 cm | 12.5" / 32 cm | 9" / 23 cm |
| 7 | 71.75" / 182 cm | 22" / 56 cm | 9" / 23 cm | 11.5" / 29 cm | 13" / 33.5 cm | 9" / 23 cm |
| 8 | 75.5" / 192 cm | 22" / 56 cm | 9" / 23 cm | 11.75" / 30 cm | 14.25" / 36 cm | 9" / 23 cm |
| 9 | 79.5" / 202 cm | 22" / 56 cm | 9" / 23 cm | 12.25" / 31 cm | 15.25" / 38.5 cm | 9" / 23 cm |

*Body ribbing measures 1.5" / 4 cm. The sweater is designed with 18 (18, 18, 17.75, 17.75) (17.75, 17.75, 17.5, 17.5)" / 46 (46, 46, 45, 45) (45, 45, 44.5, 44.5) cm positive ease. Size 2 is modeled on 30" / 77-cm bust model.*

# Ainava Landscape Sweater Pattern

**Throughout:** Ch 1 at the beginning of row counts as turning chain and is not counted as a stitch.

Ch 2: Counts as first hdc (= 1 st).

Ch 3: Counts as first tr (= 1 st).

Ch 4: Counts as double treble (= 1 st).

## Front

### Front Ribbing

With smaller hook, ch 13 (last 2 ch counts as first hdc on next row).

**Row 1:** Hdc in third ch from hook, hdc in each ch across, turn. 12 sts

**Rows 2–84 (–92, –99, –106, –114) (–121, –128, –136, –143):** Ch 2, hdc in BL across, turn. 12 sts

**After last row of the ribbing:** Don't turn. Rotate the ribbing clockwise by 90 degrees.

## Body

Change to larger hook.

**Row 1 (sizes 1, 2, 4, 5, 7, 8)(RS):** Ch 1, sc across rib rows working 3 sc in each 2 row ends, work an additional 1 (0, x, 1, 0) (x, 1, 0, x) sc in last rib row, turn. 127 (138, x, 160, 171) (x, 193, 204, x) sts

**Row 1 (sizes 3, 6, 9)(RS):** Ch 1, sc across rib rows working 3 sc in each 2 row ends to last rib row, work 2 sc in last rib row, turn. x (x, 149, x, x) (182, x, x, 215) sts

**Row 2 (all sizes):** (WS) Ch 3, tr across, turn.

**Row 3:** Ch 4, BPdtr across, turn.

**Row 4:** Ch 4, FPdtr across, turn.

Sizes 1, 2, 3: Continue to Short Rows Part 1.

Sizes 4, 5, 6: Repeat rows 3–4 one time.

Sizes 7, 8, 9: Repeat rows 3–4 twice.

### Short Rows Part 1

One side of the short rows is straight while the other decreases every two rows, creating a triangle. Start with 127 (138, 149, 160, 171) (182, 193, 204, 215) sts.

**Row 1 (RS):** Ch 4, BPdtr around next 76 (87, 98, 109, 120) (131, 142, 153, 164) sts, BPtr around next 10 sts, BPdc around next 10 sts, BPhdc around next 10 sts, BPsc around next 10 sts, mark next st and turn. Leave rem 10 sts unworked. 117 (128, 139, 150, 161) (172, 183, 194, 205) sts

**Row 2 (WS):** Ch 1, sc in first 10 sts (mark first and last [tenth] sc made), hdc in next 10 sts, FPdc around next 10 sts, FPtr around next 10 sts, FPdtr around next 77 (88, 99, 110, 121) (132, 143, 154, 165) sts, turn. 117 (128, 139, 150, 161) (172, 183, 194, 205) sts

**Row 3:** Ch 4, BPdtr around next 66 (77, 88, 99, 110) (121, 132, 143, 154) sts, BPtr around next 10 sts, BPdc around next 10 sts, BPhdc around next 10 sts, BPsc around next 10 sts, turn. Leave rem 10 sts unworked. 107 (118, 129, 140, 151) (162, 173, 184, 195) sts

**Row 4:** Ch 1, sc in first 10 sts (mark first and last [tenth] sc made), hdc in next 10 sts, FPdc around next 10 sts, FPtr around next 10 sts, FPdtr around next 67 (78, 89, 100, 111) (122, 133, 144, 155) sts, turn. 107 (118, 129, 140, 151) (162, 173, 184, 195) sts

**Row 5:** Ch 4, BPdtr around next 56 (67, 78, 89, 100) (111, 122, 133, 144) sts, BPtr around next 10 sts, BPdc around next 10 sts, BPhdc around next 10 sts, BPsc around next 10 sts, turn. Leave rem 10 sts unworked. 97 (108, 119, 130, 141) (152, 163, 174, 185) sts

**Row 6:** Ch 1, sc in first 10 sts (mark first and last [tenth] sc made), hdc in next 10 sts, FPdc around next 10 sts, FPtr around next 10 sts, FPdtr around next 57 (68, 79, 90, 101) (112, 123, 134, 145) sts, turn. 97 (108, 119, 130, 141) (152, 163, 174, 185) sts

**Row 7:** Ch 4, BPdtr around next 46 (57, 68, 79, 90) (101, 112, 123, 134) sts, BPtr around next 10 sts, BPdc around next 10 sts, BPhdc around next 10 sts, BPsc around next 10 sts, turn. Leave rem 10 sts unworked. 87 (98, 109, 120, 131) (142, 153, 164, 175) sts

**Row 8:** Ch 1, sc in first 10 sts (mark first and last [tenth] sc made), hdc in next 10 sts, FPdc around next 10 sts, FPtr around next 10 sts, FPdtr around next 47 (58, 69, 80, 91) (102, 113, 124, 135) sts, turn. 87 (98, 109, 120, 131) (142, 153, 164, 175) sts

**Row 9:** Ch 4, BPdtr around next 36 (47, 58, 69, 80) (91, 102, 113, 124) sts, BPtr around next 10 sts, BPdc around next 10 sts, BPhdc around next 10 sts, BPsc around next 10 sts, turn. Leave rem 10 sts unworked. 77 (88, 99, 110, 121) (132, 143, 154, 165) sts

**Row 10:** Ch 1, sc in first 10 sts (mark first and last [tenth] sc made), hdc in next 10 sts, FPdc around next 10 sts, FPtr around next 10 sts, FPdtr around next 37 (48, 59, 70, 81) (92, 103, 114, 125) sts, turn. 77 (88, 99, 110, 121) (132, 143, 154, 165) sts

**Row 11:** Ch 4, BPdtr around next 26 (37, 48, 59, 70) (81, 92, 103, 114) sts, BPtr around next 10 sts, BPdc around next 10 sts, BPhdc around next 10 sts, BPsc around next 10 sts, turn. Leave rem 10 sts unworked. 67 (78, 89, 100, 111) (122, 133, 144, 155) sts

**Row 12:** Ch 1, sc in first 10 sts (mark first and last [tenth] sc made), hdc in next 10 sts, FPdc around next 10 sts, FPtr around next 10 sts, FPdtr around next 27 (38, 49, 60, 71) (82, 93, 104, 115) sts, turn. 67 (78, 89, 100, 111) (122, 133, 144, 155) sts

**Row 13:** Ch 4, BPdtr around next 16 (27, 38, 49, 60) (71, 82, 93, 104) sts, BPtr around next 10 sts, BPdc around next 10 sts, BPhdc around next 10 sts, BPsc around next 10 sts, turn. Leave rem 10 sts unworked. 57 (68, 79, 90, 101) (112, 123, 134, 145) sts

**Row 14:** Ch 1, sc in first 10 sts (mark first and last [tenth] sc made), hdc in next 10 sts, FPdc around next 10 sts, FPtr around next 10 sts, FPdtr around next 17 (28, 39, 50, 61) (72, 83, 94, 105) sts, turn. 57 (68, 79, 90, 101) (112, 123, 134, 145) sts

**Row 15:** Ch 4, BPdtr around next 6 (17, 28, 39, 50) (61, 72, 83, 94) sts, BPtr around next 10 sts, BPdc around next 10 sts, BPhdc around next 10 sts, BPsc around next 10 sts, turn. Leave rem 10 sts unworked. 47 (58, 69, 80, 91) (102, 113, 124, 135) sts

**Row 16:** Ch 1, sc in first 10 sts (mark only first sc made), hdc in next 10 sts, FPdc around next 10 sts, FPtr around next 10 sts, FPdtr around next 7 (18, 29, 40, 51) (62, 73, 84, 95) sts, turn. 47 (58, 69, 80, 91) (102, 113, 124, 135) sts

The next row is worked over all short rows and over the unworked sts at the beginning of Short Rows Part 1.

**Closing row:** Ch 1, sc in first 46 (57, 68, 79, 90) (101, 112, 123, 134) sts. [Sc-hdc-tog over next 2 marked sts (remove both markers), 2 sc in next st, sc in next 7 sts] 8 times. Sc in last st, turn. 127 (138, 149, 160, 171) (182, 193, 204, 215) sts

## Short Rows Part 2

**Row 1** (WS): Ch 3, tr across, turn.

**Row 2:** Ch 4, BPdtr across, turn.

Repeat the instructions for Short Rows Part 1 starting from row 1 and ending after completing the closing row. The indicated RS will now be the WS and vice versa; therefore, work FP sts instead of BP sts and vice versa throughout.

**Next row 1** (RS): Ch 3, tr across, turn.

**Next row 2:** Ch 4, FPdtr across, turn.

**Next row 3:** Ch 4, BPdtr across, turn.

**Last row of Body:** Ch 1, BPsc across, turn and continue to work Shoulder 1.

# Shoulder 1

After finishing the Body, you have 127 (138, 149, 160, 171) (182, 193, 204, 215) sts.

With WS facing you can see two parallel rows of sts, you'll be working Shoulder 1 into the row that's farther away from you (into BPdtr sts).

**Working direction:** From side to center.

**Row 1** (RS): Ch 1, sc in first 10 sts, hdc in next 10 sts, dc in next 10 sts, tr in next 35 (40, 46, 51, 57) (62, 68, 73, 79) sts, dc in next 3 sts, hdc in next 3 sts, sc in next 2 sts, turn. Leave rem sts unworked. 73 (78, 84, 89, 95) (100, 106, 111, 117) sts

**Row 2:** (Ch 4, BPdtr2tog) over first 3 sts (here and throughout Shoulder—counts as first BPdtr3tog = 1 st), BPdtr around next 30 (35, 41, 46, 52) (57, 63, 68, 74) sts, BPtr around next 10 sts, BPdc around next 10 sts, hdc in next 10 sts, sc in last 10 sts, turn. 71 (76, 82, 87, 93) (98, 104, 109, 115) sts

**Row 3:** Ch 1, FPsc around first 10 sts, FPhdc around next 10 sts, FPdc around next 10 sts, FPtr around next 10 sts, FPdtr around next 28 (33, 39, 44, 50) (55, 61, 66, 72) sts, FPdtr3tog over last 3 sts, turn. 69 (74, 80, 85, 91) (96, 102, 107, 113) sts

**Row 4:** (Ch 4, BPdtr2tog) over first 3 sts, BPdtr around next 26 (31, 37, 42, 48) (53, 59, 64, 70) sts, BPtr around next 10 sts, BPdc around next 10 sts, hdc in next 10 sts, sc in last 10 sts, turn. 67 (72, 78, 83, 89) (94, 100, 105, 111) sts

**Row 5:** Ch 1, FPsc around first 10 sts, FPhdc around next 10 sts, FPdc around next 10 sts, FPtr around next 10 sts, FPdtr around next 24 (29, 35, 40, 46) (51, 57, 62, 68) sts, FPdtr3tog over last 3 sts, turn. 65 (70, 76, 81, 87) (92, 98, 103, 109) sts

**Row 6:** (Ch 4, BPdtr2tog) over first 3 sts, BPdtr around next 22 (27, 33, 38, 44) (49, 55, 60, 66) sts, BPtr around next 10 sts, BPdc around next 10 sts, hdc in next 10 sts, sc in last 10 sts, turn. 63 (68, 74, 79, 85) (90, 96, 101, 107) sts

**Row 7:** Ch 1, FPsc around first 10 sts, FPhdc around next 10 sts, FPdc around next 10 sts, FPtr around next 10 sts, FPdtr around next 20 (25, 31, 36, 42) (47, 53, 58, 64) sts, FPdtr3tog over last 3 sts, turn. 61 (66, 72, 77, 83) (88, 94, 99, 105) sts

**Row 8:** (Ch 4, BPdtr2tog) over first 3 sts, BPdtr around next 18 (23, 29, 34, 40) (45, 51, 56, 62) sts, BPtr around next 10 sts, BPdc around next 10 sts, hdc in next 10 sts, sc in last 10 sts, turn. 59 (64, 70, 75, 81) (86, 92, 97, 103) sts

**Row 9:** Ch 1, FPsc around first 10 sts, FPhdc around next 10 sts, FPdc around next 10 sts, FPtr around next 10 sts, FPdtr around next 16 (21, 27, 32, 38) (43, 49, 54, 60) sts, FPdtr3tog over last 3 sts, turn. 57 (62, 68, 73, 79) (84, 90, 95, 101) sts

**Row 10:** (Ch 4, BPdtr2tog) over first 3 sts, BPdtr around next 14 (19, 25, 30, 36) (41, 47, 52, 58) sts, BPtr around next 10 sts, BPdc around next 10 sts, hdc in next 10 sts, sc in last 10 sts, turn. 55 (60, 66, 71, 77) (82, 88, 93, 99) sts

**Row 11:** Ch 1, FPsc around first 10 sts, FPhdc around next 10 sts, FPdc around next 10 sts, FPtr around next 10 sts, FPdtr around next 12 (17, 23, 28, 34) (39, 45, 50, 56) sts, FPdtr3tog over last 3 sts, turn. 53 (58, 64, 69, 75) (80, 86, 91, 97) sts

**Row 12:** (Ch 4, BPdtr2tog) over first 3 sts, BPdtr around next 10 (15, 21, 26, 32) (37, 43, 48, 54) sts, BPtr around next 10 sts, BPdc around next 10 sts, hdc in next 10 sts, sc in last 10 sts, turn. 51 (56, 62, 67, 73) (78, 84, 89, 95) sts

**Row 13:** Ch 1, FPsc around first 10 sts, FPhdc around next 10 sts, FPdc around next 10 sts, FPtr around next 10 sts, FPdtr around next 8 (13, 19, 24, 30) (35, 41, 46, 52) sts, FPdtr3tog over last 3 sts, turn. 49 (54, 60, 65, 71) (76, 82, 87, 93) sts

**Row 14:** (Ch 4, BPdtr2tog) over first 3 sts, BPdtr around next 6 (11, 17, 22, 28) (33, 39, 44, 50) sts, BPtr around next 10 sts, BPdc around next 10 sts, hdc in next 10 sts, sc in last 10 sts, turn. 47 (52, 58, 63, 69) (74, 80, 85, 91) sts

**Size 1:** Fasten off.

**Sizes 2–9:** Continue to work from row 15.

**Row 15:** Ch 1, FPsc around first 10 sts, FPhdc around next 10 sts, FPdc around next 10 sts, FPtr around next 10 sts, FPdtr around next x (9, 15, 20, 26) (31, 37, 42, 48) sts, FPdtr3tog over last 3 sts, turn. x (50, 56, 61, 67) (72, 78, 83, 89) sts

**Sizes 2–3:** Fasten off.

**Sizes 4–9:** Continue to work from row 16.

**Row 16:** (Ch 4, BPdtr2tog) over first 3 sts, BPdtr around next x (x, x, 18, 24) (29, 35, 40, 46) sts, BPtr around next 10 sts, BPdc around next 10 sts, hdc in next 10 sts, sc in last 10 sts, turn. x (x, x, 59, 65) (70, 76, 81, 87) sts

**Size 4–6:** Fasten off.

**Sizes 7–9:** Continue to work from row 17.

**Row 17:** Ch 1, FPsc around first 10 sts, FPhdc around next 10 sts, FPdc around next 10 sts, FPtr around next 10 sts, FPdtr around next x (x, x, x, x) (x, 33, 38, 44) sts, FPdtr3tog over last 3 sts, turn. x (x, x, x, x) (x, 74, 79, 85) sts

**Sizes 7–9:** Fasten off.

## Shoulder 2

Attach yarn to the other end of last row of Body. With RS facing you can see two parallel rows of sts, you'll be working Shoulder 2 into the row that's farther away from you (into BPsc sts).

**Working direction:** From side to center.

**Repeat instructions for Shoulder 1:** The indicated RS will now be the WS and vice versa; therefore work FP sts instead of BP sts and vice versa throughout.

## Back

Repeat instructions for Front starting from Ribbing up through both Shoulders. Don't fasten the shoulders off.

Take the Front and put both—Front and Back—parts together with RS facing each other.

**Crochet each shoulder seam together using sl sts:** Ch 1 (turning ch), insert hook through both loops of first st of Back and through both loops of Front, yo and pull yarn through all loops on hook, continue to work like this across all sts of the shoulder, fasten off. (Or you can sew the shoulder seam if you prefer.)

**Row 2:** Ch 2, hdc in BL of next 29 sts, sc in BL of next 10 sts, mark next st, turn. Leave rem sts unworked. 40 sts

**Row 3:** Ch 1, sc in BL of first 15 sts, hdc in BL of next 25 sts, turn. 40 sts

**Row 4:** Ch 2, hdc in BL of next 19 sts, sc in BL of next 10 sts, mark next st, turn. Leave rem sts unworked. 30 sts

**Row 5:** Ch 1, sc in BL of first 15 sts, hdc in BL of next 15 sts, turn. 30 sts

**Row 6:** Ch 2, hdc in BL of next 9 sts, sc in BL of next 10 sts, mark next st, turn. Leave rem sts unworked. 20 sts

**Row 7:** Ch 1, sc in BL of next 15 sts, hdc in BL of next 5 sts, turn. 20 sts

**Row 8:** Ch 1, sc in first 19 sts. [Sc-hdc-tog over next and next marked st, 2 hdc in next st, sc in next 7 sts] 3 times. Sc in next st, turn. 50 sts

**Next 25 (27, 29, 31, 33) (35, 37, 39, 41) rows:** Ch 2, hdc in BL across, turn. 50 sts

**Rep rows 2–8:** Fasten off.

## Finishing

Crochet or sew the shoulder seams if you haven't already done so. Sew the Sleeves on, sew both side seams.

With RS facing and your larger hook, crochet 2 rows along both sides of neckline, working 2 sc in side of each row. Make sure your edge is tight and holds the neckline together.

Fasten off. Weave in all ends. Block according to fiber type.

## Sleeve

### Make 2

With larger hook, ch 51 (last 2 ch counts as first hdc on next row).

**Row 1:** Hdc in third ch from hook, hdc across, turn. 50 sts

# Zeme Earth Sweater

Zeme is the ideal compromise for any season, being neither too heavy nor too light. The variety of stitches show a good balance between solid textured fabric and filet lace. The mix of puff stitch braids and filet crochet lines form an eye-catching textural surface. Think rocky mountains, dry deserts, ravines, gorges and so much more that mother Earth has to offer from its beauty.

# Zeme Earth Sweater Construction Notes

*Zeme is a textured sweater worked top down in short rows and joined rounds. The sweater is split for body and sleeves at the bust line. A loose body ends with hem ribbing. Straight half-length sleeves are worked last.*

## Sizes

1 (2, 3, 4, 5) (6, 7, 8, 9)

**To fit bust:** 30 (34, 38, 42, 46) (50, 54, 58, 62)" / 76 (86, 97, 107, 117) (127, 137, 147, 157) cm

**Finished bust:** 45 (49.25, 52.25, 55, 58.75) (61.75, 65.75, 69, 71.25)" / 114 (125, 133, 140, 149) (157, 167, 175, 181) cm

## Gauge

15 sts x 10 rows = 4" / 10 cm in dc after blocking

## Yarn

Sport weight, Mondial Merinos Extra (50% wool, 50% acrylic), 268 yds / 245 m per 100-g ball

## Yardage/Meterage

1205 (1310, 1400, 1485, 1575) (1660, 1750, 1835, 1900) yds / 1100 (1200, 1280, 1360, 1440) (1520, 1600, 1680, 1740) m

### Shown in

Color 039

## Hook

H/8 / 5 mm, or size needed to obtain gauge

## Notions

4 stitch markers

Tapestry needle

## Skills

Experience with making crocheted sweaters

Experience with working crochet short rows

### Abbreviations (US terms)

Beg = beginning

BPdc = back post double crochet

Ch = chain

Dc = double crochet

Dc2tog = double crochet two stitches together

FPdc = front post double crochet

Fsc = foundation single crochet

Hdc = half double crochet

Inc = increase

M = marker

Prev = previous

Puff st = puff stitch

Rep = repeat

Rnd(s) = round(s)

RS = right side

Sc = single crochet

Sl st = slip stitch

St(s) = stitch(es)

WS = wrong side

Yo = yarn over

## Special stitches

**P4 puff st:** Work to create Puff on RS of fabric. Yo, insert hook in the indicated st, yo, pull loop through st and make loop same height as previous sts in working row, (yo, insert hook in same st, yo, pull loop through st and make loop same height as working row) three times, yo, draw through 8 loops on hook (2 loops remain on hook), yo, pull through both loops.

**P5 puff stitch:** Worked the same as P4, but repeat four times to have 10 loops on hook, finish with yo, pull through 9 loops on hook (2 loops remain on hook), yo, draw through both loops.

**Sc-hdc-tog:** Insert hook in indicated st, yo and pull through st (2 loops on hook), yo, insert hook in next indicated st, yo and pull through st (4 loops on hook), yo and draw through all 4 loops on hook.

**Dc-sc-tog:** Yo, insert hook in indicated st, yo and pull through st, yo and draw through 2 loops (2 loops remain on hook), insert hook in next indicated st, yo and draw through st (3 loops on hook), yo and draw through all loops on hook.

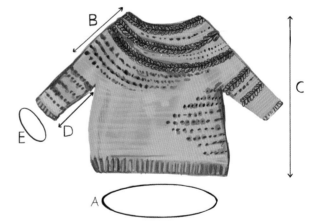

| Size | A—finished bust | B—yoke depth | C—full length | D—sleeve length | E—upper arm |
|---|---|---|---|---|---|
| 1 | 45" / 114 cm | 9" / 23 cm | 23.5" / 59.5 cm | 9" / 23 cm | 13" / 33 cm |
| 2 | 49.25" / 125 cm | 9.5" / 24 cm | 23.75" / 60.5 cm | 9" / 23 cm | 13.75" / 35 cm |
| 3 | 52.25" / 133 cm | 9.75" / 25 cm | 24.25" / 61.5 cm | 9" / 23 cm | 14.5" / 37 cm |
| 4 | 55" / 140 cm | 10.25" / 26 cm | 24.5" / 62.5 cm | 9" / 23 cm | 15.25" / 39 cm |
| 5 | 58.75" / 149 cm | 10.75" / 27 cm | 25" / 63.5 cm | 9" / 23 cm | 16.5" / 42 cm |
| 6 | 61.75" / 157 cm | 11" / 28 cm | 25.5" / 64.5 cm | 9" / 23 cm | 17" / 43 cm |
| 7 | 65.75" / 167 cm | 11.5" / 29 cm | 25.75" / 65.5 cm | 9" / 23 cm | 18.5" / 47 cm |
| 8 | 69" / 175 cm | 11.75" / 30 cm | 26.25" / 66.5 cm | 9" / 23 cm | 19" / 48 cm |
| 9 | 71.25" / 181 cm | 12.25" / 31 cm | 26.5" / 67.5 cm | 9" / 23 cm | 19.75" / 50 cm |

*Hem ribbing measures 1.25" / 3.5 cm. Sleeve ribbing measures 0.5" / 1.5 cm. The sweater is designed to be worn with 15 (15.25, 14.25, 13, 12.75) (11.75, 11.75, 11, 9.25)" / 38 (39, 36, 33, 32) (30, 30, 28, 24) cm positive ease. Size 2 modeled on 32" / 82-cm bust model.*

# Zeme Earth Sweater Pattern

Note that there will be both rounds and rows in the Yoke. Marking the first and last stitch of the round is suggested—this will make it easier to get the stitch count right.

**Throughout:** Ch 3 at the beginning of rnd/row counts as 1 dc (= 1 st); "ch 1" is a turning chain and is not counted as a stitch.

## Yoke

With RS facing, fsc 104, mark last st just made and join to first fsc with sl st to begin working in the round.

**Rnd 1 (RS):** In this round work P4. Ch 3, puff st in marked st (remove the marker). [Skip next st, dc in next st, puff st in last skipped st] 51 times. Join to top ch of beg ch-3, mark next st (puff st). Turn. 104 sts total with 52 puffs

**In second puff stitch round throughout:** Each dc is worked in dc of prev round and puff sts are worked into puff sts.

**Rnd 2 (WS):** In this round work P5. Ch 3, puff st in marked st (remove the marker). [Skip next st, dc in next dc, puff st in last skipped st] 51 times. Join to top ch of beg ch-3. Turn. 104 sts total with 52 puffs

Work 3 short rows as follows.

**Row 3 (RS):** Ch 1, [sc in next 5 sts, 2 sc in next st] twice. Hdc in next 4 sts, 2 hdc in next st. [Dc in next 9 sts, 2 dc in next st] 7 times. Hdc in next 4 sts, 2 hdc in next st, sc in next 4 sts, 2 sc in next st, mark next st, leave remaining sts unworked and turn. 109 sts

**Row 4 (WS):** Ch 1, sc in first 12 sts. [Hdc in next st, ch 1, skip next st] 3 times. [Dc in next st, ch 1, skip next st] 36 times. [Hdc in next st, ch 1, skip next st] 3 times. Sc in next 6 sts, mark next st, leave remaining sts unworked and turn. 102 sts

**Row 5 (RS):** Ch 1, [sc in next 5 sts, 2 sc in next st] twice. Hdc in next 5 sts, 2 hdc in next st. [Dc in next 10 sts, 2 dc in next st] 6 times. Hdc in next 5 sts, 2 hdc in next st, sc in next 5 sts, 2 sc in next st, sc in next 5 sts, sc-hdc-tog over next 2 sts (over next st and marked st), 2 hdc in next st, sc in next 5 sts, join to next sc. 120 sts

**Rnd 6 (RS):** Ch 1, sc in next 4 sts, hdc in next st, 2 hdc in next st, dc-sc-tog over next 2 sts (over marked st and next st), 2 sc in next st. [Sc in next 11 sts, 2 sc in next st] 7 times. Sc in next 7 sts, hdc in next 3 sts, 2 sc in next st, sc in next 11 sts, 2 sc in next st, sc in next 10 sts, 2 sc in next st, mark last st just made, join. 138 sts

**Rnd 7 (RS):** In this round work P4. Ch 3, puff st in marked st (remove the marker). [Skip next st, dc in next st, puff st in last skipped st] 68 times. Join to top ch of beg ch-3, mark next st (puff st). Turn. 138 sts total with 69 puffs.

**Rnd 8 (WS):** In this round work P5. Ch 3, puff st in marked st (remove the marker). [Skip next st, dc in next dc, puff st in last skipped st] 68 times. Join to top ch of beg ch-3. Turn. 138 sts total with 69 puffs

Work 5 short rows as follows.

**Row 9 (RS):** Ch 1, [sc in next 5 sts, 2 sc in next st] twice. Hdc in next 4 sts, 2 hdc in next st. [Dc in next 9 sts, 2 dc in next st] 10 times. Hdc in next 6 sts, 2 hdc in next st, sc in next 6 sts, 2 sc in next st, mark next st, leave remaining sts unworked and turn. 146 sts

**Row 10 (WS):** Ch 1, sc in first 12 sts. [Hdc in next st, ch 1, skip next st] 3 times. [Dc in next st, ch 1, skip next st] 54 times. [Hdc in next st, ch 1, skip next st] 3 times. Sc in next 7 sts, mark next st, leave remaining sts unworked and turn. 139 sts

**Row 11 (RS):** Ch 1, [sc in next 5 sts, 2 sc in next st] twice. Hdc in next 4 sts, 2 hdc in next st.

[Dc in next 9 sts, 2 dc in next st] 10 times. Hdc in next 7 sts, 2 hdc in next st, sc in next 7 sts, 2 sc in next st, mark next st, leave remaining sts unworked and turn. 148 sts

**Row 12 (WS):** Ch 1, sc in first 9 sts. [Hdc in next st, ch 1, skip next st] 3 times. [Dc in next st, ch 1, skip next st] 54 times. [Hdc in next st, ch 1, skip next st] 3 times. Sc in next 9 sts, mark next st, leave remaining sts unworked and turn. 138 sts

**Row 13 (RS):** Ch 1, [sc in next 5 sts, 2 sc in next st] twice. Hdc in next 4 sts, 2 hdc in next st. [Dc in next 9 sts, 2 dc in next st] 10 times. Hdc in next 5 sts, 2 hdc in next st, sc in next 5 sts, 2 sc in next st, sc in next 8 sts, sc-hdc-tog over next 2 sts (over next and marked st), 2 hdc in next st. Sc in next 3 sts, sc-hdc-tog over next 2 sts (over next and marked st), 2 hdc in next st, sc in next 5 sts, join to next sc. 166 sts

**Rnd 14 (RS):** Ch 1, sc in next 5 sts, 2 hdc in next st, dc-sc-tog over next 2 sts (over marked st and next st). 2 sc in next st, sc in next 6 sts, 2 hdc in next st, dc-sc-tog over next 2 sts (over marked st and next st). 2 sc in next st, sc in next 163 sts, 2 sc in next st, mark last st just made and join. 186 sts

**Rnd 15 (RS):** In this round work P4. Ch 3, puff st in marked st (remove the marker). [Skip next st, dc in next st, puff st in last skipped st] 92 times. Join to top ch of beg ch-3, mark next st (puff st). Turn. 186 sts total with 93 puffs

**Rnd 16 (WS):** In this round work P5. Ch 3, puff st in marked st (remove the marker). [Skip next st, dc in next dc, puff st in last skipped st] 92 times. Join to top ch of beg ch-3. Turn. 186 sts total with 93 puffs

**Rnd 17 (RS):** Ch 3, [dc in next 10 sts, 2 dc in next st] 6 times. Hdc in next 12 sts, 2 hdc in next st. [Sc in next 12 sts, 2 sc in next st] twice. Hdc in next 12 sts, 2 hdc in next st. [Dc in next 10 sts, 2 dc in next st] 6 times. Dc in next st, join. 202 sts

**Rnd 18:** Ch 4 (counts as first dc + ch 1), skip next st. [Dc in next st, ch 1, skip next st] 36 times. [Hdc in next st, ch 1, skip next st] 5 times. Sc in next 36 sts. [Hdc in next st, ch 1, skip next st] 5 times. [Dc in next st, ch 1, skip next st] 36 times, join. 202 sts

**Rnd 19:** Ch 3, [dc in next 11 sts, 2 dc in next st] 6 times. Hdc in next 10 sts, 2 hdc in next st. [Sc in next 11 sts, 2 sc in next st] 3 times. Hdc in next 10 sts, 2 hdc in next st. [Dc in next 11 sts, 2 dc in next st] 5 times. Dc in next 10 sts, 2 dc in next st, join. 219 sts

**Rnd 20:** Ch 4 (counts as first dc + ch 1), skip next st. [Dc in next st, ch 1, skip next st] 30 times. [Hdc in next st, ch 1, skip next st] 5 times. Sc in next 75 sts. [Hdc in next st, ch 1, skip next st] 5 times. [Dc in next st, ch 1, skip next st] 31 times, join. 219 sts

**Rnd 21:** Ch 3, dc in next 5 sts, 2 dc in next st. [Dc in next 12 sts, 2 dc in next st] 4 times. Hdc in next 12 sts, 2 hdc in next st. [Sc in next 12 sts, 2 sc in next st] 6 times. Hdc in next 12 sts, 2 hdc in next st. [Dc in next 12 sts, 2 dc in next st] 4 times. Dc in next 4 sts, join. 236 sts

**Rnd 22:** Ch 4 (counts as first dc + ch 1), skip next st. [Dc in next st, ch 1, skip next st] 25 times. [Hdc in next st, ch 1, skip next st] 5 times. Sc in next 112 sts. [Hdc in next st, ch 1, skip next st] 5 times. [Dc in next st, ch 1, skip next st] 26 times, join. 236 sts

**Rnd 23:** Ch 3, [dc in next 13 sts, 2 dc in next st] 3 times. Hdc in next 13 sts, 2 hdc in next st. [Sc in next 13 sts, 2 sc in next st] 8 times. Sc in next 10 sts, 2 sc in next st, hdc in next 13 sts, 2 hdc in next st. [Dc in next 13 sts, 2 dc in next st] 3 times, join. 253 sts

**Rnd 24:** Ch 4 (counts as first dc + ch 1), skip next st. [Dc in next st, ch 1, skip next st] 20 times. [Hdc in next st, ch 1, skip next st] 5 times. Sc in next 151 sts. [Hdc in next st, ch 1, skip next st] 5 times. [Dc in next st, ch 1, skip next st] 20 times, join. 253 sts

**Rnd 25:** Ch 3, dc in next 45 sts, hdc in next 15 sts, sc in next 132 sts, hdc in next 15 sts, dc in next 45 sts, join. 253 sts

**Size 1:** Fasten off and continue to Separating Body and Sleeves (page 98).

**Sizes 2–9:** Continue to work from rnd 26.

**Rnd 26:** Ch 3, dc in first st (inc), [dc in next 14 sts, 2 dc in next st] 16 times. Dc in next 12 sts, join. 270 sts

**Size 2:** Fasten off and continue to Separating Body and Sleeves (page 98).

**Sizes 3–9:** Continue to work from rnd 27.

**Rnd 27:** Ch 3, dc in next 7 sts. [2 dc in next st, dc in next 15 sts] 16 times. Dc in next 6 sts, join. 286 sts

**Size 3:** Fasten off and continue to Separating Body and Sleeves (page 98).

**Sizes 4–9:** Continue to work from rnd 28.

**Rnd 28:** Ch 3, [dc in next 16 sts, 2 dc in next st] 16 times. Dc in next 13 sts, join. 302 sts

**Size 4:** Fasten off and continue to Separating Body and Sleeves.

**Sizes 5–9:** Continue to work from rnd 29.

**Rnd 29:** Ch 3, dc in next 7 sts. [2 dc in next st, dc in next 17 sts] 16 times. Dc in next 6 sts, join. 318 sts

**Size 5:** Fasten off and continue to Separating Body and Sleeves (page 98).

**Sizes 6–9:** Continue to work from rnd 30.

**Rnd 30:** Ch 3, [dc in next 18 sts, 2 dc in next st] 16 times. Dc in next 13 sts, join. 334 sts

**Size 6:** Fasten off and continue to Separating Body and Sleeves (page 98).

**Sizes 7–9:** Continue to work from rnd 31.

**Rnd 31:** Ch 3, dc in next 7 sts. [2 dc in next st, dc in next 19 sts] 16 times. Dc in next 6 sts, join. 350 sts

**Size 7:** Fasten off and continue to Separating Body and Sleeves.

**Sizes 8–9:** Continue to work from rnd 32.

**Rnd 32:** Ch 3, dc in next 6 sts. [2 dc in next st, dc in next 20 sts] 16 times. Dc in next 7 sts, join. 366 sts

**Size 8:** Fasten off and continue to Separating Body and Sleeves (page 98).

**Size 9:** Continue to work from rnd 33.

**Rnd 33:** Ch 3, dc in next 6 sts. [2 dc in next st, dc in next 21 sts] 16 times. Dc in next 7 sts, join. 382 sts

**Size 9:** Fasten off and continue to Separating Body and Sleeves.

## Separating Body and Sleeves

With RS facing, skip next 21 (22, 23, 25, 26) (27, 29, 30, 31) sts, attach yarn with sl st to the next st.

**Rnd 1:** Ch 3 (mark last st = M1), dc in next 83 (89, 95, 100, 105) (111, 116, 122, 127) sts (mark last st = M2), ch 2 (4, 4, 4, 6) (6, 8, 8, 8), skip next 43 (45, 47, 50, 53) (55, 58, 60, 63) sts, dc in next 83 (90, 96, 101, 106) (112, 117, 123, 128) sts (mark first and last st = M3 and M4), ch 2 (4, 4, 4, 6) (6, 8, 8, 8), join to top ch of beg ch-3. 171 (188, 200, 210, 224) (236, 250, 262, 272) sts

Do not move markers up.

**Rnds 2–3:** Ch 3, dc around, join.

**Rnd 4:** Ch 3, dc in next 72 (79, 85, 90, 96) (102, 108, 114, 120) sts. [Ch 1, skip next st, dc in next st] 12 times. Dc in next 74 (84, 90, 95, 103) (109, 117, 123, 127) sts, join.

**Rnd 5:** Ch 3, dc around, join.

**Rnd 6:** Ch 3, dc in next 66 (73, 79, 84, 90) (96, 102, 108, 114) sts. [Ch 1, skip next st, dc in next st] 18 times. Dc in next 68 (78, 84, 89, 97) (103, 111, 117, 121) sts, join.

**Rnd 7:** Ch 3, dc around, join.

**Rnd 8:** Ch 3, dc in next 60 (67, 73, 78, 84) (90, 96, 102, 108) sts. [Ch 1, skip next st, dc in next st] 24 times. Dc in next 62 (72, 78, 83, 91) (97, 105, 111, 115) sts, join.

**Rnd 9:** Ch 3, dc around, join.

**Rnd 10:** Ch 3, dc in next 54 (61, 67, 72, 78) (84, 90, 96, 102) sts. [Ch 1, skip next st, dc in next st] 30 times. Dc in next 56 (66, 72, 77, 85) (91, 99, 105, 109) sts, join.

**Rnd 11:** Ch 3, dc around, join.

**Rnd 12:** Ch 3, dc in next 48 (55, 61, 66, 72) (78, 84, 90, 96) sts. [Ch 1, skip next st, dc in next st] 36 times. Dc in next 50 (60, 66, 71, 79) (85, 93, 99, 103) sts, join.

**Rnd 13:** Ch 3, dc around, join.

**Rnd 14:** Ch 3, dc in next 42 (49, 55, 60, 66) (72, 78, 84, 90) sts. [Ch 1, skip next st, dc in next st] 42 times. Dc in next 44 (54, 60, 65, 73) (79, 87, 93, 97) sts, join.

**Rnd 15:** Ch 3, dc around, join.

**Rnds 16–17:** Rep rnds 12–13.

**Rnds 18–19:** Rep rnds 10–11.

**Rnds 20–21:** Rep rnds 8–9.

**Rnds 22–23:** Rep rnds 6–7.

**Rnds 24–25:** Rep rnds 4–5.

**Rnds 26–27:** Ch 3, dc around, join.

To make the sweater longer, rep rnd 28 as desired.

**Rnd 28:** Ch 3, [Dc in next 2 sts, dc2tog over next 2 sts] 42 (46, 49, 52, 55) (58, 62, 65, 67) times. Dc in next 2 (3, 3, 1, 3) (3, 1, 1, 3) sts, join. 129 (142, 151, 158, 169) (178, 188, 197, 205) sts

**Next 4 rnds:** Ch 3, [FPdc around next st, BPdc around next st] repeat around.

**Sizes 2, 4, 6, 7:** FPdc around last st.

**All sizes:** Join.

Fasten off.

## Sleeve 1

With RS facing, attach yarn with sl st to top of M4 from beg of Separating Body and Sleeves.

**Rnd 1:** Ch 3, dc2tog around post of next horizontally lying st, dc in next 43 (45, 47, 50, 53) (55, 58, 60, 63) sts, dc2tog around next horizontally lying st, dc in next marked st (M1), dc in each of next 2 (4, 4, 4, 6) (6, 8, 8, 8) chs, join. 49 (53, 55, 58, 63) (65, 70, 72, 75) sts

**Rnd 2:** Ch 3, dc2tog over next 2 sts, dc around, join. 48 (52, 54, 57, 62) (64, 69, 71, 74) sts

**Rnd 3:** Ch 3, dc2tog over next 2 sts, dc around until the last 2 sts remain, dc2tog over last 2 sts, join. 46 (50, 52, 55, 60) (62, 67, 69, 72) sts

**Rnd 4:** Ch 4 (counts as first dc + ch 1), skip next st. [Dc in next st, ch 1, skip next st] repeat around.

**Sizes 4, 7, 8:** Dc in last st.

**All sizes:** Join.

**Rnd 5:** Ch 3, dc2tog over next 2 sts, dc around until the last 2 sts remain, dc2tog over last 2 sts, join. 44 (48, 50, 53, 58) (60, 65, 67, 70) sts

**Rnd 6:** Ch 4 (counts as first dc + ch 1), skip next st. [Dc in next st, ch 1, skip next st] repeat around.

**Sizes 4, 7, 8:** Dc in last st.

**All sizes:** Join.

**Rnd 7:** Ch 3, dc2tog over next 2 sts, dc around until the last 2 sts remain, dc2tog over last 2 sts, join. 42 (46, 48, 51, 56) (58, 63, 65, 68) sts

**Rnd 8:** Ch 3, dc2tog over next 2 sts, dc around until the last 2 sts remain, dc2tog over last 2 sts, join. 40 (44, 46, 49, 54) (56, 61, 63, 66) sts

**Rnd 9:** Ch 4 (counts as first dc + ch 1), skip next st. [Dc in next st, ch 1, skip next st] repeat around.

**Sizes 4, 7, 8:** Dc in last st.

**All sizes:** Join.

**Rnds 10–11:** Ch 3, dc around, join.

**Rnd 12:** Ch 3, dc2tog over next 2 sts, dc around until the last 2 sts remain, dc2tog over last 2 sts, join. 38 (42, 44, 47, 52) (54, 59, 61, 64) sts

**Rnd 13:** Ch 4 (counts as first dc + ch 1), skip next st. [Dc in next st, ch 1, skip next st] repeat around.

**Sizes 4, 7, 8:** Dc in last st.

**All sizes:** Join.

**Rnds 14–15:** Ch 3, dc around, join.

**Rnd 16:** Ch 3, dc2tog over next 2 sts, dc around until the last 2 sts remain, dc2tog over last 2 sts, join. 36 (40, 42, 45, 50) (52, 57, 59, 62) sts

**Rnd 17:** Ch 3, dc around, join.

**Rnd 18:** Ch 4 (counts as first dc + ch 1), skip next st. [Dc in next st, ch 1, skip next st] repeat around.

Sizes 4, 7, 8: Dc in last st.

All sizes: Join.

**Rnds 19–21:** Ch 3, dc around, join.

**Rnd 22:** Ch 3, dc2tog over next 2 sts, dc around until the last 2 sts remain, dc2tog over last 2 sts, join. 34 (38, 40, 43, 48) (50, 55, 57, 60) sts

**Last rnd:** Ch 3, [FPdc around next st, BPdc around next st] repeat around.

Sizes 1, 2, 3, 5, 6, 9: FPdc around last st.

All sizes: Join and fasten off.

## Sleeve 2

With RS facing, attach yarn with sl st to M2.

**Rnd 1:** Ch 3, dc2tog around next horizontally lying st, dc in next 43 (45, 47, 50, 53) (55, 58, 60, 63) sts, dc2tog around next horizontally lying st, dc in next marked st (M1), dc in each of next 2 (4, 4, 4, 6) (6, 8, 8, 8) chs, join. 49 (53, 55, 58, 63) (65, 70, 72, 75) sts

**Rnd 2:** Ch 3, dc2tog over next 2 sts, dc around, join. 48 (52, 54, 57, 62) (64, 69, 71, 74) sts

**Rnd 3:** Ch 3.

Sizes 1, 2, 3, 5, 6, 9 only: Dc2tog over next 2 sts.

All sizes: Dc around until last 2 sts remain, dc2tog over last 2 sts (mark last st just made), join. 46 (50, 52, 56, 60) (62, 68, 70, 72) sts

**Rnd 4 (RS):** In this round work P4. Ch 3, puff st in marked st (remove the marker). [Skip next st, dc in next st, puff st in last skipped st] 22 (24, 25, 27, 29) (30, 33, 34, 35) times. Join to top ch of beg ch-3, mark next st (puff st). Turn. 46 (50, 52, 56, 60) (62, 68, 70, 72) sts total with 23 (25, 26, 28, 30) (31, 34, 35, 36) puffs

**Rnd 5 (WS):** In this round work P5. Ch 3, puff st in marked st (remove the marker). [Skip next st, dc in next dc, puff st in last skipped st] 22 (24, 25, 27, 29) (30, 33, 34, 35) times. Join to top ch of beg ch-3. Turn. 46 (50, 52, 56, 60) (62, 68, 70, 72) sts total with 23 (25, 26, 28, 30) (31, 34, 35, 36) puffs

**Rnd 6 (RS):** Ch 3, dc2tog over next 2 sts, dc around until the last 2 sts remain, dc2tog over last 2 sts, join. 44 (48, 50, 54, 58) (60, 66, 68, 70) sts

**Rnd 7:** Ch 3, dc2tog over next 2 sts, dc around until the last 2 sts remain, dc2tog over last 2 sts, join. 42 (46, 48, 52, 56) (58, 64, 66, 68) sts

**Rnd 8:** Ch 4 (counts as first dc + ch 1), skip next st. [Dc in next st, ch 1, skip next st] repeat around, join.

**Rnd 9:** Ch 3, dc2tog over next 2 sts, dc around until the last 2 sts remain, dc2tog over last 2 sts, join. 40 (44, 46, 50, 54) (56, 62, 64, 66) sts

**Rnd 10:** Ch 3, dc around, mark last st, join.

**Rnd 11 (RS):** In this round work P4. Ch 3, puff st in marked st (remove the marker). [Skip next st, dc in next st, puff st in last skipped st] 19 (21, 22, 24, 26) (27, 30, 31, 32) times. Join to top ch of beg ch-3, mark next st (puff st). Turn. 40 (44, 46, 50, 54) (56, 62, 64, 66) sts total with 20 (22, 23, 25, 27) (28, 31, 32, 33) puffs

**Rnd 12 (WS):** In this round work P5. Ch 3, puff st in marked st (remove the marker). [Skip next st, dc in next dc, puff st in last skipped st] 19 (21, 22, 24, 26) (27, 30, 31, 32) times. Join to top ch of beg ch-3. Turn. 40 (44, 46, 50, 54) (56, 62, 64, 66) sts total with 20 (22, 23, 25, 27) (28, 31, 32, 33) puffs

**Rnd 13:** Ch 3, dc2tog over next 2 sts, dc around until the last 2 sts remain, dc2tog over last 2 sts, join. 38 (42, 44, 48, 52) (54, 60, 62, 64) sts

**Rnds 14–15:** Ch 3, dc around, join.

**Rnd 16:** Ch 3, dc2tog over next 2 sts, dc around until the last 2 sts remain, dc2tog over last 2 sts, join. 36 (40, 42, 46, 50) (52, 58, 60, 62) sts

**Rnds 17–21:** Ch 3, dc around, join.

**Rnd 22:** Ch 3, dc2tog over next 2 sts, dc around until the last 2 sts remain, dc2tog over last 2 sts, join. 34 (38, 40, 44, 48) (50, 56, 58, 60) sts

**Last rnd:** Ch 3, [FPdc around next st, BPdc around next st] repeat around, FPdc around last st, join and fasten off.

## Finishing

Weave in all ends and block according to fiber type.

# Jūra Sea Sweater

Evocative of drifting waves, Jūra features a wide variety of stitches and crochet short rows that grow harmoniously within this truly awe-worthy design. Jūra is imbued with a sense of nature's serenity and will bring about the same sense of calm while you work away on this sweater.

# Jūra Sea Sweater Construction Notes

*Jūra is worked bottom up starting with a sideways ribbing, then worked with crochet short rows in triangle-like parts—meaning rows are not crocheted until the end of the row on one side, then the next "triangle" part is worked over the first one, etc. The front and back are each worked separately, and the shoulder seams are crocheted (or sewn) together. Then the neck ribbing is worked and sewn on both parts. The sleeves are crocheted separately and sewn on afterward.*

## Sizes

1 (2, 3, 4, 5) (6, 7, 8, 9)

**To fit bust:** 30 (34, 38, 42, 46) (50, 54, 58, 62)" / 76 (86, 97, 107, 117) (127, 137, 147, 157) cm

**Finished bust:** 36.25 (40.25, 43.25, 47.25, 51.25) (54.25, 58.25, 61.5, 65.25)" / 92 (102, 110, 120, 130) (138, 148, 156, 166) cm

## Gauge

Front and back 13 sts x 9 rows = 4" / 10 cm in dc after blocking

## Yarn

Worsted weight, Paintbox Yarns Wool Mix Aran (50% Wool, 50% Acrylic), 197 yds (180 m) per 100-g skein, or use any worsted weight wool blend yarn to achieve a similar effect

## Yardage/Meterage

1180 (1325, 1455, 1625, 1770) (1870, 2125, 2225, 2360) yds / 1080 (1210, 1330, 1485, 1620) (1710, 1945, 2035, 2160) m

**Shown in**
Colorway Stormy Grey 804

## Hooks

K/10.5 / 6.5 mm for the main sections of the Body and Sleeves, or size needed to obtain gauge

J/10 / 6 mm for ribbing, or one size smaller than size needed to obtain gauge

## Notions

Tapestry needle, 10 stitch markers

## Skills

Experience with making crocheted sweaters

Experience with working crochet short rows

### Abbreviations (US terms)

BL = back loop

Ch = chain

Dc = double crochet

Dc2tog = double crochet 2 stitches together

Hdc = half double crochet

Puff st = puff stitch

RS = right side

Sc = single crochet

Sc-dc-tog = sc and dc worked together

Sl st = slip stitch

St(s) = stitch(es)

WS = wrong side

## Special stitches

**Puff st:** Yo, insert hook in the indicated st, yo, pull loop through st and make loop same height as previous sts in working row, (yo, insert hook in same st, yo, pull loop through st and make loop same height as working row) three times, pull through 8 loops on hook (2 loops left on hook), yo, pull through both loops.

**Sc-dc-tog:** Insert hook in the indicated st, yo, pull yarn through st (2 loops on hook); yo, insert hook in next indicated st, yo, pull yarn through st, yo, pull yarn through two loops, yo and pull yarn through all 3 loops on hook.

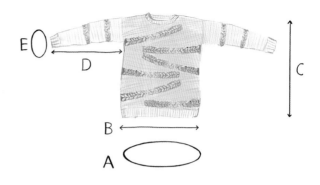

| Size | A—finished bust | B—half-bust | C—length | D—sleeve length | E—upper arm |
|---|---|---|---|---|---|
| 1 | 36.25" / 92 cm | 18" / 46 cm | 23.25" / 59 cm | 19.25" / 49 cm | 13" / 33 cm |
| 2 | 40.25" / 102 cm | 20" / 51 cm | 23.25" / 59 cm | 18.5" / 47 cm | 13.75" / 35 cm |
| 3 | 43.25" / 110 cm | 21.75" / 55 cm | 23.25" / 59 cm | 18.5" / 47 cm | 14.25" / 36 cm |
| 4 | 47.25" / 120 cm | 23.5" / 60 cm | 24.25" / 61.5 cm | 17.75" / 45 cm | 15" / 38 cm |
| 5 | 51.25" / 130 cm | 25.5" / 65 cm | 24.25" / 61.5 cm | 17.75" / 45 cm | 16.25" / 41 cm |
| 6 | 54.25" / 138 cm | 27.25" / 69 cm | 24.25" / 61.5 cm | 17" / 43 cm | 17" / 43 cm |
| 7 | 58.25" / 148 cm | 29.25" / 74 cm | 25.25" / 64 cm | 17" / 43 cm | 18.5" / 47 cm |
| 8 | 61.5" / 156 cm | 30.75" / 78 cm | 25.25" / 64 cm | 16.5" / 42 cm | 19.75" / 50 cm |
| 9 | 65.25" / 166 cm | 32.75" / 83 cm | 25.25" / 64 cm | 16.5" / 42 cm | 19.75" / 50 cm |

*Body and Sleeve ribbing measures 2.25" / 6 cm. Neck width (without ribbing) measures 7.25" / 18.5 cm. Neck ribbing measures 1" / 2.5 cm. Height of one short rows "triangle" (rows 2–12) measures 6.25" / 16 cm. The sweater is designed with 6.25 (6.25, 5, 5, 5) (4.25, 4.25, 3.5, 3.5)" / 16 (16, 13, 13, 13) (11, 11, 9, 9) cm positive ease. Size 2 is modeled on 30" / 77-cm bust model.*

# Jūra Sea Sweater Pattern

**Throughout:** Beginning ch 3 counts as first dc and counts as 1 st.

Beginning ch 4 counts as dc + ch 1 and counts as 2 sts.

Beginning ch 1 counts as turning ch and is not counted as a stitch.

## Front

### Front Ribbing

With smaller hook, ch 11 (last 2 ch counts as first hdc on next row).

**Row 1:** Hdc in third ch from hook, hdc in each ch across, turn. 10 sts

**Rows 2–40 (–44, –48, –52, –56) (–60, –64, –68, –72):** Ch 2 (counts as first hdc), hdc in BL across, turn. 10 sts

**Last row of the ribbing:** Don't turn. Rotate the ribbing clockwise by 90 degrees.

## Body

Change to your larger hook.

**For row 1 you'll be working across the side of the ribbing:** Work 3 dcs in every 2 rows of hdc to get 60 (66, 72, 78, 84) (90, 96, 102, 108) dc total.

**Row 1:** Ch 3, dc across (as described above), turn. 60 (66, 72, 78, 84) (90, 96, 102, 108) sts

Sizes 1–3: Continue to row 2.

Sizes 4–9: Work 2 more rows as [ch 3, dc across, turn], then continue to row 2.

**Row 2:** Ch 4, skip next st. [Dc in next st, puff stitch in last skipped st, skip next st] 20 (23, 26, 29, 32) (35, 38, 41, 44) times. Dc in next st, hdc in next 4 sts, sc in next 5 sts, mark next st and turn, leaving 8 sts unworked.

20 (23, 26, 29, 32) (35, 38, 41, 44) puffs and 52 (58, 64, 70, 76) (82, 88, 94, 100) sts total

**Row 3:** Ch 1, sc in next 4 sc (mark first sc), hdc in next 5 hdc, dc in next dc, ch 1, skip next st.

[Dc in next dc, puff stitch in last skipped st, skip next st] 20 (23, 26, 29, 32) (35, 38, 41, 44) times. Dc in next st, turn.

20 (23, 26, 29, 32) (35, 38, 41, 44) puffs and 52 (58, 64, 70, 76) (82, 88, 94, 100) sts total

**Row 4:** Ch 3, dc in next 31 (37, 43, 49, 55) (61, 67, 73, 79) sts, hdc in next 5 sts, sc in next 4 sts, dc one row below in the same stitch where the last puff st was made, mark next st on row you're working now, turn. 42 (48, 54, 60, 66) (72, 78, 84, 90) sts

**Row 5:** Ch 1, sc in next 5 sc (mark first sc), hdc in next 5 hdc, dc in next 32 (38, 44, 50, 56) (62, 68, 74, 80) dc, turn. 42 (48, 54, 60, 66) (72, 78, 84, 90) sts

**Row 6:** Ch 3, dc in next 21 (27, 33, 39, 45) (51, 57, 63, 69) sts, hdc in next 5 sts, sc in next 5 sts, mark next st and turn. 32 (38, 44, 50, 56) (62, 68, 74, 80) sts

**Row 7:** Ch 1, sc in next 5 sc (mark first sc), hdc in next 5 hdc, dc in next 22 (28, 34, 40, 46) (52, 58, 64, 70) dc, turn. 32 (38, 44, 50, 56) (62, 68, 74, 80) sts

**Row 8:** Ch 3, dc in next 11 (17, 23, 29, 35) (41, 47, 53, 59) sts, hdc in next 5 sts, sc in next 5 sts, mark next st and turn. 22 (28, 34, 40, 46) (52, 58, 64, 70) sts

**Row 9:** Ch 1, sc in next 5 sc (mark first sc), hdc in next 5 hdc, dc in next 12 (18, 24, 30, 36) (42, 48, 54, 60) dc, turn. 22 (28, 34, 40, 46) (52, 58, 64, 70) sts

**Row 10:** Ch 3, dc in next 1 (7, 13, 19, 25) (31, 37, 43, 49) sts, hdc in next 5 sts, sc in next 5 sts, mark next st and turn. 12 (18, 24, 30, 36) (42, 48, 54, 60) sts

**Row 11:** Ch 1, sc in next 5 sc (mark first sc), hdc in next 5 hdc, dc in next 2 (8, 14, 20, 26) (32, 38, 44, 50) dc, turn. 12 (18, 24, 30, 36) (42, 48, 54, 60) sts

Next row finishes the triangle—it goes over all of the markers all the way down to beginning of row 1.

**Row 12:** Ch 3, dc in next 5 (11, 17, 23, 29) (35, 41, 47, 53) sts, hdc in next 5 sts, sc-dc-tog over next 2 marked sts (remove markers).

[2 hdc in next st, hdc in next 7 sts, sc-dc-tog over next 2 marked sts (remove markers)] 4 times.

2 hdc in next st, hdc in next 6 sts, turn. 60 (66, 72, 78, 84) (90, 96, 102, 108) sts

**Rows 13–23:** Rep rows 2–12.

**Row 24:** Ch 1, sc across, turn. 60 (66, 72, 78, 84) (90, 96, 102, 108) sts

**Rows 25–46:** Rep rows 2–12 twice.

**Row 47:** Ch 1, sc across, turn. 60 (66, 72, 78, 84) (90, 96, 102, 108) sts

**Rows 48–69:** Rep rows 2–12 twice.

**Sizes 1–6:** Continue to Front Shoulder Part 1 and 2.

**Sizes 7–9:** Make 2 rows of dc across, then continue to Front Shoulder Parts 1 and 2.

**To make the sweater longer:** Add even rows of dcs here.

## Front Shoulder Part 1

**Row 1:** Ch 3, dc in next 19 (22, 25, 28, 31) (34, 37, 40, 43) sts, dc2tog over next 2 sts, turn. 21 (24, 27, 30, 33) (36, 39, 42, 45) sts

**Row 2:** Ch 2, dc in next st (beg ch-2 + dc counts as dc2tog), dc in next 19 (22, 25, 28, 31) (34, 37, 40, 43) sts, turn. 20 (23, 26, 29, 32) (35, 38, 41, 44) sts

**Row 3:** Ch 3, dc in next 17 (20, 23, 26, 29) (32, 35, 38, 41) sts, dc2tog over next 2 sts, turn. 19 (22, 25, 28, 31) (34, 37, 40, 43) sts

## Back

Repeat instructions for Front part until the Front Shoulder Parts.

**Next 3 rows:** Ch 3, dc across, turn. Continue to Back Shoulder Parts 1 and 2.

### Back Shoulder Part 1

**Row 1:** Ch 3, dc in next 16 (19, 22, 25, 28) (31, 34, 37, 40) sts, dc2tog over next 2 sts, turn. 18 (21, 24, 27, 30) (33, 36, 39, 42) sts

**Row 2:** Ch 3, dc in next 5 (6, 7, 8, 9) (10, 11, 12, 13) sts, hdc in next 6 (7, 8, 9, 10) (11, 12, 13, 14) sts, sc in next 6 (7, 8, 9, 10) (11, 12, 13, 14) sts, fasten off. 18 (21, 24, 27, 30) (33, 36, 39, 42) sts

Crochet the shoulder seam using sc, or leave a longer yarn end for sewing. Fasten off.

### Back Shoulder Part 2

Attach yarn with sl st to the other end of last row of Back part. Rep rows 1–2 of Back Shoulder Part 1. Crochet the shoulder seam using sc, or leave a longer yarn end for sewing. Fasten off.

### Neck Ribbing

With your smaller hook, ch 6 (last 2 ch counts as first hdc of next row).

**Row 1:** Hdc in third ch from hook, hdc across, turn. 5 sts

**Rows 2–52:** Ch 2, hdc in BL across, turn. 5 sts

**Last row of the ribbing:** Don't turn. Rotate the ribbing clockwise by 90 degrees. Ch 1, work 2 sc in side of every row of ribbing, fasten off, leaving a long yarn end for sewing the ribbing. With the WS facing, sew the ribbing onto the neckline and seam the short ends of ribbing together.

**Row 4:** Ch 2, dc in next st (counts as dc2tog), dc in next 17 (20, 23, 26, 29) (32, 35, 38, 41) sts, turn. 18 (21, 24, 27, 30) (33, 36, 39, 42) sts

**Row 5:** Ch 1, sc in next 6 (7, 8, 9, 10) (11, 12, 13, 14) sts, hdc in next 6 (7, 8, 9, 10) (11, 12, 13, 14) sts, dc in next 6 (7, 8, 9, 10) (11, 12, 13, 14) sts, fasten off. 18 (21, 24, 27, 30) (33, 36, 39, 42) sts

### Front Shoulder Part 2

Attach yarn with sl st to the other end of last row of Front part. Repeat rows 1–5 of Front Shoulder Part 1.

## Sleeve

**Make 2**

After finishing the sleeve, you may see that your sleeve stretches more vertically and your sleeve gauge most likely will be different from your body gauge (closer to 8 rows = 4" / 10 cm [if worked in wool blend yarn]). Take this information into account when choosing your sleeve length, but don't worry if your gauges differ between the Body and Sleeve.

### Ribbing

With smaller hook, ch 11 (last 2 ch counts as first hdc of next row).

**Row 1:** Hdc in third ch from hook, hdc in each ch across, turn. 10 sts

**Rows 2–17 (–18, –19, –20, –21) (–22, –23, –24, –25):** Ch 2, hdc in BL across, turn. 10 sts

**Last row of the ribbing:** Don't turn. Rotate the ribbing clockwise by 90 degrees.

**Work across the side of the ribbing:** Work 3 sc in every 2 rows of hdcs to get 25 (27, 29, 30, 32) (33, 35, 36, 38) sts total.

Change to larger hook.

### Sleeve

**Row 1:** Ch 3, dc across as described above, work 1 additional st in the last row end if needed to achieve proper st count, turn. 25 (27, 29, 30, 32) (33, 35, 36, 38) sts

**Row 2:** Ch 3, dc across, work 0 (0, 0, 1, 1) (0, 0, 1, 1) more dc in last st, turn. 25 (27, 29, 31, 33) (33, 35, 37, 39) sts

**Row 3:** Ch 3, 1 (1, 1, 1, 1) (0, 1, 1, 0) more dc in first st, dc across, 1 (1, 1, 1, 1) (0, 1, 1, 0) more dc in last st, turn. 27 (29, 31, 33, 35) (33, 37, 39, 39) sts

**Rows 4–6:** Ch 3, dc across, turn.

**Row 7:** Ch 3, 0 (1, 1, 0, 0) (0, 0, 0, 0) more dc in first st, dc across, 0 (1, 1, 0, 0) (0, 0, 0, 0) more dc in last st, turn. 27 (31, 33, 33, 35) (33, 37, 39, 39) sts

**Row 8:** Ch 3, dc across, turn.

**Row 9:** Ch 3, 1 (1, 1, 1, 1) (0, 1, 1, 1) more dc in first st, dc across, 1 (1, 1, 1, 1) (0, 1, 1, 1) more dc in last st, turn. 29 (33, 35, 35, 37) (33, 39, 41, 41) sts

**Rows 10–11:** Ch 3, dc across, turn.

**Row 12:** Ch 3, 1 more dc in first st, dc across, 1 more dc in last st, turn. 31 (35, 37, 37, 39) (35, 41, 43, 43) sts

**Rows 13–15:** Ch 3, 0 (0, 0, 0, 0) (1, 1, 1, 1) more dc in first st, dc across, 0 (0, 0, 0, 0) (1, 1, 1, 1) more dc in last st, turn. 31 (35, 37, 37, 39) (41, 47, 49, 49) sts

**Rows 16–17:** Ch 4, skip next st. [Dc in next dc, puff stitch in last skipped st, skip next st] 14 (16, 17, 17, 18) (19, 22, 23, 23) times. Dc in next st, turn.

14 (16, 17, 17, 18) (19, 22, 23, 23) puffs and 31 (35, 37, 37, 39) (41, 47, 49, 49) sts total

**Row 18:** Ch 3, 0 (0, 0, 0, 1) (1, 1, 1, 1) more dc in first st, dc across, 0 (0, 0, 0, 1) (1, 1, 1, 1) more dc in last st, turn. 31 (35, 37, 37, 41) (43, 49, 51, 51) sts

**Rows 19–20:** Ch 3, 0 (0, 0, 1, 1) (1, 1, 1, 1) more dc in first st, dc across, 0 (0, 0, 1, 1) (1, 1, 1, 1) more dc in last st, turn. 31 (35, 37, 41, 45) (47, 53, 55, 55) sts

**Rows 21–22:** Ch 3, dc across, turn.

**Row 23:** Ch 3, 1 more dc in first st, dc across, 1 more dc in last st, turn. 33 (37, 39, 43, 47) (49, 55, 57, 57) sts

**Rows 24–25:** Ch 3, 0 (0, 0, 0, 0) (0, 0, 1, 1) more dc in first st, dc across, 0 (0, 0, 0, 0) (0, 0, 1, 1) more dc in last st, turn. 33 (37, 39, 43, 47) (49, 55, 61, 61) sts

**Row 26:** Ch 3, 1 more dc in first st, dc across, 1 more dc in last st, turn. 35 (39, 41, 45, 49) (51, 57, 63, 63) sts

**Row 27:** Ch 3, 0 (0, 0, 0, 0) (1, 1, 1, 1) more dc in first st, dc across, 0 (0, 0, 0, 0) (1, 1, 1, 1) more dc in last st, turn. 35 (39, 41, 45, 49) (53, 59, 65, 65) sts

**Rows 28–29:** Ch 4, skip next st. [Dc in next dc, puff stitch in last skipped st, skip next st] 16 (18, 19, 21, 23) (25, 28, 31, 31) times. Dc in next st, turn.

16 (18, 19, 21, 23) (25, 28, 31, 31) puffs and 35 (39, 41, 45, 49) (53, 59, 65, 65) sts total

**Sizes 8 and 9:** Fasten off.

**Row 30:** Ch 3, 1 more dc in first st, dc across, 1 more dc in last st, turn. 37 (41, 43, 47, 51) (55, 61, x, x) sts

**Sizes 6 and 7:** Fasten off.

**Row 31:** Ch 3, dc across, turn.

**Row 32:** Ch 3, 1 more dc in first st, dc across, 1 more dc in last st, turn. 39 (43, 45, 49, 53) (x, x, x, x) sts

**Sizes 4 and 5:** Fasten off.

**Row 33:** Ch 3, dc across, turn.

**Row 34:** Ch 3, 1 more dc in first st, dc across, 1 more dc in last st, turn. 41 (45, 47, x, x) (x, x, x, x) sts

**Sizes 2 and 3:** Fasten off.

**Row 35:** Ch 3, dc across, turn.

**Row 36:** Ch 3, 1 more dc in first st, dc across, 1 more dc in last st, turn. 43 (x, x, x, x) (x, x, x, x) sts

**Size 1:** Fasten off.

## Finishing

Block all of the pieces of your sweater before sewing the seams. Blocking will straighten the curvy sides. Block all pieces according to fiber type (see your yarn label to decide which method is the best). Leave to dry completely. Sew both sleeves on, sew the sleeve seams and side seams. Weave in ends. Turn your sweater RS out.

# Unexpected

I've always been a firm believer in keeping things interesting, exciting and captivating. Not only should crochet not look plain and boring, but also the process of creating shouldn't just be back and forth. Luckily, this doesn't always mean complex patterns, which can sometimes take too much time and effort spent for a result that isn't that impressive.

Imagine—what if you could crochet a sweater entirely wrong side out, then turn it to the right side and suddenly the stitch pattern would appear (Rasa [page 115])? What if you could take the beautiful crochet straps that you just created and form an actual weaving with them (Saule [page 147])? What if you could wear a sweater multiple ways (Zvaigznes [page 129]) for the ultimate form of versatility? Now you can! Designing and making as I go—these unpredicted styles surprised even myself.

# Rasa Dew Sweater

It was my intention that Rasa tell the story of a calm, early morning reflection. This gorgeous sweater focuses on a simple base, displaying a texture reminiscent of dew drops on a blade of grass. By incorporating a continuous ribbing element in the solid background, the diamond-shaped post stitches bring out a subtle yet strong pattern.

# Rasa Dew Sweater Construction Notes

*Rasa is made with WS facing, revealing the stitch pattern only at the very end when the sweater is turned RS out. The sweater is worked top down in a spiral, then is split for the body and sleeves at the bust line. Post stitches form a pattern on the cropped body ending with hem ribbing. Straight half-length sleeves are worked in the round and will give a surprise moment of asymmetry depending on the yarn twist used. Rasa is worked in one piece and is seamless.*

## Sizes

1 (2, 3, 4, 5, 6) (7, 8, 9, 10, 11)

**To fit bust:** 29.5 (32.5, 35.5, 38.25, 41.25, 44.25) (47.25, 50.25, 53, 56, 59)" / 75 (82.5, 90, 97.5, 105, 112.5) (120, 127.5, 135, 142.5, 150) cm

**Finished bust:** 32.5 (35.5, 38.5, 41.25, 44.25, 47.25) (50.25, 53.25, 56, 59, 62)" / 82.5 (90, 97.5, 105, 112.5, 120) (127.5, 135, 142.5, 150, 157.5) cm

## Gauge

16 sts x 14 rows = 4" / 10 cm in hdc

## Yarn

DK weight, Concept by Katia Cotton-Yak (60% Cotton, 30% Wool, 10% Yak), 142 yds / 130 m per 50-g skein, or use any DK weight cotton-wool blend to achieve a similar effect

## Yardage/Meterage

1085 (1180, 1265, 1395, 1495, 1620) (1750, 1830, 1975, 2090, 2220) yds / 990 (1080, 1155, 1275, 1365, 1480) (1600, 1675, 1805, 1910, 2030) m

## Shown in

Colorway Brown (102)

## Hook

7 / 4.5 mm, or size needed to obtain gauge

## Notions

Tapestry needle

7 stitch markers

## Skills

Experience with making crocheted top-down sweaters

## Abbreviations (US terms)

BOR = beginning of round

BPdc = back post double crochet

BPdc2tog = back post double crochet 2 together

Ch = chain

Dc = double crochet

Fsc = foundation single crochet

Hdc = half double crochet

LL = long loop

Rnd(s) = round(s)

RS = right side

Sc = single crochet

Sl st = slip stitch

St(s) = stitch(es)

WS = wrong side

*Reduced sample of stitch diagram rounds 2–24.*

*Stitch repeat shown in grey.*

**Key**

- • sl st
- ◯ LL
- X sc
- ⊤ hdc
- BPdc
- BPdc2tog

| Size | A—finished bust | B—yoke depth | C—length | D—sleeve length from underarm | E—upper arm |
|------|-----------------|--------------|----------|-------------------------------|-------------|
| 1 | 32.5" / 82.5 cm | 7.75" / 20 cm | 16.25" / 41.5 cm | 8.75" / 22 cm | 12.5" / 32 cm |
| 2 | 35.5" / 90 cm | 8.5" / 21.5 cm | 17" / 43 cm | 8.75" / 22 cm | 13" / 33 cm |
| 3 | 38.5" / 97.5 cm | 9" / 23 cm | 17.5" / 44.5 cm | 8.75" / 22 cm | 13.5" / 34 cm |
| 4 | 41.25" / 105 cm | 9.5" / 24.5 cm | 18" / 45.5 cm | 8.75" / 22 cm | 13.75" / 35 cm |
| 5 | 44.25" / 112.5 cm | 10" / 25.5 cm | 18.5" / 47 cm | 8.75" / 22 cm | 14.5" / 37 cm |
| 6 | 47.25" / 120 cm | 10.75" / 27 cm | 19" / 48.5 cm | 8.75" / 22 cm | 15.75" / 40 cm |
| 7 | 50.25" / 127.5 cm | 11.25" / 28.5 cm | 19.75" / 50 cm | 8.75" / 22 cm | 17" / 43 cm |
| 8 | 53.25" / 135 cm | 11.75" / 30 cm | 20.25" / 51.5 cm | 8.75" / 22 cm | 17.75" / 45 cm |
| 9 | 56" / 142.5 cm | 12.25" / 31.5 cm | 20.75" / 53 cm | 8.75" / 22 cm | 18.5" / 47 cm |
| 10 | 59" / 150 cm | 13" / 33 cm | 21.5" / 54.5 cm | 8.75" / 22 cm | 19" / 48 cm |
| 11 | 62" / 157.5 cm | 13.5" / 34.5 cm | 21.75" / 55.5 cm | 8.75" / 22 cm | 19.75" / 50 cm |

*The stitch pattern on the body is 7.75" / 20 cm tall including hem ribbing. The sweater is designed to be worn with 3" / 7.5 cm of positive ease. Size 2 is modeled on 33" / 83-cm bust model.*

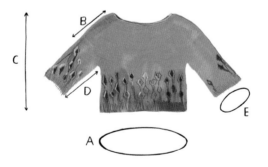

# Rasa Dew Sweater Pattern

You'll be working your sweater with WS facing throughout (except for 3 short rows on Yoke back). Turn it to the RS only when it's completely finished.

## Yoke

Using hook required for gauge and leaving approximately 6" / 15 cm-long yarn end for sewing the neck split, with WS facing fsc 98 (100, 102, 104, 106, 108) (110, 112, 114, 116, 118), turn.

Work 3 back-and-forth short rows on your foundation ch to raise the back-neck for a better fitting garment as follows.

**Row 1:** Skip first fsc, sc into next 24 (25, 26, 27, 28, 29) (30, 31, 32, 33, 34) fsc, stop here and turn work. 24 (25, 26, 27, 28, 29) (30, 31, 32, 33, 34) sts

**Row 2:** Skip first st, sc until 5 sts from previous row remain unworked, stop here and turn work. 18 (19, 20, 21, 22, 23) (24, 25, 26, 27, 28) sts

**Row 3:** Skip first st, sc until 5 sts remain unworked, stop here, do not turn. 12 (13, 14, 15, 16, 17) (18, 19, 20, 21, 22) sts

Place marker in the approximate center of row 3 to mark the center-back (will count as your BOR). Move this marker up as you work each rnd.

Place a second marker at the same position on your foundation ch to mark the true center-back.

The yoke will be worked in a spiral and your BOR will drift off-center. Replace the working marker into the approximate center stitch as often as needed, using your second marker (in the foundation ch) as a reference point.

Start working in a spiral.

Sc in next 5 sc, sc into the edge of the row (to make up for the skipped st), sc in each fsc to end of row. Join in the rnd by working 1 sc into the edge of the row at the first skipped fsc from row 1 (make sure your yoke is not twisted), sc in next 5 sc, sc into edge of row, sc in each st to BOR.

98 (100, 102, 104, 106, 108) (110, 112, 114, 116, 118) sts

Continue to work in hdc.

### Increase rnd 1

[2 hdc in next st, hdc in next st] around. 147 (150, 153, 156, 159, 162) (165, 168, 171, 174, 177) sts

**All sizes:** Continue to work evenly in hdc, in a spiral, for another 8 rnds.

### Increase rnd 2

[2 hdc in next st, hdc in next 2 sts] around. 196 (200, 204, 208, 212, 216) (220, 224, 228, 232, 236) sts

**All sizes:** Continue to work evenly in hdc, in a spiral, for another 6 rnds.

### Increase rnd 3

**Sizes 1–3:** [2 hdc in next st, hdc in next 7 sts] 24 (25, 25, x, x, x) (x, x, x, x, x) times. Hdc in next 4 (0, 4, x, x, x) (x, x, x, x, x) sts. 220 (225, 229, x, x, x) (x, x, x, x, x) sts

**Sizes 4–11:** [2 hdc in next st, hdc in next 3 sts] around. x (x, x, 260, 265, 270) (275, 280, 285, 290, 295) sts

**All sizes:** Continue to work evenly in hdc, in a spiral, for another 8 rnds.

### Increase rnd 4

**Size 1:** Hdc in next 10 sts. [2 hdc in next st, hdc in next 14 sts] 14 times. 234 sts

**Size 2:** Hdc in next 12 sts. [2 hdc in next st, hdc in next 9 sts] 21 times. Hdc in next 3 sts. 246 sts

**Size 3:** Hdc in next 10 sts. [2 hdc in next st, hdc in next 7 sts] 27 times. Hdc in next 3 sts. 256 sts

**Size 4:** Hdc in next 4 sts. [2 hdc in next st, hdc in next 31 sts] 8 times. 268 sts

**Sizes 5–11:** Hdc in next x (x, x, x, 5, 10) (15, 20, 25, 30, 35) sts. [2 hdc in next st, hdc in next 25 sts] 10 times. x (x, x, x, 275, 280) (285, 290, 295, 300, 305) sts

**Size 1:** Continue to Separating Body and Sleeves.

**Sizes 2–4:** Continue to work evenly in hdc, in a spiral, for another x (2, 4, 6, x, x) (x, x, x, x, x) rnds, then continue to Separating Body and Sleeves.

**Sizes 5–11:** Continue to work evenly in hdc, in a spiral, for another 7 rnds.

## Increase rnd 5

**Size 5:** Hdc in next 2 sts. [2 hdc in next st, hdc in next 38 sts] 7 times. 282 sts

**Size 6:** [2 hdc in next st, hdc in next 13 sts] 20 times. 300 sts

**Size 7:** Hdc in next 14 sts. [2 hdc in next st, hdc in next 7 sts] 33 times. Hdc in next 7 sts. 318 sts

**Sizes 8–11:** Hdc in next x (x, x, x, x, x) (x, 10, 15, 20, 25) sts. [2 hdc in next st, hdc in next 13 sts] 20 times. x (x, x, x, x, x) (x, 310, 315, 320, 325) sts

**Size 5:** Continue to Separating Body and Sleeves.

**Sizes 6–7:** Continue to work evenly in hdc, in a spiral, for another x (x, x, x, x, 2) (4, x, x, x, x) rnds, then continue to Separating Body and Sleeves.

**Sizes 8–11:** Continue to work evenly in hdc, in a spiral, for another 5 rnds.

## Increase rnd 6

**Size 8:** Hdc in next 2 sts. [2 hdc in next st, hdc in next 13 sts] 22 times. 332 sts

**Size 9:** Hdc in next 5 sts. [2 hdc in next st, hdc in next 9 sts] 31 times. 346 sts

**Size 10:** Hdc in next 11 sts. [2 hdc in next st, hdc in next 7 sts] 38 times. Hdc in next 5 sts. 358 sts

**Size 11:** Hdc in next 24 sts. [2 hdc in next st, hdc in next 5 sts] 47 times. Hdc in next 19 sts. 372 sts

**Size 8:** Continue to Separating Body and Sleeves.

**Sizes 9–11:** Continue to work evenly in hdc, in a spiral, for another x (x, x, x, x, x) (x, x, 2, 4, 6) rnds, then continue to Separating Body and Sleeves.

Finish Yoke with 234 (246, 256, 268, 282, 300) (318, 332, 346, 358, 372) sts.

# Separating Body and Sleeves

Re-center your working marker in the center back.

Hdc in next 33 (36, 38, 40, 43, 46) (48, 51, 53, 56, 58) sts, ch 0 (1, 2, 3, 4, 5) (6, 7, 8, 9, 10), skip next 51 (52, 52, 53, 55, 59) (63, 65, 67, 68, 70) sts, hdc in next 66 (71, 76, 81, 86, 91) (96, 101, 106, 111, 116) sts, ch 0 (1, 2, 3, 4, 5) (6, 7, 8, 9, 10), skip next 51 (52, 52, 53, 55, 59) (63, 65, 67, 68, 70) sts, hdc in next 33 (35, 38, 41, 43, 45) (48, 50, 53, 55, 58) sts.

**Size 1:** Mark first and last skipped st of each sleeve (2 markers per sleeve).

# Body

**Rnds 1–2:** Working in each st and ch, hdc around. 132 (144, 156, 168, 180, 192) (204, 216, 228, 240, 252) sts

Add rnds of hdc here to make your sweater longer, if desired.

**Stitch pattern starts here:**

**Rnd 3:** [Hdc in next 8 sts, skip next st, (2 dc in next st) twice, skip next st] around. Sl st to the first st of this rnd.

*Continue to work in joined rnds, start each rnd with a LL (long loop, pull loop up to height of hdc; doesn't count as a stitch). First hdc (or BPdc) of each rnd is made in (or around) same st as last sl st made.*

**Rnd 4:** Sl st in next st. LL, [hdc in next 6 sts, skip next st, BPdc around next dc, (2 dc in next st) twice, BPdc around next dc, skip next st] around, join.

**Rnd 5:** Sl st in next st. LL, [hdc in next 4 sts, skip next st, BPdc around next 2 sts, (2 dc in next st) twice, BPdc around next 2 sts, skip next st] around, join.

**Rnd 6:** LL, [2 hdc in next st, hdc in next 2 sts, 2 hdc in next st, BPdc around next 2 sts, skip next st, sc in next 2 sts, skip next st, BPdc around next 2 sts] around, join.

**Rnd 7:** LL, [2 hdc in next st, hdc in next 4 sts, 2 hdc in next st, BPdc around next 2 sts, skip next 2 sts, BPdc around next 2 sts] around, join.

**Rnd 8:** LL, [2 hdc in next st, hdc in next st, skip next st, (2 dc in next st) twice, skip next st, hdc in next st, 2 hdc in next st, (BPdc2tog over next 2 sts) twice] around, join.

**Rnd 9:** LL, [hdc in next 2 sts, skip next st, BPdc around next st, (2 dc in next st) twice, BPdc around next st, skip next st, hdc in next 2 sts, BPdc around next 2 sts] around, join.

**Rnd 10:** LL, [hdc in next st, skip next st, BPdc around next 2 sts, (2 dc in next st) twice, BPdc around next 2 sts, skip next st, hdc in next st, BPdc around next 2 sts] around, join.

**Rnd 11:** LL, [2 hdc in next st, BPdc around next 2 sts, skip next st, sc in next 2 sts, skip next st, BPdc around next 2 sts, 2 hdc in next st, BPdc around next 2 sts] around, join.

**Rnd 12:** LL, [hdc in next st, 2 hdc in next st, BPdc around next 2 sts, skip next 2 sts, BPdc around next 2 sts, 2 hdc in next st, hdc in next st, BPdc around next 2 sts] around, join.

**Rnd 13:** Sl st in next st. LL, [hdc in next st, 2 hdc in next st, (BPdc2tog over next 2 sts) twice, 2 hdc in next st, hdc in next st, skip next st, (2 dc in next st) twice, skip next st] around, join.

**Rnd 14:** Sl st in next st. LL, [hdc in next 2 sts, BPdc around next 2 sts, hdc in next 2 sts, skip next st, BPdc around next st, (2 dc in next st) twice, BPdc around next st, skip next st] around, join.

**Rnd 15:** Sl st in next st. LL, [hdc in next st, BPdc around next 2 sts, hdc in next st, skip next st, BPdc around next 2 sts, (2 dc in next st) twice, BPdc around next 2 sts, skip next st] around, join.

**Rnd 16:** LL, [2 hdc in next st, BPdc around next 2 sts, 2 hdc in next st, BPdc around next 2 sts, skip next st, sc in next 2 sts, skip next st, BPdc around next 2 sts] around, join.

**Rnd 17:** LL, [2 hdc in next st, hdc in next st, BPdc around next 2 sts, hdc in next st, 2 hdc in next st, BPdc around next 2 sts, skip next 2 sts, BPdc around next 2 sts] around, join.

**Rnd 18:** Rep rnd 8.

**Rnd 19:** Rep rnd 9.

**Rnd 20:** Rep rnd 10.

**Rnd 21:** LL, [BPdc around next st, hdc in next st, 2 hdc in next st, (BPdc2tog over next 2 sts) twice, 2 hdc in next st, hdc in next st, BPdc around next 3 sts] around, join.

**Rnd 22:** LL, [BPdc around next 2 sts, hdc in next 2 sts, BPdc around next 2 sts, hdc in next 2 sts, BPdc around next 4 sts] around, join.

**Rnd 23:** LL, [BPdc around next 3 sts, hdc in next st, BPdc around next 2 sts, hdc in next st, BPdc around next 5 sts] around, join.

**Rnds 24–30:** LL, BPdc around, join.

Add more repeats to make the sweater longer, if desired.

**Last rnd:** Sl st around, fasten off.

If you feel that your ribbing is not tight enough, go down a hook size for the last rnd here and on Sleeves.

## Sleeve

### Make 2

With WS facing, attach new yarn with a sl st at the center of underarm as follows:

**Size 1:** Attach in the second marked st (last st skipped).

**Sizes 2, 4, 6, 8, 10:** Attach in the middle st (ch) of underarm.

**Sizes 3, 5, 7, 9, 11:** Attach in the x (x, second, x, third, x) (fourth, x, fifth, x, sixth) st of underarm ch counting from right to left.

Work the sleeve in a spiral, marking the first stitch of the round (BOR) and moving the marker up as you go.

**Rnd 1:** Beginning in same st as join, and working into each st and ch, hdc around. 51 (53, 54, 56, 59, 64) (69, 72, 75, 77, 80) sts

**Rnd 2:** Hdc around.

Add rnds of hdc here if you want to make the sleeve longer.

**Rnd 3:** Hdc in next 23 (24, 25, 26, 27, 30) (32, 34, 35, 36, 38) sts, skip next st, (2 dc in next st) twice, skip next st, hdc in next 24 (25, 25, 26, 28, 30) (33, 34, 36, 37, 38) sts.

**Rnd 4:** Hdc in next 22 (23, 24, 25, 26, 29) (31, 33, 34, 35, 37) sts, skip next st, BPdc around next st, (2 dc in next st) twice, BPdc around next st, skip next st, hdc in next 23 (24, 24, 25, 27, 29) (32, 33, 35, 36, 37) sts.

**Rnd 5:** Hdc in next 21 (22, 23, 24, 25, 28) (30, 32, 33, 34, 36) sts, skip next st, BPdc around next 2 sts, (2 dc in next st) twice, BPdc around next 2 sts, skip next st, hdc in next 22 (23, 23, 24, 26, 28) (31, 32, 34, 35, 36) sts.

**Rnd 6:** Hdc in next 20 (21, 22, 23, 24, 27) (29, 31, 32, 33, 35) sts, 2 hdc in next st, BPdc around next 2 sts, skip next st, sc in next 2 sts, skip next st, BPdc around next 2 sts, 2 hdc in next st, hdc in next 21 (22, 22, 23, 25, 27) (30, 31, 33, 34, 35) sts.

**Rnd 7:** Hdc in next 21 (22, 23, 24, 25, 28) (30, 32, 33, 34, 36) sts, 2 hdc in next st, BPdc around next 2 sts, skip next 2 sts, BPdc around next 2 sts, 2 hdc in next st, hdc in next 22 (23, 23, 24, 26, 28) (31, 32, 34, 35, 36) sts.

**Rnd 8:** Hdc in next 17 (18, 19, 20, 21, 24) (26, 28, 29, 30, 32) sts, skip next st, (2 dc in next st) twice, skip next st, hdc in next st, 2 hdc in next st, (BPdc2tog over next 2 sts) twice, 2 hdc in next st, hdc in next st, skip next st, (2 dc in next st) twice, skip next st, hdc in next 18 (19, 19, 20, 22, 24) (27, 28, 30, 31, 32) sts.

**Rnd 9:** Hdc in next 16 (17, 18, 19, 20, 23) (25, 27, 28, 29, 31) sts, skip next st, BPdc around next st, (2 dc in next st) twice, BPdc around next st, skip next st, hdc in next 2 sts, BPdc around next 2 sts, hdc in next 2 sts, skip next st, BPdc around next st, (2 dc in next st) twice, BPdc around next st, skip next st, hdc in next 17 (18, 18, 19, 21, 23) (26, 27, 29, 30, 31) sts.

**Rnd 10:** Hdc in next 15 (16, 17, 18, 19, 22) (24, 26, 27, 28, 30) sts, skip next st, BPdc around next 2 sts, (2 dc in next st) twice, BPdc around next 2 sts, skip next st, hdc in next st, BPdc around next 2 sts, hdc in next st, skip next st, BPdc around next 2 sts, (2 dc in next st) twice, BPdc around next 2 sts, skip next st, hdc in next 16 (17, 17, 18, 20, 22) (25, 26, 28, 29, 30) sts.

**Rnd 11:** Hdc in next 14 (15, 16, 17, 18, 21) (23, 25, 26, 27, 29) sts, 2 hdc in next st, BPdc around next 2 sts, skip next st, sc in next 2 sts, skip next st, BPdc around next 2 sts, 2 hdc in next st, BPdc around next 2 sts, 2 hdc in next st, BPdc around next 2 sts, skip next st, sc in next 2 sts, skip next st, BPdc around next 2 sts, 2 hdc in next st, hdc in next 15 (16, 16, 17, 19, 21) (24, 25, 27, 28, 29) sts.

**Rnd 12:** Hdc in next 15 (16, 17, 18, 19, 22) (24, 26, 27, 28, 30) sts, 2 hdc in next st, BPdc around next 2 sts, skip next 2 sts, BPdc around next 2 sts, 2 hdc in next st, hdc in next st, BPdc around next 2 sts, hdc in next st, 2 hdc in next st, BPdc around next 2 sts, skip next 2 sts, BPdc around next 2 sts, 2 hdc in next st, hdc in next 16 (17, 17, 18, 20, 22) (25, 26, 28, 29, 30) sts.

**Rnd 13:** Hdc in next 11 (12, 13, 14, 15, 18) (20, 22, 23, 24, 26) sts, skip next st, (2 dc in next st) twice, skip next st, hdc in next st, 2 hdc in next st, (BPdc2tog over next 2 sts) twice, 2 hdc in next st, hdc in next st, skip next st, (2 dc in next st) twice, skip next st, hdc in next st, 2 hdc in next st, (BPdc2tog over next 2 sts) twice, 2 hdc in next st, hdc in next st, skip next st, (2 dc in next st) twice, skip next st, hdc in next 12 (13, 13, 14, 16, 18) (21, 22, 24, 25, 26) sts.

**Rnd 14:** Hdc in next 10 (11, 12, 13, 14, 17) (19, 21, 22, 23, 25) sts, [skip next st, BPdc around next st, (2 dc in next st) twice, BPdc around next st, skip next st, hdc in next 2 sts, BPdc around next 2 sts, hdc in next 2 sts] twice. Skip next st, BPdc around next st, (2 dc in next st) twice, BPdc around next st, skip next st, hdc in next 11 (12, 12, 13, 15, 17) (20, 21, 23, 24, 25) sts.

**Rnd 15:** Hdc in next 9 (10, 11, 12, 13, 16) (18, 20, 21, 22, 24) sts, [skip next st, BPdc around next 2 sts, (2 dc in next st) twice, BPdc around next 2 sts, skip next st, hdc in next st, BPdc around next 2 sts, hdc in next st] twice. Skip next st, BPdc around next 2 sts, (2 dc in next st) twice, BPdc around next 2 sts, skip next st, hdc in next 10 (11, 11, 12, 14, 16) (19, 20, 22, 23, 24) sts.

**Rnd 16:** Hdc in next 8 (9, 10, 11, 12, 15) (17, 19, 20, 21, 23) sts, [2 hdc in next st, BPdc around next 2 sts, skip next st, sc in next 2 sts, skip next st, BPdc around next 2 sts, 2 hdc in next st, BPdc around next 2 sts] twice. 2 hdc in next st, BPdc around next 2 sts, skip next st, sc in next 2 sts, skip next st, BPdc around next 2 sts, 2 hdc in next st, hdc in next 9 (10, 10, 11, 13, 15) (18, 19, 21, 22, 23) sts.

**Rnd 17:** Hdc in next 9 (10, 11, 12, 13, 16) (18, 20, 21, 22, 24) sts, [2 hdc in next st, BPdc around next 2 sts, skip next 2 sts, BPdc around next 2 sts, 2 hdc in next st, hdc in next st, BPdc around next 2 sts, hdc in next st] twice. 2 hdc in next st, BPdc around next 2 sts, skip next 2 sts, BPdc around next 2 sts, 2 hdc in next st, hdc in next 10 (11, 11, 12, 14, 16) (19, 20, 22, 23, 24) sts.

**Rnd 18:** Hdc in next 5 (6, 7, 8, 9, 12) (14, 16, 17, 18, 20) sts, [skip next st, (2 dc in next st) twice, skip next st, hdc in next st, 2 hdc in next st, (BPdc2tog over next 2 sts) twice, 2 hdc in next st, hdc in next st] three times. Skip next st, (2 dc in next st) twice, skip next st, hdc in next 6 (7, 7, 8, 10, 12) (15, 16, 18, 19, 20) sts.

**Rnd 19:** Hdc in next 4 (5, 6, 7, 8, 11) (13, 15, 16, 17, 19) sts, [skip next st, BPdc around next st, (2 dc in next st) twice, BPdc around next st, skip next st, hdc in next 2 sts, BPdc around next 2 sts, hdc in next 2 sts] three times. Skip next st, BPdc around next st, (2 dc in next st) twice, BPdc around next st, skip next st, hdc in next 5 (6, 6, 7, 9, 11) (14, 15, 17, 18, 19) sts.

**Rnd 20:** Hdc in next 3 (4, 5, 6, 7, 10) (12, 14, 15, 16, 18) sts, [skip next st, BPdc around next 2 sts, (2 dc in next st) twice, BPdc around next 2 sts, skip next st, hdc in next st, BPdc around next 2 sts, hdc in next st] three times. Skip next st, BPdc around next 2 sts, (2 dc in next st) twice, BPdc around next 2 sts, skip next st, hdc in next 4 (5, 5, 6, 8, 10) (13, 14, 16, 17, 18) sts.

**Rnd 21:** Hdc in next 2 (3, 4, 5, 6, 9) (11, 13, 14, 15, 17) sts, [2 hdc in next st, BPdc around next 2 sts, skip next st, sc in next 2 sts, skip next st, BPdc around next 2 sts, 2 hdc in next st, BPdc around next 2 sts] three times. 2 hdc in next st, BPdc around next 2 sts, skip next st, sc in next 2 sts, skip next st, BPdc around next 2 sts, 2 hdc in next st, hdc in next 3 (4, 4, 5, 7, 9) (12, 13, 15, 16, 17) sts.

**Rnd 22:** Hdc in next 3 (4, 5, 6, 7, 10) (12, 14, 15, 16, 18) sts, [2 hdc in next st, BPdc around next 2 sts, skip next 2 sts, BPdc around next 2 sts, 2 hdc in next st, hdc in next st, BPdc around next 2 sts, hdc in next st] three times. 2 hdc in next st, BPdc around next 2 sts, skip next 2 sts, BPdc around next 2 sts, 2 hdc in next st, hdc in next 4 (5, 5, 6, 8, 10) (13, 14, 16, 17, 18) sts.

**Rnd 23:** Hdc in next 4 (5, 6, 7, 8, 11) (13, 15, 16, 17, 19) sts, [2 hdc in next st, (BPdc2tog over next 2 sts) twice, 2 hdc in next st, hdc in next st, skip next st, (2 dc in next st) twice, skip next st, hdc in next st] three times. 2 hdc in next st, (BPdc2tog over next 2 sts) twice, 2 hdc in next st, hdc in next 5 (6, 6, 7, 9, 11) (14, 15, 17, 18, 19) sts.

**Rnd 24:** Hdc in next 6 (7, 8, 9, 10, 13) (15, 17, 18, 19, 21) sts, [BPdc around next 2 sts, hdc in next 2 sts, skip next st, BPdc around next st, (2 dc in next st) twice, BPdc around next st, skip next st, hdc in next 2 sts] three times. BPdc around next 2 sts, hdc in next 7 (8, 8, 9, 11, 13) (16, 17, 19, 20, 21) sts.

**Rnd 25:** Hdc in next 6 (7, 8, 9, 10, 13) (15, 17, 18, 19, 21) sts, [BPdc around next 2 sts, hdc in next st, skip next st, BPdc around next 2 sts, (2 dc in next st) twice, BPdc around next 2 sts, skip next st, hdc in next st] three times. BPdc around next 2 sts, hdc in next 7 (8, 8, 9, 11, 13) (16, 17, 19, 20, 21) sts.

**Rnd 26:** Hdc in next 6 (7, 8, 9, 10, 13) (15, 17, 18, 19, 21) sts, [BPdc around next 2 sts, 2 hdc in next st, BPdc around next 2 sts, skip next st, sc in next 2 sts, skip next st, BPdc around next 2 sts, 2 hdc in next st] three times. BPdc around next 2 sts, hdc in next 7 (8, 8, 9, 11, 13) (16, 17, 19, 20, 21) sts.

**Rnd 27:** Hdc in next 6 (7, 8, 9, 10, 13) (15, 17, 18, 19, 21) sts, [BPdc around next 2 sts, hdc in next st, 2 hdc in next st, BPdc around next 2 sts, skip next 2 sts, BPdc around next 2 sts, 2 hdc in next st, hdc in next st] three times. BPdc around next 2 sts, hdc in next 7 (8, 8, 9, 11, 13) (16, 17, 19, 20, 21) sts.

**Rnd 28:** Hdc in next 6 (7, 8, 9, 10, 13) (15, 17, 18, 19, 21) sts, [BPdc around next 2 sts, hdc in next 2 sts, 2 hdc in next st, (BPdc2tog over next 2 sts) twice, 2 hdc in next st, hdc in next 2 sts] three times. BPdc around next 2 sts, hdc in next 7 (8, 8, 9, 11, 13) (16, 17, 19, 20, 21) sts.

**Rnds 29–32:** BPdc around.

**Last rnd:** Sc in next st, sl st around, fasten off.

## Finishing

Remove markers, sew the neck split (if not done already) and weave in all ends. Block according to fiber type. Turn the sweater RS out.

# Zvaigznes Stars Wrap Sweater

A wrap sweater revealing a bit of the back and accentuating the tied waist, Zvaigznes deserves the title of a timeless closet staple. Its versatility doesn't stop there—turn it back side to the front and wear Zvaigznes as a cardigan, if desired. The alpine stitch embodies a soft texture while the finer details demand attention and leave nobody indifferent.

# Zvaigznes Stars Wrap Sweater Construction Notes

*Zvaigznes is worked bottom up starting with the front, and continuing over one shoulder and down the back. The second half of the back is then made over the second shoulder. Long ties finish the back pieces. The front panel and both back panels are worked in one piece with no seaming. The sleeves are crocheted separately and sewn in.*

## Sizes

1 (2, 3, 4, 5) (6, 7, 8, 9)

**To fit bust:** 30 (34, 38, 42, 46) (50, 54, 58, 62)" / 76 (86, 97, 107, 117) (127, 137, 147, 157) cm

**Finished bust:** 32.25 (36.25, 40.25, 44, 48) (52, 56, 59.75, 63.75)" / 82 (92, 102, 112, 122) (132, 142, 152, 162) cm

## Gauge

16 sts x 10 rows = 4" / 10 cm in dc after blocking with H/8 / 5 mm

16 sts x 18 rows = 4" / 10 cm over main stitch pattern after blocking

## Yarn

DK weight, Hedgehog Fibers Tweedy (50% Falkland merino wool, 38% recycled wool, 12% HHF thread waste), 252 yds / 230 m per 100-g skein, or use any DK weight wool yarn to achieve a similar effect

## Yardage/Meterage

1535 (1660, 1860, 2010, 2265) (2400, 2720, 2830, 3210) yds / 1405 (1520, 1700, 1840, 2070) (2195, 2485, 2590, 2935) m

## Shown in

Colorway Tweedy

## Hooks

H/8 / 5 mm for Body, Sleeves and Tie, or size needed to obtain gauge

G/6 / 4 mm for Ribbing

## Notions

Tapestry needle for sewing seams and ribbing

3 stitch markers

## Skills

Experience with making and sewing crocheted sweaters

### Abbreviations (US terms)

Ch = chain

Dc = double crochet

Dc2tog = double crochet 2 stitches together

Fdc = foundation double crochet

FPdc = front post double crochet

Rep = repeat

RS = right side

Sc = single crochet

Sl st = slip stitch

St(s) = stitch(es)

WS = wrong side

| Size | Finished bust | Finished half-bust | Length | Sleeve length from underarm | Upper arm |
|------|---------------|--------------------|--------|----------------------------|-----------|
| 1 | 32.25" / 82 cm | 16.25" / 41 cm | 16.25" / 41 cm | 19.5" / 50 cm | 13" / 33 cm |
| 2 | 36.25" / 92 cm | 18" / 46 cm | 17" / 43 cm | 19.25" / 49 cm | 13" / 33 cm |
| 3 | 40.25" / 102 cm | 20" / 51 cm | 17.75" / 45 cm | 19" / 48 cm | 13.5" / 34 cm |
| 4 | 44" / 112 cm | 22" / 56 cm | 18.5" / 47 cm | 18.5" / 47 cm | 14.25" / 36 cm |
| 5 | 48" / 122 cm | 24" / 61 cm | 19.25" / 49 cm | 18" / 46 cm | 14.5" / 37 cm |
| 6 | 52" / 132 cm | 26" / 66 cm | 20.5" / 52 cm | 17.5" / 44.5 cm | 15" / 38 cm |
| 7 | 56" / 142 cm | 28" / 71 cm | 21.25" / 54 cm | 17" / 43 cm | 15.25" / 39 cm |
| 8 | 59.75" / 152 cm | 30" / 76 cm | 22" / 56 cm | 16.5" / 42 cm | 16.25" / 41 cm |
| 9 | 63.75" / 162 cm | 32" / 81 cm | 22.75" / 58 cm | 16" / 40.5 cm | 16.5" / 42 cm |

*Hem ribbing measures 2" / 5 cm. Back-Neck-Back ribbing measures 1.25" / 3 cm. The sweater is designed to be worn with 2.25 (2.25, 2, 2, 2) (2, 2, 2, 2)" / 6 (6, 5, 5, 5) (5, 5, 5, 5) cm of positive ease. Size 2 is modeled on 35" / 89-cm bust model.*

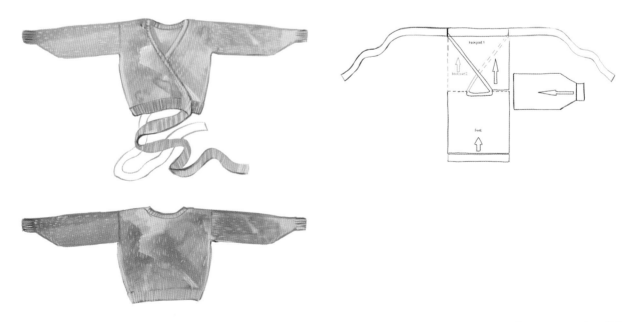

# Zvaigznes Stars Wrap Sweater Pattern

**Throughout:** Ch 2 at the beginning of row counts as first dc (=1 st).

Ch 1 at the beginning of a row counts as turning ch and is not counted as a stitch.

## Front

With larger hook, fdc 65 (73, 81, 89, 97) (105, 113, 121, 129).

**Row 1:** With RS facing, ch 2, [dc in next st, FPdc around next st] across until 2 sts left. Dc in next 2 sts, turn.

**Row 2:** Ch 1, sc across, turn.

**Row 3:** Ch 2, [FPdc around next dc 2 rows down, dc in next st] across, turn.

**Row 4:** Ch 1, sc across, turn.

**Row 5:** Ch 2, [dc in next st, FPdc around next dc 2 rows down] across until 2 sts left. Dc in next 2 sts, turn.

Rep rows 2–5 another 14 (15, 16, 17, 18) (19, 20, 21, 22) times.

Rep rows 2–4 one time.

64 (68, 72, 76, 80) (84, 88, 92, 96) rows

Don't fasten off, continue to Shoulder 1.

## Shoulder 1

**Row 1:** Ch 2, [dc in next st, FPdc around next dc 2 rows down] 8 (10, 12, 14, 16) (18, 20, 22, 24) times, dc2tog over next 2 sts, turn. 18 (22, 26, 30, 34) (38, 42, 46, 50) sts

**Row 2:** Ch 1, sc across, turn.

**Row 3:** Ch 2, [FPdc around next dc 2 rows down, dc in next st] 7 (9, 11, 13, 15) (17, 19, 21, 23) times. FPdc around next dc 2 rows down, dc2tog over next 2 sts, turn. 17 (21, 25, 29, 33) (37, 41, 45, 49) sts

**Row 4:** Ch 1, sc across, turn.

**Row 5:** Ch 2, [dc in next st, FPdc around next dc 2 rows down] 7 (9, 11, 13, 15) (17, 19, 21, 23) times, dc2tog over next 2 sts, turn. 16 (20, 24, 28, 32) (36, 40, 44, 48) sts

**Row 6:** Ch 1, sc across, turn.

**Row 7:** Ch 2, [FPdc around next dc 2 rows down, dc in next st] 6 (8, 10, 12, 14) (16, 18, 20, 22) times. FPdc around next dc 2 rows down, dc2tog over next 2 sts, turn. 15 (19, 23, 27, 31) (35, 39, 43, 47) sts

**Row 8:** Ch 1, sc across, turn. Mark this row as your shoulder seam.

Don't fasten off and continue to Back Part 1.

## Back Part 1

**Row 1:** Ch 2, [dc in next st, FPdc around next dc 2 rows down] 6 (8, 10, 12, 14) (16, 18, 20, 22) times. Dc in next 2 sts, turn. 15 (19, 23, 27, 31) (35, 39, 43, 47) sts

**Row 2:** Ch 1, sc across, turn.

**Row 3:** Ch 2, [FPdc around next dc 2 rows down, dc in next st] 6 (8, 10, 12, 14) (16, 18, 20, 22) times. FPdc around next dc 2 rows down, 2 dc in next st, turn. 16 (20, 24, 28, 32) (36, 40, 44, 48) sts

**Row 4:** Ch 1, sc across, turn.

**Row 5:** Ch 2, [dc in next st, FPdc around next dc 2 rows down] 7 (9, 11, 13, 15) (17, 19, 21, 23) times. 2 dc in next st, turn. 17 (21, 25, 29, 33) (37, 41, 45, 49) sts

**Row 6:** Ch 1, sc across, turn.

**Row 7:** Ch 2, [FPdc around next dc 2 rows down, dc in next st] 7 (9, 11, 13, 15) (17, 19, 21, 23) times. FPdc around next dc 2 rows down, 2 dc in next st, turn. 18 (22, 26, 30, 34) (38, 42, 46, 50) sts

**Row 8:** Ch 1, sc across, turn.

**Row 9:** Ch 2, [dc in next st, FPdc around next dc 2 rows down] 8 (10, 12, 14, 16) (18, 20, 22, 24) times. 2 dc in next st, turn. 19 (23, 27, 31, 35) (39, 43, 47, 51) sts

**Row 10:** Ch 1, sc across, turn.

**Row 11:** Ch 2, [FPdc around next dc 2 rows down, dc in next st] 8 (10, 12, 14, 16) (18, 20, 22, 24) times. FPdc around next dc 2 rows down, 2 dc in next st, turn. 20 (24, 28, 32, 36) (40, 44, 48, 52) sts

**Row 12:** Ch 1, sc across, turn.

**Row 13:** Ch 2, [dc in next st, FPdc around next dc 2 rows down] 9 (11, 13, 15, 17) (19, 21, 23, 25) times. 2 dc in next st, turn. 21 (25, 29, 33, 37) (41, 45, 49, 53) sts

**Row 14:** Ch 1, sc across, turn.

**Row 15:** Ch 2, [FPdc around next dc 2 rows down, dc in next st] 9 (11, 13, 15, 17) (19, 21, 23, 25) times. FPdc around next dc 2 rows down, 2 dc in next st, turn. 22 (26, 30, 34, 38) (42, 46, 50, 54) sts

**Row 16:** Ch 1, sc across, turn.

**Row 17:** Ch 2, [dc in next st, FPdc around next dc 2 rows down] 10 (12, 14, 16, 18) (20, 22, 24, 26) times. 2 dc in next st, turn. 23 (27, 31, 35, 39) (43, 47, 51, 55) sts

**Row 18:** Ch 1, sc across, turn.

**Row 19:** Ch 2, [FPdc around next dc 2 rows down, dc in next st] 10 (12, 14, 16, 18) (20, 22, 24, 26) times. FPdc around next dc 2 rows down, 2 dc in next st, turn. 24 (28, 32, 36, 40) (44, 48, 52, 56) sts

**Row 20:** Ch 1, sc across, turn.

**Row 21:** Ch 2, [dc in next st, FPdc around next dc 2 rows down] 11 (13, 15, 17, 19) (21, 23, 25, 27) times. 2 dc in next st, turn. 25 (29, 33, 37, 41) (45, 49, 53, 57) sts

**Row 22:** Ch 1, sc across, turn.

**Row 23:** Ch 2, [FPdc around next dc 2 rows down, dc in next st] 11 (13, 15, 17, 19) (21, 23, 25, 27) times. FPdc around next dc 2 rows down, 2 dc in next st, turn. 26 (30, 34, 38, 42) (46, 50, 54, 58) sts

**Row 24:** Ch 1, sc across, turn.

**Row 25:** Ch 2, [dc in next st, FPdc around next dc 2 rows down] 12 (14, 16, 18, 20) (22, 24, 26, 28) times. 2 dc in next st, turn. 27 (31, 35, 39, 43) (47, 51, 55, 59) sts

**Row 26:** Ch 1, sc across, turn.

**Row 27:** Ch 2, [FPdc around next dc 2 rows down, dc in next st] 12 (14, 16, 18, 20) (22, 24, 26, 28) times. FPdc around next dc 2 rows down, 2 dc in next st, turn. 28 (32, 36, 40, 44) (48, 52, 56, 60) sts

**Row 28:** Ch 1, sc across, turn.

**Row 29:** Ch 2, [dc in next st, FPdc around next dc 2 rows down] 13 (15, 17, 19, 21) (23, 25, 27, 29) times. 2 dc in next st, turn. 29 (33, 37, 41, 45) (49, 53, 57, 61) sts

**Row 30:** Ch 1, sc across, turn.

**Row 31:** Ch 2, [FPdc around next dc 2 rows down, dc in next st] 13 (15, 17, 19, 21) (23, 25, 27, 29) times. FPdc around next dc 2 rows down, 2 dc in next st, turn. 30 (34, 38, 42, 46) (50, 54, 58, 62) sts

**Row 32:** Ch 1, sc across, turn.

**Row 33:** Ch 2, [dc in next st, FPdc around next dc 2 rows down] 14 (16, 18, 20, 22) (24, 26, 28, 30) times. 2 dc in next st, turn. 31 (35, 39, 43, 47) (51, 55, 59, 63) sts

**Row 34:** Ch 1, sc across, turn.

**Row 35:** Ch 2, [FPdc around next dc 2 rows down, dc in next st] 14 (16, 18, 20, 22) (24, 26, 28, 30) times. FPdc around next dc 2 rows down, 2 dc in next st, turn. 32 (36, 40, 44, 48) (52, 56, 60, 64) sts

**Row 36:** Ch 1, sc across, turn.

**Row 37:** Ch 2, [dc in next st, FPdc around next dc 2 rows down] 15 (17, 19, 21, 23) (25, 27, 29, 31) times. 2 dc in next st, turn. 33 (37, 41, 45, 49) (53, 57, 61, 65) sts

**Row 38:** Ch 1, sc across, turn.

**Row 39:** Ch 2, [FPdc around next dc 2 rows down, dc in next st] 15 (17, 19, 21, 23) (25, 27, 29, 31) times. FPdc around next dc 2 rows down, 2 dc in next st, turn. 34 (38, 42, 46, 50) (54, 58, 62, 66) sts

**Row 40:** Ch 1, sc across, turn.

**Row 41:** Ch 2, [dc in next st, FPdc around next dc 2 rows down] 16 (18, 20, 22, 24) (26, 28, 30, 32) times. 2 dc in next st, turn. 35 (39, 43, 47, 51) (55, 59, 63, 67) sts

**Row 42:** Ch 1, sc across, turn.

**Row 43:** Ch 2, [FPdc around next dc 2 rows down, dc in next st] 16 (18, 20, 22, 24) (26, 28, 30, 32) times. FPdc around next dc 2 rows down, 2 dc in next st, turn. 36 (40, 44, 48, 52) (56, 60, 64, 68) sts

**Row 44:** Ch 1, sc across, turn.

**Row 45:** Ch 2, [dc in next st, FPdc around next dc 2 rows down] 17 (19, 21, 23, 25) (27, 29, 31, 33) times. 2 dc in next st, turn. 37 (41, 45, 49, 53) (57, 61, 65, 69) sts

**Row 46:** Ch 1, sc across, turn.

**Row 47:** Ch 2, [FPdc around next dc 2 rows down, dc in next st] 17 (19, 21, 23, 25) (27, 29, 31, 33) times. FPdc around next dc 2 rows down, 2 dc in next st, turn. 38 (42, 46, 50, 54) (58, 62, 66, 70) sts

**Row 48:** Ch 1, sc across, turn.

**Row 49:** Ch 2, [dc in next st, FPdc around next dc 2 rows down] 18 (20, 22, 24, 26) (28, 30, 32, 34) times. 2 dc in next st, turn. 39 (43, 47, 51, 55) (59, 63, 67, 71) sts

**Row 50:** Ch 1, sc across, turn.

**Row 51:** Ch 2, [FPdc around next dc 2 rows down, dc in next st] 18 (20, 22, 24, 26) (28, 30, 32, 34) times. FPdc around next dc 2 rows down, 2 dc in next st, turn. 40 (44, 48, 52, 56) (60, 64, 68, 72) sts

**Row 52:** Ch 1, sc across, turn.

**Row 53:** Ch 2, [dc in next st, FPdc around next dc 2 rows down] 19 (21, 23, 25, 27) (29, 31, 33, 35) times. 2 dc in next st, turn. 41 (45, 49, 53, 57) (61, 65, 69, 73) sts

**Row 54:** Ch 1, sc across, turn.

**Row 55:** Ch 2, [FPdc around next dc 2 rows down, dc in next st] 19 (21, 23, 25, 27) (29, 31, 33, 35) times. FPdc around next dc 2 rows down, 2 dc in next st, turn. 42 (46, 50, 54, 58) (62, 66, 70, 74) sts

**Row 56:** Ch 1, sc across, turn.

**Row 57:** Ch 2, [dc in next st, FPdc around next dc 2 rows down] 20 (22, 24, 26, 28) (30, 32, 34, 36) times. 2 dc in next st, turn. 43 (47, 51, 55, 59) (63, 67, 71, 75) sts

**Row 58:** Ch 1, sc across, turn.

**Row 59:** Ch 2, [FPdc around next dc 2 rows down, dc in next st] 20 (22, 24, 26, 28) (30, 32, 34, 36) times. FPdc around next dc 2 rows down, 2 dc in next st, turn. 44 (48, 52, 56, 60) (64, 68, 72, 76) sts

**Row 60:** Ch 1, sc across, turn.

**Row 61:** Ch 2, [dc in next st, FPdc around next dc 2 rows down] 21 (23, 25, 27, 29) (31, 33, 35, 37) times. 2 dc in next st, turn. 45 (49, 53, 57, 61) (65, 69, 73, 77) sts

**Row 62:** Ch 1, sc across, turn.

**Row 63:** Ch 2, [FPdc around next dc 2 rows down, dc in next st] 21 (23, 25, 27, 29) (31, 33, 35, 37) times. FPdc around next dc 2 rows down, 2 dc in next st, turn. 46 (50, 54, 58, 62) (66, 70, 74, 78) sts

**Row 64:** Ch 1, sc across, turn.

Size 1: Fasten off

Sizes 2–9: Continue to work from row 65.

**Row 65:** Ch 2, [dc in next st, FPdc around next dc 2 rows down] x (24, 26, 28, 30) (32, 34, 36, 38) times. 2 dc in next st, turn. x (51, 55, 59, 63) (67, 71, 75, 79) sts

**Row 66:** Ch 1, sc across, turn.

**Row 67:** Ch 2, [FPdc around next dc 2 rows down, dc in next st] x (24, 26, 28, 30) (32, 34, 36, 38) times. FPdc around next dc 2 rows down, 2 dc in next st, turn. x (52, 56, 60, 64) (68, 72, 76, 80) sts

**Row 68:** Ch 1, sc across, turn.

Size 2: Fasten off.

Sizes 3–9: Continue to work from row 69.

**Row 69:** Ch 2, [dc in next st, FPdc around next dc 2 rows down] x (x, 27, 29, 31) (33, 35, 37, 39) times. 2 dc in next st, turn. x (x, 57, 61, 65) (69, 73, 77, 81) sts

**Row 70:** Ch 1, sc across, turn.

**Row 71:** Ch 2, [FPdc around next dc 2 rows down, dc in next st] x (x, 27, 29, 31) (33, 35, 37, 39) times. FPdc around next dc 2 rows down, 2 dc in next st, turn. x (x, 58, 62, 66) (70, 74, 78, 82) sts

**Row 72:** Ch 1, sc across, turn.

Size 3: Fasten off.

Sizes 4–9: Continue to work from row 73.

**Row 73:** Ch 2, [dc in next st, FPdc around next dc 2 rows down] x (x, x, 30, 32) (34, 36, 38, 40) times. 2 dc in next st, turn. x (x, x, 63, 67) (71, 75, 79, 83) sts

**Row 74:** Ch 1, sc across, turn.

**Row 75:** Ch 2, [FPdc around next dc 2 rows down, dc in next st] x (x, x, 30, 32) (34, 36, 38, 40) times. FPdc around next dc 2 rows down, 2 dc in next st, turn. x (x, x, 64, 68) (72, 76, 80, 84) sts

**Row 76:** Ch 1, sc across, turn.

**Size 4:** Fasten off.

**Sizes 5–9:** Continue to work from row 77.

**Row 77:** Ch 2, [dc in next st, FPdc around next dc 2 rows down] x (x, x, x, 33) (35, 37, 39, 41) times. 2 dc in next st, turn. x (x, x, x, 69) (73, 77, 81, 85) sts

**Row 78:** Ch 1, sc across, turn.

**Row 79:** Ch 2, [FPdc around next dc 2 rows down, dc in next st] x (x, x, x, 33) (35, 37, 39, 41) times. FPdc around next dc 2 rows down, 2 dc in next st, turn. x (x, x, x, 70) (74, 78, 82, 86) sts

**Row 80:** Ch 1, sc across, turn.

**Size 5:** Fasten off.

**Sizes 6–9:** Continue to work from row 81.

**Row 81:** Ch 2, [dc in next st, FPdc around next dc 2 rows down] x (x, x, x, x) (36, 38, 40, 42) times. 2 dc in next st, turn. x (x, x, x, x) (75, 79, 83, 87) sts

**Row 82:** Ch 1, sc across, turn.

**Row 83:** Ch 2, [FPdc around next dc 2 rows down, dc in next st] x (x, x, x, x) (36, 38, 40, 42) times. FPdc around next dc 2 rows down, 2 dc in next st, turn. x (x, x, x, x) (76, 80, 84, 88) sts

**Row 84:** Ch 1, sc across, turn.

**Size 6:** Fasten off.

**Sizes 7–9:** Continue to work from row 85.

**Row 85:** Ch 2, [dc in next st, FPdc around next dc 2 rows down] x (x, x, x, x) (x, 39, 41, 43) times. 2 dc in next st, turn. x (x, x, x, x) (x, 81, 85, 89) sts

**Row 86:** Ch 1, sc across, turn.

**Row 87:** Ch 2, [FPdc around next dc 2 rows down, dc in next st] x (x, x, x, x) (x, 39, 41, 43) times. FPdc around next dc 2 rows down, 2 dc in next st, turn. x (x, x, x, x) (x, 82, 86, 90) sts

**Row 88:** Ch 1, sc across, turn.

**Size 7:** Fasten off.

**Sizes 8–9:** Continue to work from row 89.

**Row 89:** Ch 2, [dc in next st, FPdc around next dc 2 rows down] x (x, x, x, x) (x, x, 42, 44) times. 2 dc in next st, turn. x (x, x, x, x) (x, x, 87, 91) sts

**Row 90:** Ch 1, sc across, turn.

**Row 91:** Ch 2, [FPdc around next dc 2 rows down, dc in next st] x (x, x, x, x) (x, x, 42, 44) times. FPdc around next dc 2 rows down, 2 dc in next st, turn. x (x, x, x, x) (x, x, 88, 92) sts

**Row 92:** Ch 1, sc across, turn.

**Size 8:** Fasten off.

**Size 9:** Continue to work from row 93.

**Row 93:** Ch 2, [dc in next st, FPdc around next dc 2 rows down] x (x, x, x, x) (x, x, x, 45) times. 2 dc in next st, turn. x (x, x, x, x) (x, x, x, 93) sts

**Row 94:** Ch 1, sc across, turn.

**Row 95:** Ch 2, [FPdc around next dc 2 rows down, dc in next st] x (x, x, x, x) (x, x, x, 45) times. FPdc around next dc 2 rows down, 2 dc in next st, turn. x (x, x, x, x) (x, x, x, 94) sts

**Row 96:** Ch 1, sc across, turn.

**Size 9:** Fasten off.

**All sizes:** Continue to Shoulder 2.

## Shoulder 2

With RS facing, count in 19 (23, 27, 31, 35) (39, 43, 47, 51) sts from side opposite Shoulder 1 on last row of Front, attach yarn with sl st to last st counted.

**Row 1:** Ch 2, dc in next st (counts as dc2tog). [FPdc around next dc 2 rows down, dc in next st] 8 (10, 12, 14, 16) (18, 20, 22, 24) times, dc in next st, turn. 18 (22, 26, 30, 34) (38, 42, 46, 50) sts

**Row 2:** Ch 1, sc across, turn.

**Row 3:** Ch 2, dc in next st (counts as dc2tog). [FPdc around next dc 2 rows down, dc in next st] 8 (10, 12, 14, 16) (18, 20, 22, 24) times, turn. 17 (21, 25, 29, 33) (37, 41, 45, 49) sts

**Row 4:** Ch 1, sc across, turn.

**Row 5:** Ch 2, dc in next st (counts as dc2tog). [FPdc around next dc 2 rows down, dc in next st] 7 (9, 11, 13, 15) (17, 19, 21, 23) times, dc in next st, turn. 16 (20, 24, 28, 32) (36, 40, 44, 48) sts

**Row 6:** Ch 1, sc across, turn.

**Row 7:** Ch 2, dc in next st (counts as dc2tog). [FPdc around next dc 2 rows down, dc in next st] 7 (9, 11, 13, 15) (17, 19, 21, 23) times, turn. 15 (19, 23, 27, 31) (35, 39, 43, 47) sts

**Row 8:** Ch 1, sc across, turn. Mark this row as your shoulder seam.

Don't fasten off, continue to work Back Part 2.

## Back Part 2

**Row 1:** Ch 2, [dc in next st, FPdc around next dc 2 rows down] 6 (8, 10, 12, 14) (16, 18, 20, 22) times. Dc in next 2 sts, turn. 15 (19, 23, 27, 31) (35, 39, 43, 47) sts

**Row 2:** Ch 1, sc across, turn.

**Row 3:** (Ch 2, dc) in first st (counts as 2 dc in first st). [FPdc around next dc 2 rows down, dc in next st] 7 (9, 11, 13, 15) (17, 19, 21, 23) times, turn. 16 (20, 24, 28, 32) (36, 40, 44, 48) sts

**Row 4:** Ch 1, sc across, turn.

**Row 5:** (Ch 2, dc) in first st (counts as 2 dc in first st). [FPdc around next dc 2 rows down, dc in next st] 7 (9, 11, 13, 15) (17, 19, 21, 23) times, dc in next st, turn. 17 (21, 25, 29, 33) (37, 41, 45, 49) sts

**Row 6:** Ch 1, sc across, turn.

**Row 7:** (Ch 2, dc) in first st (counts as 2 dc in first st). [FPdc around next dc 2 rows down, dc in next st] 8 (10, 12, 14, 16) (18, 20, 22, 24) times, turn. 18 (22, 26, 30, 34) (38, 42, 46, 50) sts

**Row 8:** Ch 1, sc across, turn.

**Row 9:** (Ch 2, dc) in first st (counts as 2 dc in first st). [FPdc around next dc 2 rows down, dc in next st] 8 (10, 12, 14, 16) (18, 20, 22, 24) times, dc in next st, turn. 19 (23, 27, 31, 35) (39, 43, 47, 51) sts

**Row 10:** Ch 1, sc across, turn.

**Row 11:** (Ch 2, dc) in first st (counts as 2 dc in first st). [FPdc around next dc 2 rows down, dc in next st] 9 (11, 13, 15, 17) (19, 21, 23, 25) times, turn. 20 (24, 28, 32, 36) (40, 44, 48, 52) sts

**Row 12:** Ch 1, sc across, turn.

**Row 13:** (Ch 2, dc) in first st (counts as 2 dc in first st). [FPdc around next dc 2 rows down, dc in next st] 9 (11, 13, 15, 17) (19, 21, 23, 25) times, dc in next st, turn. 21 (25, 29, 33, 37) (41, 45, 49, 53) sts

**Row 14:** Ch 1, sc across, turn.

**Row 15:** (Ch 2, dc) in first st (counts as 2 dc in first st). [FPdc around next dc 2 rows down, dc in next st] 10 (12, 14, 16, 18) (20, 22, 24, 26) times, turn. 22 (26, 30, 34, 38) (42, 46, 50, 54) sts

**Row 16:** Ch 1, sc across, turn.

**Row 17:** (Ch 2, dc) in first st (counts as 2 dc in first st). [FPdc around next dc 2 rows down, dc in next st] 10 (12, 14, 16, 18) (20, 22, 24, 26) times, dc in next st, turn. 23 (27, 31, 35, 39) (43, 47, 51, 55) sts

**Row 18:** Ch 1, sc across, turn.

**Row 19:** (Ch 2, dc) in first st (counts as 2 dc in first st). [FPdc around next dc 2 rows down, dc in next st] 11 (13, 15, 17, 19) (21, 23, 25, 27) times, turn. 24 (28, 32, 36, 40) (44, 48, 52, 56) sts

**Row 20:** Ch 1, sc across, turn.

**Row 21:** (Ch 2, dc) in first st (counts as 2 dc in first st). [FPdc around next dc 2 rows down, dc in next st] 11 (13, 15, 17, 19) (21, 23, 25, 27) times, dc in next st, turn. 25 (29, 33, 37, 41) (45, 49, 53, 57) sts

**Row 22:** Ch 1, sc across, turn.

**Row 23:** (Ch 2, dc) in first st (counts as 2 dc in first st). [FPdc around next dc 2 rows down, dc in next st] 12 (14, 16, 18, 20) (22, 24, 26, 28) times, turn. 26 (30, 34, 38, 42) (46, 50, 54, 58) sts

**Row 24:** Ch 1, sc across, turn.

**Row 25:** (Ch 2, dc) in first st (counts as 2 dc in first st). [FPdc around next dc 2 rows down, dc in next st] 12 (14, 16, 18, 20) (22, 24, 26, 28) times, dc in next st, turn. 27 (31, 35, 39, 43) (47, 51, 55, 59) sts

**Row 26:** Ch 1, sc across, turn.

**Row 27:** (Ch 2, dc) in first st (counts as 2 dc in first st). [FPdc around next dc 2 rows down, dc in next st] 13 (15, 17, 19, 21) (23, 25, 27, 29) times, turn. 28 (32, 36, 40, 44) (48, 52, 56, 60) sts

**Row 28:** Ch 1, sc across, turn.

**Row 29:** (Ch 2, dc) in first st (counts as 2 dc in first st). [FPdc around next dc 2 rows down, dc in next st] 13 (15, 17, 19, 21) (23, 25, 27, 29) times, dc in next st, turn. 29 (33, 37, 41, 45) (49, 53, 57, 61) sts

**Row 30:** Ch 1, sc across, turn.

**Row 31:** (Ch 2, dc) in first st (counts as 2 dc in first st). [FPdc around next dc 2 rows down, dc in next st] 14 (16, 18, 20, 22) (24, 26, 28, 30) times, turn. 30 (34, 38, 42, 46) (50, 54, 58, 62) sts

**Row 32:** Ch 1, sc across, turn.

**Row 33:** (Ch 2, dc) in first st (counts as 2 dc in first st). [FPdc around next dc 2 rows down, dc in next st] 14 (16, 18, 20, 22) (24, 26, 28, 30) times, dc in next st, turn. 31 (35, 39, 43, 47) (51, 55, 59, 63) sts

**Row 34:** Ch 1, sc across, turn.

**Row 35:** (Ch 2, dc) in first st (counts as 2 dc in first st). [FPdc around next dc 2 rows down, dc in next st] 15 (17, 19, 21, 23) (25, 27, 29, 31) times, turn. 32 (36, 40, 44, 48) (52, 56, 60, 64) sts

**Row 36:** Ch 1, sc across, turn.

**Row 37:** (Ch 2, dc) in first st (counts as 2 dc in first st). [FPdc around next dc 2 rows down, dc in next st] 15 (17, 19, 21, 23) (25, 27, 29, 31) times, dc in next st, turn. 33 (37, 41, 45, 49) (53, 57, 61, 65) sts

**Row 38:** Ch 1, sc across, turn.

**Row 39:** (Ch 2, dc) in first st (counts as 2 dc in first st). [FPdc around next dc 2 rows down, dc in next st] 16 (18, 20, 22, 24) (26, 28, 30, 32) times, turn. 34 (38, 42, 46, 50) (54, 58, 62, 66) sts

**Row 40:** Ch 1, sc across, turn.

**Row 41:** (Ch 2, dc) in first st (counts as 2 dc in first st). [FPdc around next dc 2 rows down, dc in next st] 16 (18, 20, 22, 24) (26, 28, 30, 32) times, dc in next st, turn. 35 (39, 43, 47, 51) (55, 59, 63, 67) sts

**Row 42:** Ch 1, sc across, turn.

**Row 43:** (Ch 2, dc) in first st (counts as 2 dc in first st). [FPdc around next dc 2 rows down, dc in next st] 17 (19, 21, 23, 25) (27, 29, 31, 33) times, turn. 36 (40, 44, 48, 52) (56, 60, 64, 68) sts

**Row 44:** Ch 1, sc across, turn.

**Row 45:** (Ch 2, dc) in first st (counts as 2 dc in first st). [FPdc around next dc 2 rows down, dc in next st] 17 (19, 21, 23, 25) (27, 29, 31, 33) times, dc in next st, turn. 37 (41, 45, 49, 53) (57, 61, 65, 69) sts

**Row 46:** Ch 1, sc across, turn.

**Row 47:** (Ch 2, dc) in first st (counts as 2 dc in first st). [FPdc around next dc 2 rows down, dc in next st] 18 (20, 22, 24, 26) (28, 30, 32, 34) times, turn. 38 (42, 46, 50, 54) (58, 62, 66, 70) sts

**Row 48:** Ch 1, sc across, turn.

**Row 49:** (Ch 2, dc) in first st (counts as 2 dc in first st). [FPdc around next dc 2 rows down, dc in next st] 18 (20, 22, 24, 26) (28, 30, 32, 34) times, dc in next st, turn. 39 (43, 47, 51, 55) (59, 63, 67, 71) sts

**Row 50:** Ch 1, sc across, turn.

**Row 51:** (Ch 2, dc) in first st (counts as 2 dc in first st). [FPdc around next dc 2 rows down, dc in next st] 19 (21, 23, 25, 27) (29, 31, 33, 35) times, turn. 40 (44, 48, 52, 56) (60, 64, 68, 72) sts

**Row 52:** Ch 1, sc across, turn.

**Row 53:** (Ch 2, dc) in first st (counts as 2 dc in first st). [FPdc around next dc 2 rows down, dc in next st] 19 (21, 23, 25, 27) (29, 31, 33, 35) times, dc in next st, turn. 41 (45, 49, 53, 57) (61, 65, 69, 73) sts

**Row 54:** Ch 1, sc across, turn.

**Row 55:** (Ch 2, dc) in first st (counts as 2 dc in first st). [FPdc around next dc 2 rows down, dc in next st] 20 (22, 24, 26, 28) (30, 32, 34, 36) times, turn. 42 (46, 50, 54, 58) (62, 66, 70, 74) sts

**Row 56:** Ch 1, sc across, turn.

**Row 57:** (Ch 2, dc) in first st (counts as 2 dc in first st). [FPdc around next dc 2 rows down, dc in next st] 20 (22, 24, 26, 28) (30, 32, 34, 36) times, dc in next st, turn. 43 (47, 51, 55, 59) (63, 67, 71, 75) sts

**Row 58:** Ch 1, sc across, turn.

**Row 59:** (Ch 2, dc) in first st (counts as 2 dc in first st). [FPdc around next dc 2 rows down, dc in next st] 21 (23, 25, 27, 29) (31, 33, 35, 37) times, turn. 44 (48, 52, 56, 60) (64, 68, 72, 76) sts

**Row 60:** Ch 1, sc across, turn.

**Row 64:** Ch 1, sc across, turn.

**Size 1:** Fasten off.

**Sizes 2–9:** Continue to work from row 65.

**Row 65:** (Ch 2, dc) in first st (counts as 2 dc in first st). [FPdc around next dc 2 rows down, dc in next st] x (24, 26, 28, 30) (32, 34, 36, 38) times, dc in next st, turn. x (51, 55, 59, 63) (67, 71, 75, 79) sts

**Row 66:** Ch 1, sc across, turn.

**Row 67:** (Ch 2, dc) in first st (counts as 2 dc in first st). [FPdc around next dc 2 rows down, dc in next st] x (25, 27, 29, 31) (33, 35, 37, 39) times, turn. x (52, 56, 60, 64) (68, 72, 76, 80) sts

**Row 68:** Ch 1, sc across, turn.

**Size 2:** Fasten off.

**Sizes 3–9:** Continue to work from row 69.

**Row 69:** (Ch 2, dc) in first st (counts as 2 dc in first st). [FPdc around next dc 2 rows down, dc in next st] x (x, 27, 29, 31) (33, 35, 37, 39) times, dc in next st, turn. x (x, 57, 61, 65) (69, 73, 77, 81) sts

**Row 70:** Ch 1, sc across, turn.

**Row 71:** (Ch 2, dc) in first st (counts as 2 dc in first st). [FPdc around next dc 2 rows down, dc in next st] x (x, 28, 30, 32) (34, 36, 38, 40) times, turn. x (x, 58, 62, 66) (70, 74, 78, 82) sts

**Row 72:** Ch 1, sc across, turn.

**Size 3:** Fasten off.

**Sizes 4–9:** Continue to work from row 73.

**Row 73:** (Ch 2, dc) in first st (counts as 2 dc in first st). [FPdc around next dc 2 rows down, dc in next st] x (x, x, 30, 32) (34, 36, 38, 40) times, dc in next st, turn. x (x, x, 63, 67) (71, 75, 79, 83) sts

**Row 61:** (Ch 2, dc) in first st (counts as 2 dc in first st). [FPdc around next dc 2 rows down, dc in next st] 21 (23, 25, 27, 29) (31, 33, 35, 37) times, dc in next st, turn. 45 (49, 53, 57, 61) (65, 69, 73, 77) sts

**Row 62:** Ch 1, sc across, turn.

**Row 63:** (Ch 2, dc) in first st (counts as 2 dc in first st). [FPdc around next dc 2 rows down, dc in next st] 22 (24, 26, 28, 30) (32, 34, 36, 38) times, turn. 46 (50, 54, 58, 62) (66, 70, 74, 78) sts

**Row 74:** Ch 1, sc across, turn.

**Row 75:** (Ch 2, dc) in first st (counts as 2 dc in first st). [FPdc around next dc 2 rows down, dc in next st] x (x, x, 31, 33) (35, 37, 39, 41) times, turn. x (x, x, 64, 68) (72, 76, 80, 84) sts

**Row 76:** Ch 1, sc across, turn.

**Size 4:** Fasten off.

**Sizes 5–9:** Continue to work from row 77.

**Row 77:** (Ch 2, dc) in first st (counts as 2 dc in first st). [FPdc around next dc 2 rows down, dc in next st] x (x, x, x, 33) (35, 37, 39, 41) times, dc in next st, turn. x (x, x, x, 69) (73, 77, 81, 85) sts

**Row 78:** Ch 1, sc across, turn.

**Row 79:** (Ch 2, dc) in first st (counts as 2 dc in first st). [FPdc around next dc 2 rows down, dc in next st] x (x, x, x, 34) (36, 38, 40, 42) times, turn. x (x, x, x, 70) (74, 78, 82, 86) sts

**Row 80:** Ch 1, sc across, turn.

**Size 5:** Fasten off.

**Sizes 6–9:** Continue to work from row 81.

**Row 81:** (Ch 2, dc) in first st (counts as 2 dc in first st). [FPdc around next dc 2 rows down, dc in next st] x (x, x, x, x) (36, 38, 40, 42) times, dc in next st, turn. x (x, x, x, x) (75, 79, 83, 87) sts

**Row 82:** Ch 1, sc across, turn.

**Row 83:** (Ch 2, dc) in first st (counts as 2 dc in first st). [FPdc around next dc 2 rows down, dc in next st] x (x, x, x, x) (37, 39, 41, 43) times, turn. x (x, x, x, x) (76, 80, 84, 88) sts

**Row 84:** Ch 1, sc across, turn.

**Size 6:** Fasten off.

**Sizes 7–9:** Continue to work from row 85.

**Row 85:** (Ch 2, dc) in first st (counts as 2 dc in first st). [FPdc around next dc 2 rows down, dc in next st] x (x, x, x, x) (x, 39, 41, 43) times, dc in next st, turn. x (x, x, x, x) (x, 81, 85, 89) sts

**Row 86:** Ch 1, sc across, turn.

**Row 87:** (Ch 2, dc) in first st (counts as 2 dc in first st). [FPdc around next dc 2 rows down, dc in next st] x (x, x, x, x) (x, 40, 42, 44) times, turn. x (x, x, x, x) (x, 82, 86, 90) sts

**Row 88:** Ch 1, sc across, turn.

**Size 7:** Fasten off.

**Sizes 8–9:** Continue to work from row 89.

**Row 89:** (Ch 2, dc) in first st (counts as 2 dc in first st). [FPdc around next dc 2 rows down, dc in next st] x (x, x, x, x) (x, x, 42, 44) times, dc in next st, turn. x (x, x, x, x) (x, x, 87, 91) sts

**Row 90:** Ch 1, sc across, turn.

**Row 91:** (Ch 2, dc) in first st (counts as 2 dc in first st). [FPdc around next dc 2 rows down, dc in next st] x (x, x, x, x) (x, x, 43, 45) times, turn. x (x, x, x, x) (x, x, 88, 92) sts

**Row 92:** Ch 1, sc across, turn.

**Size 8:** Fasten off.

**Size 9:** Continue to work from row 93.

**Row 93:** (Ch 2, dc) in first st (counts as 2 dc in first st). [FPdc around next dc 2 rows down, dc in next st] x (x, x, x, x) (x, x, x, 45) times, dc in next st, turn. x (x, x, x, x) (x, x, x, 93) sts

**Row 94:** Ch 1, sc across, turn.

**Row 95:** (Ch 2, dc) in first st (counts as 2 dc in first st). [FPdc around next dc 2 rows down, dc in next st] x (x, x, x, x) (x, x, x, 46) times, turn. x (x, x, x, x) (x, x, x, 94) sts

**Row 96:** Ch 1, sc across, turn.

**Size 9:** Fasten off.

## Hem Ribbing

Mark the last sc of your last row—this will be the start of your Hem Ribbing and Back-Neck-Back Ribbing.

With RS facing, pin the side seams together at the hem.

Change to smaller hook.

**Row 1:** Ch 2, dc across Back part, continue working in dc across Front, then continue in dc across other Back part, turn. 157 (177, 197, 217, 237) (257, 277, 297, 317) sts

**Row 2:** WS facing. Ch 2, [FPdc around next st, BPdc around next st] across, turn.

Work 6 more rows of ribbing, making FPdc around each FPdc of previous row, and BPdc around each BPdc of previous row. Fasten off.

## Back-Neck-Back Ribbing

With WS facing and smaller hook, attach yarn with sl st to the marked st of Back Part 2.

**Row 1:** Dc across one back opening, then across front neckline, then across the other back opening edge, making approx 2 sts in the side of each row at the back openings, and 1 st in each st across the front neckline. Turn.

**Rows 2–4:** Ch 2, [FPdc around next st, BPdc around next st] across, turn.

**Last row:** Don't turn or fasten off, continue to work Tie.

## Tie

### With RS facing and larger hook:

**Row 1:** Rotate to crochet along the side of both ribbing sections. Ch 2, dc in next row end (counts as dc2tog over 2 sts = 1 st), [dc in next row end, 2 dc in next row end, dc in next row end] 3 times, 2 dc in last row end, turn. 15 sts

**Row 2:** RS facing. Ch 2, dc across until 2 sts left, dc2tog over last 2 sts, turn. 14 sts

**Row 3:** Ch 2, dc in next st (counts as dc2tog over 2 sts = 1 st), dc across, turn. 13 sts

**Row 4:** Rep row 2. 12 sts

**Row 5:** Rep row 3. 11 sts

**Row 6:** Ch 2, dc across, turn. 11 sts

Rep row 6 until your Tie reaches 46.5 (48.5, 50.5, 52.5, 54.5) (56.5, 58.5, 60.5, 62.5)" / 118 (123, 128, 133, 138) (143, 149, 154, 159) cm long, or until your desired tie length is reached.

## Sleeve

### Make 2

Choose a size that is closest to your wrist measurement: 5 (5.5, 6, 6.25, 6.75) (7, 7.5, 7.75, 8.25)" / 13 (14, 15, 16, 17) (18, 19, 20, 21) cm. You will be able to adjust the sleeve circumference later as you work.

## Cuff

With smaller hook, ch 30 (30, 32, 34, 36) (38, 40, 42, 44).

**Row 1:** Dc in third ch from hook (first ch 2 counts as first dc), dc across, turn. 29 (29, 31, 33, 35) (37, 39, 41, 43) sts

**Row 2:** Ch 2, (BPdc around next st, FPdc around next st) across, turn.

**Row 3:** Ch 2, (FPdc around next st, BPdc around next st) across, turn.

**Rows 4–7:** Rep rows 2–3 two times.

**Row 8:** Rep row 2.

## Sleeve

Change to larger hook.

**Row 1:** (Ch 2, dc) in first st. [FPdc around next st, dc in next st] until last 2 sts. FPdc around next st, 2 dc in last st, turn. 31 (31, 33, 35, 37) (39, 41, 43, 45) sts

**Row 2:** Ch 1, sc across, turn.

**Row 3:** (Ch 2, dc) in first st. [FPdc around next dc 2 rows down, dc in next st] until last 2 sts. FPdc around next st, 2 dc in last st, turn. 33 (33, 35, 37, 39) (41, 43, 45, 47) sts

**Row 4:** Ch 1, sc across, turn.

Rep rows 3–4, increasing by 2 sts every next row until your Sleeve reaches 53 (53, 55, 57, 59) (61, 63, 65, 67) sts, or your desired sleeve circumference. Be sure that the circumference corresponds at least to your upper arm measurement.

**Next row 1:** Ch 2. [FPdc around next dc 2 rows down, dc in next st] across, turn. 53 (53, 55, 57, 59) (61, 63, 65, 67) sts

**Next row 2:** Ch 1, sc across, turn.

**Next row 3:** Ch 2. [Dc in next st, FPdc around next dc 2 rows down] until last 2 sts. Dc in next 2 sts, turn.

**Next row 4:** Ch 1, sc across, turn.

Continue to rep next rows 1–4 until your Sleeve (including Cuff) measures 19.5 (19.25, 19, 18.5, 18) (17.5, 17, 16.5, 16)" / 50 (49, 48, 47, 46) (44.5, 43, 42, 40.5) cm, or until your desired sleeve length is reached. Fasten off.

## Finishing

Block all parts according to fiber type. Sew both sleeves to the shoulder, then sew the side seam and sleeve seam. Weave in all ends. Wear the sweater with the wrap in the back or front.

# Saule Sun Sweater

Crochet and weaving are both crafts that blend artistry with technical skills. Merging the two is not just a unique crafting technique, but a way of working with textiles that truly celebrates texture. Saule is a more unusual, unexpected and intriguing choice due to the uniqueness inherent in this extraordinary design. You'll be surprised how interesting and satisfying it is to weave the crocheted straps into a voluminous basketweave fabric.

# Saule Sun Sweater Construction Notes

*Saule is designed to be worn with either side as the RS. The sweater is worked top down in a spiral, then is split for the body and sleeves at the bust line. Voluminous crisscross straps are formed on the body while the sleeves remain plain. Saule is worked in one piece and is seamless. It comes in nine sizes and the sleeve length is easily adjusted.*

## Sizes

1 (2, 3, 4, 5) (6, 7, 8, 9)

**To fit bust:** 30 (34, 38, 42, 46) (50, 54, 58, 62)" / 76 (86, 97, 107, 117) (127, 137, 147, 157) cm

**Finished bust:** 35.75 (40.25, 44, 48, 52) (56, 59.75, 64.25, 68)" / 91 (102, 112, 122, 132) (142, 152, 163, 173) cm

## Gauge

13 sts x 11 rows = 4" / 10 cm in hdc

## Yarn

Worsted weight, Hobbii Mohair Delight (50% Mohair, 50% Acrylic), 164 yds / 150 m per 50-g skein, or use any worsted weight wool yarn with a fuzzy texture to achieve a similar effect

## Yardage/Meterage

1100 (1200, 1295, 1380, 1475) (1395, 1675, 1790, 1885) yds / 1005 (1095, 1185, 1260, 1350) (1275, 1530, 1635, 1725) m

## Shown in

Colorway Curry (24)

## Hook

H/8 / 5 mm, or size needed to obtain gauge

## Notions

Tapestry needle

2 stitch markers

## Skills

Experience with making crocheted top-down sweaters

## Abbreviations (US terms)

BOR = beginning of round

Ch = chain

FPhdc = front post half double crochet

Fsc = foundation single crochet

Hdc = half double crochet

Hdc2tog = half double crochet 2 together

LL = long loop

Rnd(s) = round(s)

RS = right side

Sc = single crochet

Sl st = slip stitch

St(s) = stitch(es)

WS = wrong side

| Size | A—finished bust | B—yoke depth | C—length | D—sleeve length from underarm | E—upper arm |
|---|---|---|---|---|---|
| 1 | 35.75" / 91 cm | 8.5" / 21.5 cm | 24.5" / 62.5 cm | 19.5" / 50 cm | 13.5" / 34 cm |
| 2 | 40.25" / 102 cm | 9.25" / 23.5 cm | 25.5" / 64.5 cm | 19" / 48 cm | 14.25" / 36 cm |
| 3 | 44" / 112 cm | 9.75" / 25 cm | 26" / 66 cm | 18.5" / 47 cm | 15" / 38 cm |
| 4 | 48" / 122 cm | 10.25" / 26 cm | 26.25" / 67 cm | 18" / 46 cm | 15.75" / 40 cm |
| 5 | 52" / 132 cm | 11" / 28 cm | 27.25" / 69 cm | 17.5" / 44.5 cm | 16.5" / 42 cm |
| 6 | 56" / 142 cm | 11.5" / 29.5 cm | 27.75" / 70.5 cm | 17" / 43 cm | 17.25" / 44 cm |
| 7 | 59.75" / 152 cm | 12" / 30.5 cm | 28.25" / 71.5 cm | 16.5" / 42 cm | 18" / 46 cm |
| 8 | 64.25" / 163 cm | 12.75" / 32.5 cm | 29" / 73.5 cm | 16" / 40.5 cm | 19" / 48 cm |
| 9 | 68" / 173 cm | 13.5" / 34 cm | 29.5" / 75 cm | 15.5" / 39 cm | 19.75" / 50 cm |

*One crisscross tier is ~5" / 12.5 cm tall. Hem measures 1.5" / 3.5 cm deep. Neckline measures 0.5" / 1.5 cm. The oversized sweater is designed to be worn with 5.75 (6.25, 6, 6, 6) (6, 5.75, 6.25, 6)" / 14.5 (15.5, 15, 15, 15) (15, 14.5, 15.5, 15) cm of positive ease. Size 2 is modeled on 33" / 83-cm bust model. The sweater is being worn WS out.*

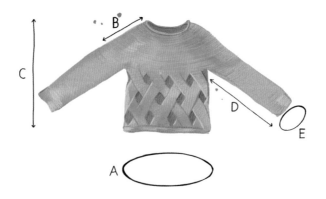

# Saule Sun Sweater Pattern

## Yoke

Using hook required for gauge and leaving approximately 6" / 15 cm-long yarn end for sewing the neck split, with WS facing fsc 74 (76, 78, 80, 82) (84, 86, 88, 90), turn.

Work 3 back-and-forth short rows on your foundation ch to raise the back-neck for a better fitting garment.

**Row 1:** Skip first fsc, sc into next 24 (25, 26, 27, 28) (29, 30, 31, 32) fsc, stop here and turn work. 24 (25, 26, 27, 28) (29, 30, 31, 32) sts

**Row 2:** Skip first st, sc until 5 sts remain unworked, stop here and turn work. 18 (19, 20, 21, 22) (23, 24, 25, 26) sts

**Row 3:** Skip first st, sc until 5 sts remain unworked, stop here, do not turn. 12 (13, 14, 15, 16) (17, 18, 19, 20) sts

Place marker in the approximate center of row 3 to mark center-back (will count as your BOR). Move this marker up as you work each rnd.

Place the second marker at the same position on your foundation ch to mark the true center-back.

The yoke will be worked in spiral and your BOR will drift off-center. Replace the working marker into the approximate center stitch as often as needed, using your second marker (in the foundation ch) as a reference point.

Start working in a spiral.

Sc in next 5 sc, sc into the edge of the row (to make up for the skipped st), sc in each fsc to end of row. Join in the rnd by working 1 sc into the edge of the row at the first skipped fsc from row 1 (make sure your yoke is not twisted), sc in next 5 sc, sc into edge of row, sc in each st to BOR.

74 (76, 78, 80, 82) (84, 86, 88, 90) sts

Continue to work in hdc.

### Increase rnd 1

[2 hdc in next st, hdc in next st] around. 111 (114, 117, 120, 123) (126, 129, 132, 135) sts

**Sizes 1–6:** Continue to work evenly in hdc, in a spiral, for another 6 rnds.

**Sizes 7–9:** Continue to work evenly in hdc, in a spiral, for another 7 rnds.

### Increase rnd 2

[2 hdc in next st, hdc in next 2 sts] around. 148 (152, 156, 160, 164) (168, 172, 176, 180) sts

**Sizes 1–6:** Continue to work evenly in hdc, in a spiral, for another 5 rnds.

**Sizes 7–9:** Continue to work evenly in hdc, in a spiral, for another 4 rnds.

### Increase rnd 3

**Size 1:** [2 hdc in next st, hdc in next 2 sts] 49 times. 2 hdc in next st. 198 sts

**Size 2:** [2 hdc in next st, hdc in next 2 sts] 50 times. Hdc in next 2 sts. 202 sts

**Size 3:** [2 hdc in next st, hdc in next 2 sts] 50 times. Hdc in next 6 sts. 206 sts

**Sizes 4–9:** [2 hdc in next st, hdc in next 3 sts] around. x (x, x, 200, 205) (210, 215, 220, 225) sts

**Size 1:** Continue to work evenly in hdc, in a spiral, for another 7 rnds, then continue to Separating Body and Sleeves (page 153).

**Sizes 2–9:** Continue to work evenly in hdc, in a spiral, for another 5 rnds.

## Increase rnd 4

**Size 2:** [Hdc in next 15 sts, 2 hdc in next st] 12 times. Hdc in next 10 sts. 214 sts

**Size 3:** [Hdc in next 8 sts, 2 hdc in next st] 22 times. Hdc in next 8 sts. 228 sts

**Sizes 4–9:** [2 hdc in next st, hdc in next 4 sts] around. x (x, x, 240, 246) (252, 258, 264, 270) sts

**Size 2:** Continue to work evenly in hdc, in a spiral, for another 3 rnds, then continue to Separating Body and Sleeves (page 153).

**Sizes 3–9:** Continue to work evenly in hdc, in a spiral, for another 5 rnds.

**Size 3:** Continue to Separating Body and Sleeves (page 153).

## Increase rnd 5

**Size 4:** [Hdc in next 119 sts, 2 hdc in next st] twice. 242 sts

**Size 5:** [Hdc in next 19 sts, 2 hdc in next st] 12 times. Hdc in next 6 sts. 258 sts

**Size 6:** [Hdc in next 13 sts, 2 hdc in next st] 18 times. 270 sts

**Sizes 7–9:** [Hdc in next 11 sts, 2 hdc in next st] 21 times. Hdc in next x (x, x, x, x) (x, 6, 12, 18) sts. x (x, x, x, x) (x, 279, 285, 291) sts

**Size 4:** Continue to Separating Body and Sleeves (page 153).

**Size 5:** Continue to work evenly in hdc, in a spiral, for another 2 rnds, then continue to Separating Body and Sleeves (page 153).

**Sizes 6–9:** Continue to work evenly in hdc, in a spiral, for another 4 rnds.

**Size 6:** Continue to Separating Body and Sleeves (page 153).

## Increase rnd 6

**Size 7:** [Hdc in next 38 sts, 2 hdc in next st] 7 times. Hdc in next 6 sts. 286 sts

**Size 8:** [Hdc in next 18 sts, 2 hdc in next st] 15 times. 300 sts

**Size 9:** [Hdc in next 11 sts, 2 hdc in next st] 23 times. Hdc in next 15 sts. 314 sts

**Size 7:** Continue to Separating Body and Sleeves (page 153).

## Separating Body and Sleeves

Place your BOR marker into the center-back of your last row.

**Base rnd:** Hdc in next 29 (32, 35, 37, 40) (43, 46, 49, 51) sts, ch 2 (3, 4, 5, 6) (7, 8, 9, 10), skip next 42 (44, 45, 47, 49) (50, 52, 53, 55) sts, hdc in next 57 (63, 69, 74, 80) (85, 91, 97, 102) sts, ch 2 (3, 4, 5, 6) (7, 8, 9, 10), skip next 42 (44, 45, 47, 49) (50, 52, 53, 55) sts, hdc in next 28 (31, 34, 37, 40) (42, 45, 48, 51) sts to BOR.

## Body

Start Body with 118 (132, 146, 158, 172) (184, 198, 212, 224) sts. Place marker in the last st of Base rnd. You will be creating 16 (16, 16, 18, 18) (18, 20, 20, 20) straps all around the Body.

### Number of sts per Strap

**Size 1:** 8-7-7-8-7-7-8-7-7-8-7-7-8-7-7-8 sts per strap

(Strap 1 = 8 sts, Strap 2 = 7 sts, Strap 3= 7 sts, etc.)

**Size 2:** 8-8-8-9-8-8-8-9-8-8-8-9-8-8-8-9

**Size 3:** 9-9-9-9-9-9-9-10-9-9-9-9-9-9-9-10

**Size 4:** 9-9-9-8-9-9-9-8-9-9-9-8-9-9-9-8-9-9

**Size 5:** 9-10-10-9-9-10-10-9-9-10-10-9-9-10-10-9-10-10

**Size 6:** 10-10-10-11-10-10-10-11-10-10-10-11-10-10-10-11-10-10

**Size 7:** 10-10-10-10-10-10-10-9-10-10-10-10-10-10-10-9-10-10-10-10

**Size 8:** 10-11-10-11-11-10-11-11-10-11-11-10-11-11-10-11-10-11-11-10

**Size 9:** 11-11-11-11-12-11-11-11-11-12-11-11-11-11-12-11-11-11-11-12

**Size 8:** Continue to work evenly in hdc, in a spiral, for another 2 rnds, then continue to Separating Body and Sleeves.

**Size 9:** Continue to work evenly in hdc, in a spiral, for another 4 rnds, then continue to Separating Body and Sleeves.

## Tier 1

### Strap 1

**Row 1:** Hdc in next 8 (8, 9, 9, 9) (10, 10, 10, 11) sts, turn.

**Row 2:** LL, hdc in next 8 (8, 9, 9, 9) (10, 10, 10, 11) sts, turn.

Continue to repeat row 2 for another 10 rows (12 rows total per strap) and fasten off.

Make all other Straps around the Body. Start each Strap in the next unused st on the base rnd. No sts are skipped between Straps. Work the number of sts necessary for each Strap following the st count given on the left. Don't fasten off your last Strap, turn.

### Connection Rounds

You'll be crossing the two straps that are next to each other, using a pin to secure the straps together—for example, cross Strap 1 and Strap 2, cross Strap 3 and Strap 4, etc. If Strap 1 goes over Strap 2, make sure Strap 3 also goes over Strap 4. Odd numbered straps go over even numbered straps in Tier 1.

Your last Strap will now be your first Strap.

Work hdc in each st of the current Strap, cross the previous Strap over the one you're currently attached to, continue to work hdc across the previous Strap.

[Skip next Strap, work hdc in each st of the next Strap, cross the skipped Strap over the one you're currently attached to, continue to work hdc across the skipped Strap] repeat around, join with sl st to the first st of connection rnd.

Work one more rnd of hdc, join.

## Tier 2

Work another 16 (16, 16, 18, 18) (18, 20, 20, 20) straps around the Body, each with 12 rows. Make sure the current Strap you're working on is the same width (has the same number of sts) as the Strap that is right under it (on the previous Tier).

Fasten off the last Strap. Attach yarn with sl st to the first Strap of this Tier and work hdc across this first Strap. Place the last Strap *under* the first Strap and hdc across this last Strap. [Skip next Strap, work hdc across the next Strap, cross the skipped Strap *under* the one you're currently attached to, continue to work hdc across the skipped Strap] repeat around, join with sl st to the first st of the current connection rnd.

Work one more rnd of hdc, join.

## Tier 3

Work another 16 (16, 16, 18, 18) (18, 20, 20, 20) straps around the Body, each with 12 rows. Make sure the current Strap is same width as the Strap below it.

Fasten off the last Strap. Attach yarn with sl st to the first Strap of this Tier and work hdc across this first Strap. Place the last Strap *over* the first Strap and hdc across this last Strap. [Skip next Strap, work hdc across the next Strap, cross the skipped Strap *over* the one you're currently attached to, continue to work hdc across the skipped Strap] repeat around, join with sl st to the first st of the current connection rnd.

Work one more rnd of hdc, join.

**Finishing rnd:** LL, FPhdc around, join.

Repeat last rnd 5 times for a total of 6 finishing rnds. Fasten off.

## Neckline

Attach yarn with sl st anywhere on the neckline.

**Rnd 1:** With RS facing, LL, hdc around, do not join, continue in a spiral.

**Rnds 2 and 3:** FPhdc around each st.

Fasten off.

## Sleeve

### Make 2

With RS facing, attach yarn with sl st at approximate center-bottom of underarm, place marker in this st to mark beginning of rnd. Since you are working in a spiral, this marker will eventually look off-center. Simply replace it into the approximate center st as often as needed.

**Rnd 1:** LL, hdc around. 44 (47, 49, 52, 55) (57, 60, 62, 65) sts

**For the rest of the Sleeve:** Work the rnds as written for your size, starting with decrease rnd.

**Decrease rnd:** Hdc in first st, hdc2tog, hdc in each st around until 3 sts remain, hdc2tog, hdc in last st. (decreases rnd by 2 sts)

**Size 1:** Starting with the decrease rnd, work 55 rnds total decreasing every 8th rnd, or until your desired sleeve length is reached.

**Size 2:** Starting with the decrease rnd, work 53 rnds total, decreasing every 8th rnd, or until your desired sleeve length is reached.

**Size 3:** Starting with the decrease rnd, work 52 rnds total, decreasing every 8th rnd, or until your desired sleeve length is reached.

**Size 4:** Starting with the decrease rnd, work 51 rnds total, decreasing every 7th rnd, or until your desired sleeve length is reached.

**Size 5:** Starting with the decrease rnd, work 49 rnds total, decreasing every 7th rnd, or until your desired sleeve length is reached.

**Size 6:** Starting with the decrease rnd, work 47 rnds total, decreasing every 7th rnd, or until your desired sleeve length is reached.

**Size 7:** Starting with the decrease rnd, work 46 rnds total, decreasing every 6th rnd, or until your desired sleeve length is reached.

**Size 8:** Starting with the decrease rnd, work 45 rnds total, decreasing every 6th rnd, or until your desired sleeve length is reached.

**Size 9:** Starting with the decrease rnd, work 43 rnds total, decreasing every 6th rnd, or until your desired sleeve length is reached.

55 (53, 52, 51, 49) (47, 46, 45, 43) rnds total

**Finishing rnd:** Sl sl around, fasten off.

Choose which side—Right or Wrong—will be your Right Side for wearing your sweater. Weave in all ends. Sew the neck split. Block according to fiber type.

# Thoughtful

Revealing the past, present and future of your personal style, crochet can tell your authentic story. Full of curiosity, intrigue and texture, this wonderful craft is a combination of old and new swirling together. More than ever, it is important for creatives to share their story in a more personal and genuine way. The designs in this chapter encourage and celebrate a more complete and comprehensive guide to showcase the true fabrics of an inventive wardrobe.

All four patterns in this chapter will make you want to take a closer look to admire their attention to detail, while the process of creating these pieces is meditative and thoughtful. You'll find an eclectic fusion of fragile broomstick strands and bold, deep Tunisian cables, filigree post stitch "drawing" and delicate graphic patterns. One thing's for sure, these designs won't leave anyone indifferent.

# Mēness Moon Sweater

Mixing athleisure with graphic lacework is probably the last thing one might expect from crochet, yet here it is—Mēness, a perfect, everyday throw-it-on piece that is as dynamic and captivating as the stitches it features. From the flattest slip stitches up to the tall double trebles ending with short row shoulder lines, this light sweater embodies effortlessness and easiness.

# Mēness Moon Sweater Construction Notes

*Mēness is worked bottom up starting with a sideways ribbing. The front and back are each worked separately, and the shoulder seams are crocheted (or sewn) together. Then both sleeves, cuffs and neck ribbing are worked and sewn on.*

## Sizes

1 (2, 3, 4, 5) (6, 7, 8, 9)

**To fit bust:** 30 (34, 38, 42, 46) (50, 54, 58, 62)" / 76 (86, 97, 107, 117) (127, 137, 147, 157) cm

**Finished bust:** 36.25 (40.25, 44, 48, 52) (56, 59.75, 63.75, 67.75)" / 92 (102, 112, 122, 132) (142, 152, 162, 172)

## Gauge

18 sts x 12 rows = 4" / 10 cm in dc after blocking

4 squares x 4 squares = 4" / 10 cm in both Body stitch patterns after blocking

## Yarn

Light Fingering weight held double, Holst Garn Coast (55% lambs wool, 45% cotton), 383 yds / 350 m per 50-g skein, or use any light fingering weight wool-cotton blend to achieve a similar effect

## Yardage/Meterage

MC 1455 (1610, 1760, 1875, 2030) (2410, 2565, 2720, 2870) yds / 1330 (1470, 1610, 1715, 1855) (2205, 2345, 2485, 2625) m

CC 575 (650, 690, 765, 805) (880, 920, 995, 1035) yds / 525 (595, 630, 700, 735) (805, 840, 910, 945) m

## Total yardage/meterage (MC + CC)

2030 (2260, 2450, 2640, 2835) (3290, 3485, 3715, 3905) yds / 1855 (2065, 2240, 2415, 2590) (3010, 3185, 3395, 3570) m

The total yardage/meterage is shown for yarn held double.

**To use a single strand:** Use Sport weight yarn and note that the yardage/meterage will be half what is listed above.

## Shown in

Colorways Charcoal (MC) and Old Gold (CC)

## Hooks

G/6 / 4 mm for the main sections of the Body and Sleeves, or size needed to obtain gauge

F/5 / 3.75 mm for ribbing, or one size smaller than size needed to obtain gauge

## Notions

Stitch markers

Tapestry needle for sewing seams and ribbing

## Skills

Experience with making crocheted sweaters

## Abbreviations (US terms)

BL = back loop

CC = contrast color

Ch = chain

Dc = double crochet

Dtr = double treble (yo 3 times before working st in indicated st/sp)

Dtr2tog = double treble two stitches together

Hdc = half double crochet

Hdc2tog = half double crochet two stitches together

MC = main color

Rnd(s) = round(s)

RS = right side

Sc = single crochet

Sc-hdc-tog = single crochet and half double crochet together

Sl st = slip stitch

St(s) = stitch(es)

WS = wrong side

Yo = yarn over

## Special stitches

**Sc-hdc-tog:** Insert hook in indicated st, yo, draw yarn through stitch, yo, insert hook in next indicated st, yo, draw yarn through st, yo, draw yarn through all 4 loops on hook.

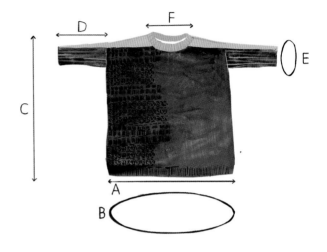

| Size | A—finished half-bust | B—finished bust | C—length | D—sleeve length | E—upper arm | F—neck width (without ribbing) |
|---|---|---|---|---|---|---|
| 1 | 18" / 46 cm | 36.25" / 92 cm | 22" / 56 cm | 9" / 23 cm | 10" / 25.5 cm | 8.75" / 22 cm |
| 2 | 20" / 51 cm | 40.25" / 102 cm | 22" / 56 cm | 9" / 23 cm | 10.5" / 27 cm | 8.75" / 22 cm |
| 3 | 22" / 56 cm | 44" / 112 cm | 22" / 56 cm | 9" / 23 cm | 11.25" / 28.5 cm | 8.75" / 22 cm |
| 4 | 24" / 61 cm | 48" / 122 cm | 22" / 56 cm | 9" / 23 cm | 11.75" / 30 cm | 8.75" / 22 cm |
| 5 | 26" / 66 cm | 52" / 132 cm | 22" / 56 cm | 9" / 23 cm | 12.5" / 31.5 cm | 8.75" / 22 cm |
| 6 | 28" / 71 cm | 56" / 142 cm | 25.25" / 64 cm | 9" / 23 cm | 13" / 33 cm | 8.75" / 22 cm |
| 7 | 30" / 76 cm | 59.75" / 152 cm | 25.25" / 64 cm | 9" / 23 cm | 13.5" / 34.5 cm | 8.75" / 22 cm |
| 8 | 32" / 81 cm | 63.75" / 162 cm | 25.25" / 64 cm | 9" / 23 cm | 14.25" / 36 cm | 8.75" / 22 cm |
| 9 | 33.75" / 86 cm | 67.75" / 172 cm | 25.25" / 64 cm | 9" / 23 cm | 14.75" / 37.5 cm | 8.75" / 22 cm |

*Body ribbing measures 1.5" / 3.5 cm. Neck ribbing measures 1.25" / 3 cm. The sweater is designed with 6.25 (6.25, 6, 6, 6) (6, 6, 6, 6)" / 16 (16, 15, 15, 15) (15, 15, 15, 15) cm positive ease. Size 2 is modeled on 33" / 83-cm bust model.*

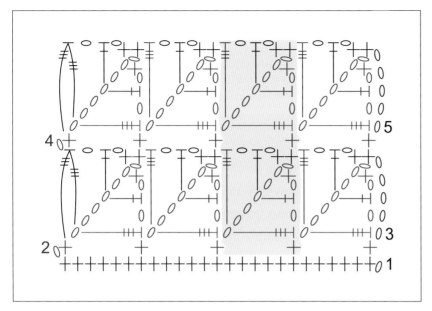

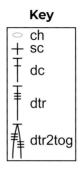

**Key**

| | |
|---|---|
| ⬭ | ch |
| + | sc |
| ⊤ | dc |
| ⊤̄ | dtr |
| ⊤̄⊤̄ | dtr2tog |

*Reduced sample of stitch diagram rows 1–5 of Front Body.*

*Stitch repeat is shown in gray.*

# Mēness Moon Sweater Pattern

Yarn is held double throughout the pattern.

**Throughout:** Ch 1 at the beginning of row counts as turning chain and is not counted as a stitch.

Ch 2: Counts as first hdc (= 1 st).

Ch 5: Counts as first dtr (= 1 st).

## Front

### Front Ribbing

With MC held double and smaller hook, ch 11 (last 2 ch counts as first hdc on next row).

**Row 1:** Hdc in third ch from hook, hdc in each ch across, turn. 10 sts

**Rows 2–68 (–76, –84, –92, –100) (–108, –116, –124, –132):** Ch 2 (counts as first hdc), hdc in BL across, turn. 10 sts

**Last row of the ribbing:** Don't turn. Rotate the ribbing clockwise by 90 degrees.

### Front Body

Change to larger hook.

**Row 1:** Ch 1, sc across rib rows working 3 sc in each 2 row ends, work 1 more sc in last row end, turn. 103 (115, 127, 139, 151) (163, 175, 187, 199) sts

**Row 2:** Ch 1, sc in first st. [Ch 7 (mark last ch just made), sc in second ch from hook, ch 1, skip next ch, dc in next ch, ch 1, skip next 2 chs, dtr in next ch, skip next 5 sts on previous row, sc in next st] 17 (19, 21, 23, 25) (27, 29, 31, 33) times, turn. 17 (19, 21, 23, 25) (27, 29, 31, 33) triangles

**Row 8:** Ch 1, sc in first st. [Ch 5, skip next 5 sts, sc in next st] 17 (19, 21, 23, 25) (27, 29, 31, 33) times, turn. 103 (115, 127, 139, 151) (163, 175, 187, 199) sts

**Row 9:** Ch 5. [5 dtr in next ch-5 sp, ch 1, skip next sc] 16 (18, 20, 22, 24) (26, 28, 30, 32) times total. 5 dtr in next ch-5 sp, dtr in next sc, turn. 103 (115, 127, 139, 151) (163, 175, 187, 199) sts

**Rows 10–13:** Rep rows 8–9 twice.

**Rows 14–19:** Rep rows 2–3 three times.

**Rows 20–25:** Rep rows 8–9 three times.

**Rows 26–31:** Rep rows 2–3 three times.

**Rows 32–37:** Rep rows 8–9 three times.

Sizes 1–5: Continue to Front Shoulder 1.

Sizes 6–9: Rep rows 2–3 three times, then continue to Front Shoulder 1.

## Front Shoulder 1

With CC held double and larger hook.

**Row 1:** Ch 2, hdc in next 37 (43, 49, 55, 61) (67, 73, 79, 85) sts, hdc2tog over next 2 sts, turn. 39 (45, 51, 57, 63) (69, 75, 81, 87) sts

**Row 2:** Ch 2, hdc in next st (counts as hdc-2tog over 2 sts), hdc in BL of next 37 (43, 49, 55, 61) (67, 73, 79, 85) sts, turn. 38 (44, 50, 56, 62) (68, 74, 80, 86) sts

**Row 3:** Ch 2, hdc in BL of next 35 (41, 47, 53, 59) (65, 71, 77, 83) sts, hdc2tog over next 2 sts, turn. 37 (43, 49, 55, 61) (67, 73, 79, 85) sts

**Row 4:** Ch 2, hdc in next st (counts as hdc-2tog over 2 sts), hdc in BL of next 19 (22, 25, 28, 31) (34, 37, 40, 43) hdc, sc in BL of next 3 (6, 9, 12, 15) (18, 21, 24, 27) sts, (mark next st), turn. 23 (29, 35, 41, 47) (53, 59, 65, 71) sts

**Row 5:** Ch 1, sc in BL of next 9 (12, 15, 18, 21) (24, 27, 30, 33) sts, hdc in BL of next 12 (15, 18, 21, 24) (27, 30, 33, 36) sts, hdc2tog over next 2 sts, turn. 22 (28, 34, 40, 46) (52, 58, 64, 70) sts

**Row 3:** You will be working on the opposite side of the chains of each triangle and work the same st in the same ch. You will work a sc in the same ch that holds the sc, a dc in the same ch that holds the dc, and a dtr in the same ch that holds the dtr.

Ch 5. [Sc in the marked st and in next ch (remove marker), ch 1, skip next ch, dc in next ch, ch 1, skip next 2 chs, dtr in next ch] across all triangles omitting dtr in last triangle, work dtr2tog in last ch and last st, turn. 103 (115, 127, 139, 151) (163, 175, 187, 199) sts

**Rows 4–7:** Rep rows 2–3 twice.

**Row 6:** Ch 2, hdc in next st (counts as hdc2tog over 2 sts), hdc in BL of next 11 (14, 17, 20, 23) (26, 29, 32, 35) hdc, sc in BL of next 3 (6, 9, 12, 15) (18, 21, 24, 27) sts, (mark next st), turn. 15 (21, 27, 33, 39) (45, 51, 57, 63) sts

**Row 7:** Ch 1, sc in BL of next 9 (12, 15, 18, 21) (24, 27, 30, 33) sts, hdc in BL of next 4 (7, 10, 13, 16) (19, 22, 25, 28) sts, hdc2tog over next 2 sts, turn. 14 (20, 26, 32, 38) (44, 50, 56, 62) sts

**Row 8:** Ch 2, hdc in next st (counts as hdc2tog over 2 sts), hdc in BL of next 3 (6, 9, 12, 15) (18, 21, 24, 27) hdc, sc in BL of next 3 (6, 9, 12, 15) (18, 21, 24, 27) sts, (mark next st), turn. 7 (13, 19, 25, 31) (37, 43, 49, 55) sts

**Row 9:** Ch 1, sc in BL of next 3 (6, 9, 12, 15) (18, 21, 24, 27) sts, hdc in BL of next 2 (5, 8, 11, 14) (17, 20, 23, 26) sts, hdc2tog over next 2 sts, turn. 6 (12, 18, 24, 30) (36, 42, 48, 54) sts

**Row 10:** Ch 1, sc in next 5 (11, 17, 23, 29) (35, 41, 47, 53) sts, sc-hdc-tog over next st and next marked st, 2 hdc in next st. [Sc in next 3 sts, sc-hdc-tog over next st and next marked st, 2 hdc in next st] twice. Sc in next 11 sts, fasten off. 31 (37, 43, 49, 55) (61, 67, 73, 79) sts

## Front Shoulder 2

With CC held double and larger hook, attach yarn with sl st to the other side of last row of Front Body. Work Rows 1–10 of Front Shoulder 1.

# Back

Repeat Front Ribbing and Front Body part and stop right before the Shoulder parts.

## Upper Back

With CC held double and larger hook:

**Row 1:** Ch 2, hdc across, turn. 103 (115, 127, 139, 151) (163, 175, 187, 199) sts

**Rows 2–3:** Ch 2, hdc in BL across, turn. 103 (115, 127, 139, 151) (163, 175, 187, 199) sts

**Row 4:** Sl st in next 13 sts, mark last st just made. (sl sts are not counted in the total stitch count)

Sc in BL of next 3 (6, 9, 12, 15) (18, 21, 24, 27) sts, hdc in BL of next 71 (77, 83, 89, 95) (101, 107, 113, 119) sts, sc in BL of next 3 (6, 9, 12, 15) (18, 21, 24, 27) sts, mark next st, turn. 77 (89, 101, 113, 125) (137, 149, 161, 173) sts not counting sl sts

**Row 5:** Ch 1, sc in BL of next 9 (12, 15, 18, 21) (24, 27, 30, 33) sts, hdc in BL of next 59 (65, 71, 77, 83) (89, 95, 101, 107) sts, sc in BL of next 3 (6, 9, 12, 15) (18, 21, 24, 27) sts, mark next st, turn. 71 (83, 95, 107, 119) (131, 143, 155, 167) sts

**Row 6:** Ch 1, sc in BL of next 9 (12, 15, 18, 21) (24, 27, 30, 33) sts, hdc in BL of next 53 (59, 65, 71, 77) (83, 89, 95, 101) sts, sc in BL of next 3 (6, 9, 12, 15) (18, 21, 24, 27) sts, mark next st, turn. 65 (77, 89, 101, 113) (125, 137, 149, 161) sts

**Row 7:** Ch 1, sc in BL of next 9 (12, 15, 18, 21) (24, 27, 30, 33) sts, hdc in BL of next 47 (53, 59, 65, 71) (77, 83, 89, 95) sts, sc in BL of next 3 (6, 9, 12, 15) (18, 21, 24, 27) sts, mark next st, turn. 59 (71, 83, 95, 107) (119, 131, 143, 155) sts

## Back Shoulder 1

**Row 8:** Ch 1, sc in BL of next 3 (6, 9, 12, 15) (18, 21, 24, 27) sts, hdc in BL of next 3 (6, 9, 12, 15) (18, 21, 24, 27) hdc, hdc2tog over next 2 sts, turn. 7 (13, 19, 25, 31) (37, 43, 49, 55) sts

**Row 9:** Ch 2, hdc in next st (counts as hdc2tog over 2 sts), hdc in BL of next 2 (5, 8, 11, 14) (17, 20, 23, 26) sts, sc in BL of next 2 (5, 8, 11, 14) (17, 20, 23, 26) sts, sc-hdc-tog over next st and next marked st, 2 hdc in next st. Sc in next 3 sts, sc-hdc-tog over next st and next marked st, 2 hdc in next st. Sc in next 4 sts, sc in next (marked) st, sc in next 12 sts.

Fasten off, leaving a longer yarn end for sewing or crochet the shoulder seam right away—take the Front and put both (Front and Back) parts together with RS facing each other (WS out).

**Crochet the shoulder seam together using sl sts:** Ch 1 (turning ch), insert hook through both loops of first st of Back and through both loops of Front, yo and pull yarn through all loops on hook, continue to work like this across all sts of the shoulder, fasten off. 31 (37, 43, 49, 55) (61, 67, 73, 79) sts

## Back Shoulder 2

Attach yarn with sl st to the other end of row 7 of Upper Back.

**Row 8:** Ch 1, sc in BL of next 9 (12, 15, 18, 21) (24, 27, 30, 33) sts, hdc in BL of next 3 (6, 9, 12, 15) (18, 21, 24, 27) hdc, hdc2tog over next 2 sts, turn. 13 (19, 25, 31, 37) (43, 49, 55, 61) sts

**Row 9:** Ch 2, hdc in next st (counts as hdc2tog over 2 sts), hdc in BL of next 2 (5, 8, 11, 14) (17, 20, 23, 26) sts, sc in BL of next 8 (11, 14, 17, 20) (23, 26, 29, 32) sts, sc-hdc-tog over next st and next marked st, 2 hdc in next st. Sc in next 3 sts, sc-hdc-tog over next st and next marked st, 2 hdc in next st, sc in next 11 sts, fasten off, leaving a longer yarn end for sewing, or crochet the shoulder seam right away (put Front and Back detail together with WS out and crochet the shoulder seam with sl st). 31 (37, 43, 49, 55) (61, 67, 73, 79) sts

# Sleeve

## Make 2

With MC held double and larger hook, ch 51 (last 2 ch counts as first hdc on next row).

**Row 1:** Hdc in third ch from hook, hdc across, turn. 50 sts

**Row 2:** Ch 2, hdc in BL of next 29 sts, sc in BL of next 10 sts, mark next st, turn. 40 sts

**Row 3:** Ch 1, sc in BL of next 15 sts, hdc in BL of next 25 sts, turn. 40 sts

**Row 4:** Ch 2, hdc in BL of next 19 sts, sc in BL of next 10 sts, mark next st, turn. 30 sts

**Row 5:** Ch 1, sc in BL of next 15 sts, hdc in BL of next 15 sts, turn. 30 sts

**Row 6:** Ch 2, hdc in BL of next 9 sts, sc in BL of next 10 sts, mark next st, turn. 20 sts

**Row 7:** Ch 1, sc in BL of next 15 sts, hdc in BL of next 5 sts, turn. 20 sts

**Row 8:** Ch 1, sc in next 19 sts. [Sc-hdc-tog over next and next marked st, 2 hdc in next st, sc in next 7 sts] 3 times. Sc in next st, turn. 50 sts

**Next 10 (11, 12, 13, 14) (15, 16, 17, 18) rows:** Ch 2, hdc in BL across, turn. 50 sts

Change to CC.

**Next 7 rows:** Ch 2, hdc in BL across, turn. 50 sts

Change back to MC.

**Next 10 (11, 12, 13, 14) (15, 16, 17, 18) rows:** Ch 2, hdc in BL across, turn. 50 sts

Rep rows 2–8, fasten off.

## Neckline Ribbing

With CC held double and smaller hook, ch 9 (last 2 ch counts as first hdc on next row).

**Row 1:** Hdc in third ch from hook, hdc in each ch across, turn. 8 sts

**Rows 2–67:** Ch 2 (counts as first hdc), hdc in BL across, turn. 8 sts

**Last row of the ribbing:** Don't turn. Rotate the ribbing clockwise by 90 degrees and work across the side of the ribbing: work 3 sc in every 2 rows of hdc, leave a longer yarn end for sewing the ribbing to the neckline.

## Finishing

Block all parts according to fiber type. Sew both Shoulder seams (if not already done). Sew the Neckline Ribbing on to the neckline starting from the side seam. Sew both ends of the Neckline Ribbing together. Sew the Sleeves on and sew both side seams. Weave in ends.

# Nora Forest Meadow Sweater

Just as dew drops cling to the finest grass stalks at dawn, ethereal broomstick lace strands meet the lively herringbone braids in the sophisticated Nora sweater. Slanted drop stitch braids accompany the broomstick loops, coming together in this intricate piece, giving it a sense of delicate fragility and meticulous beauty.

# Nora Forest Meadow Sweater Construction Notes

*The round yoke Nora sweater is worked top down in joined rounds, then is split for the body and sleeves at the bust line. The sweater is worked in one piece and is seamless. Nora comes in nine sizes and includes instructions for adjusting the length of the body and straight sleeves.*

## Sizes

1 (2, 3, 4, 5) (6, 7, 8, 9)

**Finished bust:** 30 (34, 38, 42, 46) (50, 54, 58, 62)" / 76 (86, 97, 107, 117) (127, 137, 147, 157) cm

## Gauge

20 sts x 13 rows = 4" / 10 cm in dc after blocking

One stitch pattern repeat (13 rows) measures 3.75" / 9.5 cm

## Yarn

Sport weight, Go Handmade Tencel Bamboo Double (60% Bamboo, 40% Tencel™), 142 yds / 130 m per 50-g skein, or use any sport weight bamboo blend to achieve a similar effect

## Yardage/Meterage

1080 (1135, 1225, 1450, 1535) (1650, 1760, 1850, 1900) yds / 990 (1040, 1120, 1325, 1405) (1510, 1610, 1690, 1740) m

## Shown in

Colorway Hunting Green (17715)

## Hook

G/6 / 4 mm for the main sections of the Yoke, Body and Sleeves, or size needed to obtain gauge

## Notions

**Broomstick Lace Tool that creates 1.25" / 3.2-cm tall loops:**

>   ruler (1.5" / 3.7 cm wide)

>   or rectangular piece of cardboard

>   or large knitting needle 50mm

Tapestry needle

4 stitch markers

## Skills

Experience with making crocheted top-down sweaters

Experience with broomstick lace

## Special stitches

**Slanted drop stitch:** [Yo, insert hook into indicated ch-sp, yo, draw yarn through ch-sp and pull up a longer loop to the height of your working row] twice, yo, draw through 4 loops on hook, yo, draw through last 2 loops on hook.

**Broomstick loop:** Insert your crochet hook into the indicated st, yarn over and draw through the stitch, yo, draw through both loops on the hook. Continue to draw up a long loop, insert the ruler (or other tool you use for making the loops)—from right to left, pull the working yarn back to tighten the loop. [Insert hook in next st, yo, draw through the stitch, yo, draw through the loop and continue to draw up a long loop, place it on the ruler next to the previous loop, release the hook. Pull back to tighten the loop] in each designated stitch.

## Abbreviations (US terms)

Ch = chain

Ch-sp = chain space

Dc = double crochet

Fsc = foundation single crochet

Hdc = half double crochet

Rnd(s) = round(s)

RS = right side

Sc = single crochet

Sl st = slip stitch

St(s) = stitch(es)

Tr = treble

WS = wrong side

| Size | A—finished bust | B—yoke depth | C—body length (armhole to hem) | D—full length | E—sleeve length | F—upper arm |
|---|---|---|---|---|---|---|
| 1 | 30" / 76 cm | 7.75" / 20 cm | 8.25" / 21 cm | 16.25" / 41 cm | 18.5" / 47 cm | 11.5" / 29 cm |
| 2 | 34" / 86 cm | 8.25" / 21 cm | 8.75" / 22 cm | 17" / 43 cm | 17.75" / 45 cm | 11.75" / 30 cm |
| 3 | 38" / 97 cm | 9" / 23 cm | 9.5" / 24 cm | 18.5" / 47 cm | 17.25" / 44 cm | 12.5" / 32 cm |
| 4 | 42" / 107 cm | 9.5" / 24 cm | 9" / 23 cm | 18.5" / 47 cm | 17" / 43 cm | 13.75" / 35 cm |
| 5 | 46" / 117 cm | 9.75" / 25 cm | 9.25" / 23.5 cm | 19" / 48.5 cm | 16.25" / 41.5 cm | 15" / 38 cm |
| 6 | 50" / 127 cm | 10.5" / 27 cm | 10" / 25.5 cm | 20.5" / 52.5 cm | 15.75" / 40 cm | 17" / 43 cm |
| 7 | 54" / 137 cm | 11" / 28 cm | 8.25" / 21 cm | 19.25" / 49 cm | 14.75" / 37.5 cm | 18.5" / 47 cm |
| 8 | 58" / 147 cm | 11.5" / 29 cm | 8.75" / 22 cm | 20" / 51 cm | 14" / 35.5 cm | 19.75" / 50 cm |
| 9 | 62" / 157 cm | 12.25" / 31 cm | 9.5" / 24 cm | 21.75" / 55 cm | 13.5" / 34.5 cm | 19.75" / 50 cm |

*The sweater is designed to be worn with no ease. Size 2 is modeled on 32" / 82-cm bust model.*

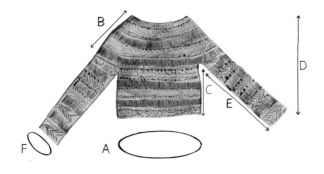

# Nora Forest Meadow Sweater Pattern

## Yoke

Using your main gauge hook and leaving approximately 6" / 15 cm long yarn end for sewing the neck split, with WS facing, fsc 106 (108, 108, 110, 112) (114, 116, 118, 120), turn.

**Throughout:** Beginning ch 3 counts as first dc.

**Rnd 1 (sizes 1, 4, 7):** With RS facing, ch 2, hdc in each fsc across (mark last hdc), join with sl st to the top ch of beg ch-2 and continue to work in rounds.

**Rnd 1 (sizes 2, 5, 8):** With RS facing, ch 3, dc in each fsc across (mark last dc), join with sl st to the top ch of beg ch-3 and continue to work in rounds.

**Rnd 1 (sizes 3, 6, 9):** With RS facing, ch 4, tr in each fsc across (mark last tr), join with sl st to the top ch of beg ch-4 and continue to work in rounds.

**Rnd 2 (increase rnd):** [Sc in first st, 2 sc in next st] around, join to the first st (counts as join here and throughout). 159 (162, 162, 165, 168) (171, 174, 177, 180) sts

**Rnd 3:** Ch 4 (counts as first dc + ch 1), skip next st. [Dc in next st, ch 1, skip next st] across until 1 (0, 0, 1, 0) (1, 0, 1, 0) st left, dc in next 1 (0, 0, 1, 0) (1, 0, 1, 0) st, join. Mark second ch-sp from end of the rnd.

**Rnd 4:** Ch 3, dc around, join.

**Rnd 5:** Sc in first st, slanted drop st in marked ch-sp (remove marker). [Sc in next st, slanted drop st in next ch-sp from Rnd 3] around, skip 1 (0, 0, 1, 0) (1, 0, 1, 0) next st, join. 158 (162, 162, 164, 168) (170, 174, 176, 180) sts

**Rnd 6:** [Sc in next st, ch 1, skip next st] around, join.

**Rnd 7:** Ch 3, dc around, join and turn to the WS. Mark second ch-sp (of rnd 6) counting from left to right.

**Rnd 8:** With WS facing, sc in next st, slanted drop st in marked ch-sp (remove marker). [Sc in next st, drop st in next ch-sp] around, join and turn back to RS.

**Rnd 9:** Ch 4, skip next st. [Dc in next st, ch 1, skip next st] around, join.

**Rnd 10 (increase rnd):** [Sc in next 2 sts, 2 sc in next st] 52 (54, 54, 54, 56) (56, 58, 58, 60) times. Dc in next 2 (0, 0, 2, 0) (2, 0, 2, 0) sts, join. 210 (216, 216, 218, 224) (226, 232, 234, 240) sts

**Rnd 11 (sizes 1, 4, 7):** Ch 2, hdc around, join.

**Rnd 11 (sizes 2, 5, 8):** Ch 3, dc around, join.

**Rnd 11 (sizes 3, 6, 9):** Ch 4, tr around, join.

**Rnd 12:** Make broomstick loops in each st around: Insert your crochet hook into the first st of the round. Yarn over and draw through the stitch, yo, draw through both loops on the hook. Continue to draw up a long loop, insert the ruler (or other tool you use for making the loops)—from right to left, pull the working yarn back to tighten the loop. [Insert hook in next st, yo, draw through the stitch, yo, draw through the loop and continue to draw up a long loop, place it on the ruler next to the previous loop, release the hook. Pull back to tighten the loop] around. 210 (216, 216, 218, 224) (226, 232, 234, 240) loops made.

It will become difficult to keep all loops on your tool when working in the round. Release some loops from the right side of the tool as needed. Leave the hook inserted in the last loop. Make sure your loops are not twisted, and always insert the tool in all loops the same way.

**Rnd 13:** With your hook already inserted in the last loop—yo, draw hook through loop, yo, draw through. SC in each broomstick loop around, join.

**Rnd 14 (sizes 1, 4, 7):** Ch 2, hdc around, join.

**Rnd 14 (sizes 2, 5, 8):** Ch 3, dc around, join.

**Rnd 14 (sizes 3, 6, 9):** Ch 4, tr around, join.

**Rnd 15 (increase rnd):** [Sc in next 5 (5, 4, 3, 3) (3, 3, 3, 3) sts, 2 sc in next st] 35 (36, 43, 54, 56) (56, 58, 58, 60) times. Sc in next 0 (0, 1, 2, 0) (2, 0, 2, 0) sts, join. 245 (252, 259, 272, 280) (282, 290, 292, 300) sts

**Rnd 16:** Ch 4 (counts as first dc + ch 1), skip next st. [Dc in next st, ch 1, skip next st] across until 1 (0, 1, 0, 0) (0, 0, 0, 0) st left, dc in next 1 (0, 1, 0, 0) (0, 0, 0, 0) st, join. Mark second ch-sp from end of the rnd.

**Rnd 17:** Ch 3, dc around, join.

**Rnd 18:** Sc in first st, slanted drop st in marked ch-sp (remove marker). [Sc in next st, slanted drop st in next ch-sp] around, skip 1 (0, 1, 0, 0) (0, 0, 0, 0) next st, join. 244 (252, 258, 272, 280) (282, 290, 292, 300) sts

**Rnd 19:** [Sc in next st, ch 1, skip next st] around, join.

**Rnd 20:** Ch 3, dc around, join and turn to the WS. Mark second ch-sp (of rnd 19) counting from left to right.

**Rnd 21:** With WS facing, sc in next st, slanted drop st in marked ch-sp (remove marker). [Sc in next st, drop st in next ch-sp] around, join and turn back to RS.

**Rnd 22:** Ch 4, skip next st. [Dc in next st, ch 1, skip next st] around, join.

## Increase rnd

**Rnd 23 (size 1):** 2 sc in each of next 2 sts. [Sc in next 29 sts, 2 sc in next st] 8 times. 2 sc in each of next 2 sts, join. 256 sts

**Rnd 23 (size 2):** [Sc in next 10 sts, 2 sc in next st] 22 times. Sc in next 10 sts, join. 274 sts

**Rnd 23 (size 3):** [Sc in next 6 sts, 2 sc in next st] 36 times. Sc in next 6 sts, join. 294 sts

**Rnd 23 (sizes 4–9):** [Sc in next 10 sts, 2 sc in next st] x (x, x, 24, 25) (25, 26, 26, 27) times. Sc in next x (x, x, 8, 5) (7, 4, 6, 3) sts, join. x (x, x, 296, 305) (307, 316, 318, 327) sts

**Rnd 24 (sizes 1, 4, 7):** Ch 2, hdc around, join.

**Rnd 24 (sizes 2, 5, 8):** Ch 3, dc around, join.

**Rnd 24 (sizes 3, 6, 9):** Ch 4, tr around, join.

**Rnd 25:** Repeat rnd 12.

**Rnd 26:** Repeat rnd 13.

**Rnd 27 (sizes 1, 4, 7):** Ch 2, hdc around, join.

**Rnd 27 (sizes 2, 5, 8):** Ch 3, dc around, join.

**Rnd 27 (sizes 3, 6, 9):** Ch 4, tr around, join.

**Sizes 1–3:** Continue to Separating Body and Sleeves (page 180).

**Sizes 4–9:** Continue to work from rnd 28.

**Rnd 28 (increase rnd):** [Sc in next 21 sts, 2 sc in next st] x (x, x, 13, 13) (13, 14, 14, 14) times. Sc in next x (x, x, 10, 19) (21, 8, 10, 19) sts, join. x (x, x, 309, 318) (320, 330, 332, 341) sts

**Rnd 29:** Ch 4 (counts as first dc + ch 1), skip next st. [Dc in next st, ch 1, skip next st] across until x (x, x, 1, 0) (0, 0, 0, 1) st left, dc in next x (x, x, 1, 0) (0, 0 , 0, 1) st, join. Mark second ch-sp from end of the rnd.

**Rnd 30:** Ch 3, dc around, join.

**Rnd 31:** Sc in first st, slanted drop st in marked ch-sp (remove marker). [Sc in next st, slanted drop st in next ch-sp] around, skip x (x, x, 1, 0) (0, 0, 0, 1) next st, join. x (x, x, 308, 318) (320, 330, 332, 340) sts

**Rnd 32:** [Sc in next st, ch 1, skip next st] around, join. Mark third ch-sp of this rnd.

**Rnd 33:** Ch 3, dc around, join and turn to the WS. Mark second ch-sp (of rnd 32) counting from left to right.

**Rnd 34:** With WS facing, sc in next st, slanted drop st in marked ch-sp (remove marker). [Sc in next st, drop st in next ch-sp] around, join and turn back to RS.

**Rnd 35:** Ch 4, skip next st. [Dc in next st, ch 1, skip next st] around, join.

## Increase rnd

**Rnd 36 (size 4):** [Sc in next 29 sts, 2 sc in next st] 10 times. Sc in next 8 sts, join. 318 sts

**Rnd 36 (size 5):** [Sc in next 12 sts, 2 sc in next st] 24 times. Sc in next 6 sts, join. 342 sts

**Rnd 36 (size 6):** [Sc in next 4 sts, 2 sc in next st] 54 times. Sc in next 50 sts, join. 374 sts

**Rnd 36 (sizes 7–9):** [Sc in next x (x, x, x, x) (x, 3, 2, 2) sts, 2 sc in next st] x (x, x, x, x) (x, 72, 94, 98) times. Sc in next x (x, x, x, x) (x, 42, 50, 46) sts, join. x (x, x, x, x) (x, 402, 426, 438) sts

**Sizes 4–6:** Continue to Separating Body and Sleeves (page 180).

**Sizes 7–9:** Continue to work from rnd 37.

**Rnd 37 (size 7):** Ch 2, hdc around, join.

**Rnd 37 (size 8):** Ch 3, dc around, join.

**Rnd 37 (size 9):** Ch 4, tr around, join.

**Rnds 38–39 (sizes 7–9):** Repeat rnds 12–13.

**Rnd 40 (size 7):** Ch 2, hdc around, join.

**Rnd 40 (size 8):** Ch 3, dc around, join.

**Rnd 40 (size 9):** Ch 4, tr around, join.

**Sizes 7–9:** Continue to Separating Body and Sleeves.

# Body

Continue to work Body in joined rounds. Add more repeats if you wish to make the top longer. Make sure to end the Body with one or two slanted drop stitch braids.

## Body (Sizes 1–3 and 7–9)

Start with 152 (172, 194, x, x) (x, 274, 294, 314) sts

**Rnd 1:** Ch 4 (counts as first dc + ch 1), skip next st. [Dc in next st, ch 1, skip next st] across, join. Mark second ch-sp from end of the rnd.

**Rnd 2:** Ch 3, dc around, join.

**Rnd 3:** Sc in first st, slanted drop st in marked ch-sp (remove marker). [Sc in next st, slanted drop st in next ch-sp] around, join.

**Rnd 4:** [Sc in next st, ch 1, skip next st] around, join.

**Rnd 5:** Ch 3, dc around, join and turn to the WS. Mark second ch-sp (of rnd 4) counting from left to right.

**Rnd 6:** With WS facing, sc in next st, slanted drop st in marked ch-sp (remove marker). [Sc in next st, drop st in next ch-sp] around, join and turn back to RS.

**Rnd 7:** Ch 4, skip next st. [Dc in next st, ch 1, skip next st] around, join.

**Rnd 8:** Sc around, join.

**Rnd 9 (sizes 1, 7):** Ch 2, hdc around, join.

**Rnd 9 (sizes 2, 8):** Ch 3, dc around, join.

**Rnd 9 (sizes 3, 9):** Ch 4, tr around, join.

# Separating Body and Sleeves

You should have 256 (274, 294, 318, 342) (374, 402, 426, 438) sts when the Yoke is finished.

You can use stitch markers to mark the skipped stitches for sleeves.

Sc in next 36 (40, 45, 49, 53) (57, 61, 65, 69) sts, ch 3 (5, 7, 9, 11) (13, 15, 17, 19), skip next 55 (56, 57, 61, 65) (73, 79, 83, 81) sts for one sleeve, sc in next 73 (81, 90, 98, 106) (114, 122, 130, 138) sts, ch 3 (5, 7, 9, 11) (13, 15, 17, 19), skip next 55 (56, 57, 61, 65) (73, 79, 83, 81) sts for other sleeve, sc in next 37 (41, 45, 49, 53) (57, 61, 65, 69) sts, join and continue to Body.

**Rnd 10:** Make broomstick loops in each st around. Leave the hook inserted in the last loop. Make sure your loops are not twisted and always insert hook in all loops the same way.

**Rnd 11:** With your hook already inserted in the last loop, yo, draw hook through loop, yo, draw through. SC in each broomstick loop around, join.

**Rnd 12 (sizes 1, 7):** Ch 2, hdc around, join.

**Rnd 12 (sizes 2, 8):** Ch 3, dc around, join.

**Rnd 12 (sizes 3, 9):** Ch 4, tr around, join.

**Rnd 13:** Sc around, join.

Rep rnds 1–13 one more time.

To make longer—repeat rnds 1–13 more times if you want to add length to your sweater. One repeat measures 3.75" / 9.5 cm.

Repeat rnds 1–6 one more time.

**Next rnd:** Sc around, join.

**Last rnd:** Sl st around, fasten off.

## Body (Sizes 4–6)

Start with x (x, x, 214, 234) (254, x, x, x) sts

**Rnd 1 (size 4):** Ch 2, hdc around, join.

**Rnd 1 (size 5):** Ch 3, dc around, join.

**Rnd 1 (size 6):** Ch 4, tr around, join.

**Rnd 2:** Make broomstick loops in each st around.

**Rnd 3:** With your hook already inserted in the last loop, yo, draw hook through loop, yo, draw through. SC in each broomstick loop around, join.

**Rnd 4 (size 4):** Ch 2, hdc around, join.

**Rnd 4 (size 5):** Ch 3, dc around, join.

**Rnd 4 (size 6):** Ch 4, tr around, join.

**Rnd 5:** Sc around, join.

**Rnd 6:** Ch 4 (counts as first dc + ch 1), skip next st. [Dc in next st, ch 1, skip next st] across, join. Mark second ch-sp from end of the rnd.

**Rnd 7:** Ch 3, dc around, join.

**Rnd 8:** Sc in first st, slanted drop st in marked ch-sp (remove marker). [Sc in next st, slanted drop st in next ch-sp] around, join.

**Rnd 9:** [Sc in next st, ch 1, skip next st] around, join.

**Rnd 10:** Ch 3, dc around, join and turn to the WS. Mark second ch-sp counting from left to right.

**Rnd 11:** With WS facing, sc in next st, slanted drop st in marked ch-sp (remove marker). [Sc in next st, drop st in next ch-sp] around, join and turn back to RS.

**Rnd 12:** Ch 4, skip next st. [Dc in next st, ch 1, skip next st] around, join.

**Rnd 13:** Sc around, join.

Rep rnds 1–13 one more time.

To make longer—repeat rnds 1–13 more times if you want to add length to your sweater. One repeat measures 3.75" / 9.5 cm.

Repeat rnds 4–11 one more time.

**Next rnd:** Sc around, join.

**Last rnd:** Sl st around, fasten off.

# Sleeves

The sleeves are designed straight. As sleeves are always such an individual measurement, aim to finish your sleeve with the slanted drop stitch braid—either one braid, or two.

You can opt for a short-sleeved top and finish the armholes with a rnd of sc and a rnd of sl sts.

Or if you wish to narrow the sleeves, decrease 4 sts in every rnd of sc (work 4 sc2tog, spreading the sts evenly) until you reach the desired circumference, then continue to work straight.

## Sleeve (sizes 1–3 and 7–9)

### Make 2

Start with 58 (61, 64, x, x) (x, 94, 100, 100) sts

With your main gauge hook, attach yarn with sl st anywhere in the underarm.

**Rnd 1:** Ch 4 (counts as first dc + ch 1), skip next st. [Dc in next st, ch 1, skip next st] across.

**Size 2 only:** Make dc, ch 1 in last st.

**All sizes:** Join. Mark second ch-sp from end of the rnd.

**Rnd 2:** Ch 3, dc around, join.

**Rnd 3:** Sc in first st, slanted drop st in marked ch-sp (remove marker). [Sc in next st, slanted drop st in next ch-sp] around, join.

**Rnd 4:** [Sc in next st, ch 1, skip next st] around, join.

**Rnd 5:** Ch 3, dc around, join and turn to the WS. Mark second ch-sp (of rnd 4) counting from left to right.

**Rnd 6:** With WS facing, sc in next st, slanted drop st in marked ch-sp (remove marker). [Sc in next st, drop st in next ch-sp] around, join and turn back to RS.

**Rnd 7:** Ch 4, skip next st. [Dc in next st, ch 1, skip next st] around, join.

**Rnd 8:** Sc around, join.

**Rnd 9 (sizes 1, 7):** Ch 4, tr around, join.

**Rnd 9 (sizes 2, 8):** Ch 3, dc around, join.

**Rnd 9 (sizes 3, 9):** Ch 2, hdc around, join.

**Rnd 10:** Make broomstick loops in each st around. Leave the hook inserted in the last loop. Make sure your loops are not twisted and always insert hook in all loops the same way.

**Rnd 11:** With your hook already inserted in the last loop, yo, draw hook through loop, yo, draw through. Sc in each broomstick loop around, join.

**Rnd 12 (sizes 1, 7):** Ch 4, tr around, join.

**Rnd 12 (sizes 2, 8):** Ch 3, dc around, join.

**Rnd 12 (sizes 3, 9):** Ch 2, hdc around, join.

**Rnd 13:** Sc around, join.

Rep rnds 1–13 another 3 (3, 3, x, x) (x, 2, 2, 2) times.

Rep rnds 1–6 two times.

**Next rnd:** Sc around, join.

**Last rnd:** Sl st around, fasten off.

Or finish when the desired sleeve length is reached, preferably finishing right after the second slanted drop stitch rnd. If you're close to the end of your individual sleeve length and if it will be reached right after the broomstick loops, I suggest skipping the last broomstick loops rnd and working the second group of slanted drop stitches instead.

## Sleeve (sizes 4–6)

Make 2

Start with x (x, x, 70, 76) (86, x, x, x) sts

With your main gauge hook, attach yarn with sl st anywhere in the underarm.

**Rnd 1 (size 4):** Ch 4, tr around, join.

**Rnd 1 (size 5):** Ch 3, dc around, join.

**Rnd 1 (size 6):** Ch 2, hdc around, join.

**Rnd 2:** Make broomstick loops in each st around.

**Rnd 3:** With your hook already inserted in the last loop, yo, draw hook through loop, yo, draw through. SC in each broomstick loop around, join.

**Rnd 4 (size 4):** Ch 4, tr around, join.

**Rnd 4 (size 5):** Ch 3, dc around, join.

**Rnd 4 (size 6):** Ch 2, hdc around, join.

**Rnd 5:** Sc around, join.

**Rnd 6:** Ch 4 (counts as first dc + ch 1), skip next st. [Dc in next st, ch 1, skip next st] across, join. Mark second ch-sp from end of the rnd.

**Rnd 7:** Ch 3, dc around, join.

**Rnd 8:** Sc in first st, slanted drop st in marked ch-sp (remove marker). [Sc in next st, slanted drop st in next ch-sp] around, join.

**Rnd 9:** [Sc in next st, ch 1, skip next st] around, join.

**Rnd 10:** Ch 3, dc around, join and turn to the WS. Mark second ch-sp counting from left to right.

**Rnd 11:** With WS facing, sc in next st, slanted drop st in marked ch-sp (remove marker). [Sc in next st, drop st in next ch-sp] around, join and turn back to RS.

**Rnd 12:** Ch 4, skip next st. [Dc in next st, ch 1, skip next st] around, join.

**Rnd 13:** Sc around, join.

Rep rnds 1–13 another 3 times.

Rep rnds 7–11 one time.

**Next rnd:** Sc around, join.

**Last rnd:** Sl st around, fasten off.

## Finishing

Turn the sweater to the WS and weave in all ends. Sew the little opening on foundation row of neck if you haven't already done so. Block the sweater according to fiber type, and turn the sweater back to RS.

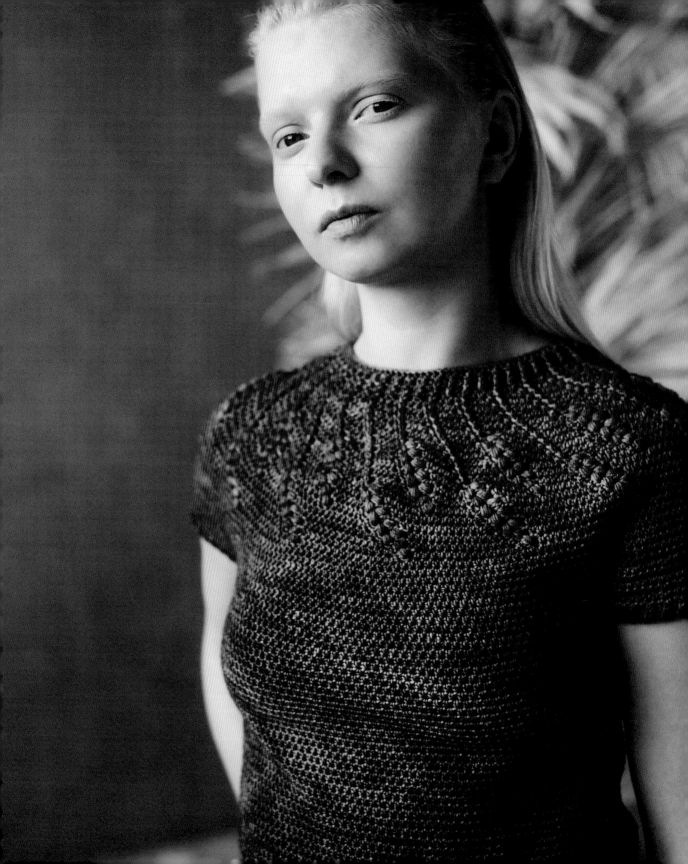

# Malduguns Fen Fire Sweater

In this sweater, you can imagine yourself as an artist "drawing" with post stitches and adding texture with puff stitch accents! The sophisticated yoke works as a lovely additional detail and balances the solid body. Using a hand-dyed yarn adds more interest and excitement to the alluring Malduguns sweater, creating a piece you'll truly be proud to show off.

# Malduguns Fen Fire
## Construction Notes

*Malduguns is worked top down in joined rounds, then is split for the body and sleeves at the bust line. The straight body ends with a ribbed edge. Instructions for both a cropped and regular body length, as well as for adjusting the length of the sleeves, are available. The sweater is worked in one piece and is seamless.*

## Sizes

1 (2, 3, 4, 5) (6, 7, 8, 9)

**To fit bust:** 30 (34, 38, 42, 46) (50, 54, 58, 62)" / 76 (86, 97, 107, 117) (127, 137, 147, 157) cm

**Finished bust:** 28.25 (32, 35.75, 39.75, 43.75) (47.25, 50.75, 54.75, 58.25)" / 72 (81, 91, 101, 111) (120, 129, 139, 148) cm

## Gauge

19 sts x 18 rows = 4" / 10 cm in hdc after blocking

## Yarn

Sport weight, The Yarn Collective Fleurville 4 Ply (100% Merino Wool), 382 yds / 350 m per 100-g skein, or use any sport weight merino wool to achieve a similar effect

## Yardage/Meterage

Amounts shown are for the regular length.

**Short sleeved:** 975 (1065, 1180, 1335, 1430) (1565, 1715, 1815, 1985) yds / 890 (975, 1080, 1220, 1310) (1430, 1570, 1660, 1815) m

**Long sleeved:** 1220 (1320, 1450, 1600, 1715) (1870, 2060, 2175, 2330) yds / 1115 (1205, 1325, 1465, 1570) (1710, 1885, 1990, 2130) m

## Shown in

Colorway Hibiscus (602)

## Hook

G/6 / 4 mm, or size needed to obtain gauge

## Notions

Tapestry needle

2 stitch markers

## Skills

Experience with making crocheted top-down sweaters

Experience with working post stitches

## Abbreviations (US terms)

Beg = beginning

BPdc = back post double crochet

Ch = chain

Dc = double crochet

Dc2tog = double crochet 2 together

FPdc = front post double crochet

Fsc = foundation single crochet

Hdc = half double crochet

Hdc2tog = half double crochet 2 together

LL = long loop

Prev = previous

Puff st = puff stitch

Rnd(s) = round(s)

RS = right side

Sc = single crochet

Sl st = slip stitch

St(s) = stitch(es)

WS = wrong side

## Special stitches

**Puff stitch:** Yo, insert hook in the indicated st, yo, pull loop through st and make loop same height as previous sts in working row, (yo, insert hook in same st, yo, pull loop through st and make loop same height as working row) three times, yo, pull through 8 loops on hook (2 loops left on hook), yo, pull through both loops.

**V-puff:** (Puff st, ch 1, puff st) all in same stitch.

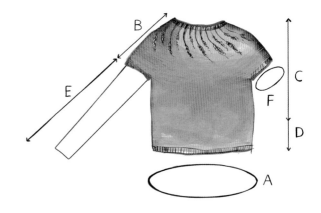

| Size | A—finished bust | B—yoke depth | C—cropped length | D—regular length | E—sleeve length from underarm | F—upper arm |
|---|---|---|---|---|---|---|
| 1 | 28.25" / 72 cm | 7.75" / 20 cm | 14.5" / 37 cm | 19.75" / 50 cm | 19.75" / 50 cm | 10.75" / 27.5 cm |
| 2 | 32" / 81 cm | 8.25" / 21 cm | 15" / 38 cm | 20" / 51 cm | 19" / 48 cm | 11.25" / 28.5 cm |
| 3 | 35.75" / 91 cm | 9" / 23 cm | 16.25" / 41 cm | 20.75" / 53 cm | 18.5" / 47 cm | 12" / 30.5 cm |
| 4 | 39.75" / 101 cm | 9.5" / 24 cm | 16.5" / 42 cm | 21.25" / 54 cm | 18" / 46 cm | 13" / 33 cm |
| 5 | 43.75" / 111 cm | 9.75" / 25 cm | 17.75" / 45 cm | 21.75" / 55 cm | 17.5" / 44.5 cm | 14.25" / 36 cm |
| 6 | 47.25" / 120 cm | 10.5" / 27 cm | 18.5" / 47 cm | 22.5" / 57 cm | 17" / 43 cm | 16" / 40.5 cm |
| 7 | 50.75" / 129 cm | 11" / 28 cm | 19.25" / 49 cm | 22.75" / 58 cm | 16.5" / 42 cm | 17.25" / 44 cm |
| 8 | 54.75" / 139 cm | 11.5" / 29 cm | 19.75" / 50 cm | 23.25" / 59 cm | 16" / 40.5 cm | 18.75" / 47.5 cm |
| 9 | 58.25" / 148 cm | 12.25" / 31 cm | 20.75" / 53 cm | 24" / 61 cm | 15.25" / 39 cm | 19.25" / 49 cm |

*This sweater is designed to fit with 1.5 (2, 2.25, 2.25, 2.25) (2.75, 3.25, 3.25, 3.5)" / 4 (5, 6, 6, 6) (7, 8, 8, 9) cm of negative ease. Size 2 is modeled on 35" / 89-cm bust model.*

# Malduguns Fen Fire Sweater Pattern

## Yoke

Using your main gauge hook and leaving an approximately 6" / 15-cm long yarn end for sewing the neck split, with WS facing, fsc 104 (104, 104, 112, 112) (112, 120, 120, 120), turn.

Beginning ch 2 counts as first dc/hdc (= 1 st).

**Rnd 1:** RS facing, dc across, join with sl st in first dc. 104 (104, 104, 112, 112) (112, 120, 120, 120) sts

**Rnds 2–3:** Ch 2 (counts as first BPdc), [FPdc around next st, BPdc around next st] around to last st, FPdc around last st, join with sl st to the top ch of beg ch-2.

Make a ch 2 as your first hdc of the rnd.

**Rnd 4:** [Hdc in next 3 sts, FPdc around next st] around, join.

**Rnd 5:** Sl st in next st. Starting in same st as last sl st, [hdc in next st, 3 hdc in next st, FPdc around next st, skip next st] around, join. 130 (130, 130, 140, 140) (140, 150, 150, 150) sts

**Rnd 6:** Sl st in next st. Starting in same st as last sl st, [hdc in next 2 sts, 3 hdc in next st, FPdc around next st, skip next st] around, join. 156 (156, 156, 168, 168) (168, 180, 180, 180) sts

**Rnds 7–9:** Sl st in next 2 sts. Starting in same st as last sl st, [hdc in next 2 sts, 3 hdc in next st, FPdc around next st, skip next 2 sts] around, join.

**Rnd 10:** Sl st in next 2 sts. Starting in same st as last sl st, [hdc in next st, 2 hdc in next st, 3 hdc in next st, FPdc around next st, skip next 2 sts] around, join. 182 (182, 182, 196, 196) (196, 210, 210, 210) sts

When working the V-puff on next rnd, make sure to insert the hook in **front most loop** (see image on page 195) to make sure your V-puff is more stable.

**Rnd 11:** Sl st in next 2 sts. Starting in same st as last sl st, [hdc in next 3 sts, 3 hdc in next st, V-puff in next st, skip next 2 sts, hdc in next 3 sts, 3 hdc in next st, FPdc around next st, skip next 2 sts] around, join. 208 (208, 208, 224, 224) (224, 240, 240, 240) sts

**Rnds 12–15:** Sl st in next 2 sts. Starting in same st as last sl st, [hdc in next 3 sts, 3 hdc in next st, V-puff in next ch-sp, skip next 2 hdc, hdc in next 3 sts, 3 hdc in next st, FPdc around next st, skip next 2 sts] around, join. 208 (208, 208, 224, 224) (224, 240, 240, 240) sts

**Rnd 16:** Sl st in next 2 sts. Starting in same st as last sl st, [hdc in next 4 sts, 2 hdc in next puff st, puff st in next ch-sp, skip next puff st and hdc, hdc in next 4 sts, 3 hdc in next st, V-puff in front most loop of next st, skip next 2 sts] around, join. 221 (221, 221, 238, 238) (238, 255, 255, 255) sts

**In rnds 17 and 22:** When working the puff st over the puff st of prev rnd, insert the hook also under the loops that are right under the top ch of that st—this way your puff st will be more stable.

**Rnd 17:** Sl st in next st. Starting in same st as last sl st, [hdc in next 4 sts, 2 hdc in next st, puff st in next puff st, skip next 2 sts, hdc in next 4 sts, 3 hdc in next st, V-puff in next ch-sp, skip next hdc] around, join.

**Rnds 18–20:** Sl st in next 2 sts. Starting in same st as last sl st, [hdc in next 11 sts, 3 hdc in next st, V-puff in next ch-sp, skip next 2 hdc] around, join.

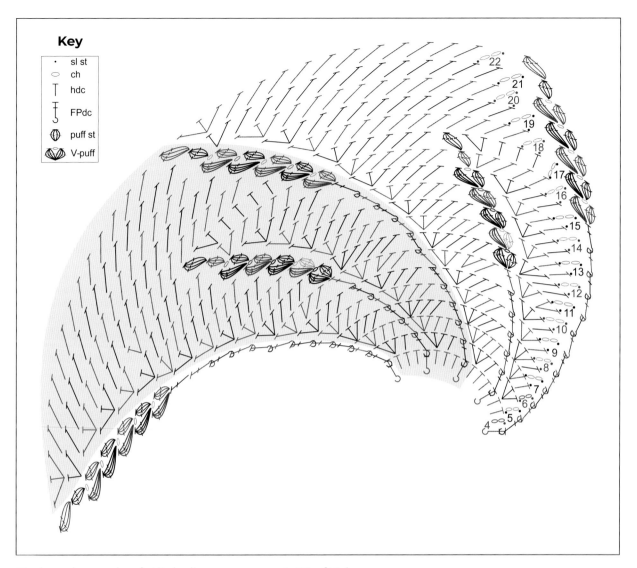

## Key

| | |
|---|---|
| • | sl st |
| ⬭ | ch |
| T | hdc |
| Ŧ | FPdc |
| ◍ | puff st |
| ⬯ | V-puff |

*Reduced sample of stitch diagram, rows 4–22 of Yoke*

*Stitch repeat is shown in gray.*

**Rnd 21:** Sl st in next st. Starting in same st as last sl st, [hdc in next 13 sts, 2 hdc in next puff st, puff st in next ch-sp, skip next puff st and hdc] around, join. 208 (208, 208, 224, 224) (224, 240, 240, 240) sts

**Rnd 22:** Sl st in next 2 sts. Starting in same st as last sl st, [hdc in next 12 sts, 3 hdc in next st, puff st in next puff st, skip next 2 sts] around, join.

**Rnd 30** (sizes 4–6): Hdc. [Hdc in next 17 sts, 2 hdc in next st] 13 times. Hdc in next 3 sts, join. x (x, x, 251, 251) (251, x, x, x) sts

**Rnd 30** (sizes 7–9): [Hdc in next 16 sts, 2 hdc in next st] 15 times, join. x (x, x, x, x) (x, 270, 270, 270) sts

**Rnds 31–32:** Hdc around, join. 232 (232, 232, 251, 251) (251, 270, 270, 270) sts

**Size 1:** Continue to Separating Body and Sleeves.

**Sizes 2–9:** Continue to work from rnd 33.

**Rnd 33:** Hdc around, join. x (232, 232, 251, 251) (251, 270, 270, 270) sts

**Rnd 34:** [Hdc in next x (15, 15, 14, 14) (14, 14, 14, 14) sts, 2 hdc in next st] x (14, 14, 16, 16) (16, 18, 18, 18) times. Hdc in next x (8, 8, 11, 11) (11, 0, 0, 0) sts, join. x (246, 246, 267, 267) (267, 288, 288, 288) sts

**Size 2:** Continue to Separating Body and Sleeves.

**Sizes 3–9:** Continue to work from rnd 35.

**Rnds 35–36:** Hdc around, join.

**Rnd 37:** [Hdc in next x (x, 11, 25, 25) (25, 27, 27, 27) sts, 2 hdc in next st] x (x, 20, 10, 10) (10, 10, 10, 10) times. Hdc in next x (x, 6, 7, 7) (7, 8, 8, 8) sts, join. x (x, 266, 277, 277) (277, 298, 298, 298) sts

**Size 3:** Continue to Separating Body and Sleeves.

**Sizes 4–9:** Continue to work from rnd 38.

**Rnd 38:** Hdc around, join.

**Rnd 39:** [Hdc in next x (x, x, 29, 29) (29, 32, 32, 32) sts, 2 hdc in next st] 9 times. Hdc in next x (x, x, 7, 7) (7, 1, 1, 1) sts, join. x (x, x, 286, 286) (286, 307, 307, 307) sts

**From now on throughout Yoke:** Make your first st as LL, hdc2tog (over 2 first sts) and make 1 more hdc in your last st of the rnd.

**Rnd 23:** Hdc around, join.

**Rnd 24:** [Hdc in next 7 sts, 2 hdc in next st, hdc in next 8 sts] around, join. 221 (221, 221, 238, 238) (238, 255, 255, 255) sts

**Rnds 25–29:** Hdc around, join.

**Rnd 30** (sizes 1–3): Hdc. [Hdc in next 19 sts, 2 hdc in next st] 11 times, join. 232 (232, 232, x, x) (x, x, x, x) sts

**Size 4:** Continue to Separating Body and Sleeves.

**Sizes 5–9:** Continue to work from rnd 40.

**Rnd 40:** Hdc around, join.

**Rnd 41:** [Hdc in next x (x, x, x, 13) (13, 14, 14, 14) sts, 2 hdc in next st] 20 times. Hdc in next x (x, x, x, 6) (6, 7, 7, 7) sts, join. x (x, x, x, 306) (306, 327, 327, 327) sts

**Size 5:** Continue to Separating Body and Sleeves.

**Sizes 6–9:** Continue to work from rnd 42.

**Rnds 42–43:** Hdc around, join.

**Rnd 44:** [Hdc in next x (x, x, x, x) (9, 12, 12, 12) sts, 2 hdc in next st] x (x, x, x, x) (28, 24, 24, 24) times. Hdc in next x (x, x, x, x) (26, 15, 15, 15) sts, join. x (x, x, x, x) (334, 351, 351, 351) sts

**Size 6:** Continue to Separating Body and Sleeves.

**Sizes 7–9:** Continue to work from rnd 45.

**Rnd 45:** Hdc around, join.

**Rnd 46:** [Hdc in next x (x, x, x, x) (x, 49, 38, 30) sts, 2 hdc in next st] x (x, x, x, x) (x, 7, 9, 11) times. Hdc in next x (x, x, x, x) (x, 1, 0, 10) sts, join. x (x, x, x, x) (x, 358, 360, 362) sts

**Size 7:** Continue to Separating Body and Sleeves.

**Sizes 8 and 9:** Continue to work from rnd 47.

**Rnd 47:** Hdc around, join.

**Rnd 48:** [Hdc in next x (x, x, x, x) (x, x, 17, 15) sts, 2 hdc in next st] x (x, x, x, x) (x, x, 20, 22) times. Hdc in next x (x, x, x, x) (x, x, 0, 10) sts, join. x (x, x, x, x) (x, x, 380, 384) sts

**Size 8:** Continue to Separating Body and Sleeves.

**Size 9:** Continue to work from rnd 49.

**Rnds 49–50:** Hdc around, join.

**Rnd 51:** [Hdc in next 31 sts, 2 hdc in next st] 12 times, join. x (x, x, x, x) (x, x, x, 396) sts

**Size 9:** Continue to Separating Body and Sleeves.

Finish Yoke with 232 (246, 266, 286, 306) (334, 358, 380, 396) sts

## Separating Body and Sleeves

Hdc in next st, ch 2 (4, 6, 8, 10) (12, 14, 16, 18), skip next 50 (50, 52, 55, 58) (65, 70, 74, 75) sts, hdc in next 66 (73, 81, 88, 95) (102, 109, 116, 123) sts, ch 2 (4, 6, 8, 10) (12, 14, 16, 18), skip next 50 (50, 52, 55, 58) (65, 70, 74, 75) sts, hdc in next 65 (72, 80, 87, 94) (101, 108, 115, 122) sts, join.

## Body

136 (154, 174, 192, 210) (228, 246, 264, 282) sts for the body

Work hdc around in spiral for 6.75 (6.75, 7, 7, 7.75) (7.75, 8.25, 8.25, 8.75)" / 17 (17, 18, 18, 20) (20, 21, 21, 22) cm for the cropped body, or 11" / 28 cm for regular body, or when your desired length is achieved, minus 0.75" / 2 cm for the hem ribbing.

**To work in spiral:** Hdc around for the first rnd as usual (working into each st and ch), don't join. Work sc on the first hdc of body rnd 1 (mark), then continue to work hdc in a spiral until the desired length is achieved. (The marker will show you the approximate place to start your Hem Ribbing.)

End your spiral beneath the marked underarm with a sc. Continue to work the Hem Ribbing in rounds.

## Hem Ribbing

**Rnd 1:** Ch 3 (counts as first dc), dc around, join.

**Rnds 2–3:** Ch 2 (counts as first BPdc). [FPdc around next st, BPdc around next st] around to last st, FPdc around last st, join.

**Rnd 4:** Sl st around, fasten off.

## Short Sleeve

Make 2

Start with 52 (54, 58, 63, 68) (77, 84, 90, 93) sts

### Sleeve Ribbing

With RS facing, attach yarn with sl st at approximate center of underarm.

**For more stability in rnd 1:** At the underarm work stitches between the sts of the body, work stitches as usual for the rest of the sleeve. You'll have a space between the underarm and sleeve—make last st in underarm as unfinished dc, make next unfnished dc in that space (between underarm and sleeve) and finish both unfinished sts (dc2tog = 1 st), do the same when finished working sts on the sleeve. Start with unfinished dc in the space/side of a stitch between sleeve and underarm, make next unfinished st in the next underarm st (between the sts), finish both unfinished sts.

**Rnd 1:** Ch 3 (counts as first dc), dc around, join. 52 (54, 58, 63, 68) (77, 84, 90, 93) sts

**Rnds 2–3:** [FPdc in next st, BPdc in next st] around, join.

**Rnd 4:** Sl st around, fasten off. Repeat the same for the other sleeve.

## Long Sleeve

Make 2

With RS facing, attach yarn with sl st at approximate center of underarm.

**For more stability in rnd 1:** See instructions at Short Sleeve Sleeve Ribbing.

**Rnd 1:** Ch 2 (counts as first hdc), hdc around. 52 (54, 58, 63, 68) (77, 84, 90, 93) sts

Sc into first hdc from rnd 1 to begin working in a spiral, place marker in this st to mark beginning of rnd, moving up as you go. Since you are working in a spiral, this marker will eventually look off-center. Simply replace it into the approximate center st as often as needed.

**For the rest of the Sleeve:** Work the rnds as written for your size, where decreasing is worked as follows:

**Decrease rnd:** Hdc in first st, hdc2tog, hdc in each st around until 3 sts remain, hdc2tog, hdc in last st. (decreases rnd by 2 sts)

**Size 1:** Work 90 rnds total, decreasing every 15th rnd, or when your desired sleeve length is reached.

**Size 2:** Work 86 rnds total, decreasing every 14th rnd, or when your desired sleeve length is reached.

**Size 3:** Work 84 rnds total, decreasing every 13th rnd, or when your desired sleeve length is reached.

**Size 4:** Work 82 rnds total, decreasing every 12th rnd, or when your desired sleeve length is reached.

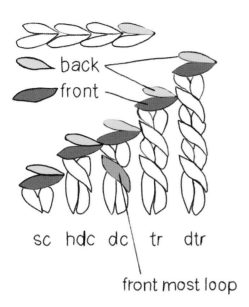

sc    hdc    dc    tr    dtr

front most loop

**Size 5:** Work 80 rnds total, decreasing every 10th rnd, or when your desired sleeve length is reached.

**Size 6:** Work 77 rnds total, decreasing every 9th rnd, or when your desired sleeve length is reached.

**Size 7:** Work 75 rnds total, decreasing every 8th rnd, or when your desired sleeve length is reached.

**Size 8:** Work 73 rnds total, decreasing every 8th rnd, or when your desired sleeve length is reached.

**Size 9:** Work 70 rnds total, decreasing every 7th rnd, or when your desired sleeve length is reached.

90 (86, 84, 82, 80) (77, 75, 73, 70) rnds total, 40 (42, 46, 51, 52) (61, 66, 72, 73) sts

**Last rnd:** Sl sl around, fasten off.

## Finishing

Weave in all ends. Block according to fiber type.

# Nakts Night Tunisian Sweater

Classic crochet cables get a contemporary upgrade in the Nakts Tunisian sweater. The design is beguilingly simple, but upon closer inspection, the ribbing sections and asymmetrical cables reveal themselves for an added layer of interest. The straight boat neck is mirrored in the front and back ribbing, and the deeply, gorgeously textured cables will have you asking the age-old question—is this really crochet?

# Nakts Night Tunisian Sweater Construction Notes

*The Nakts Tunisian sweater has a boat neck and is worked top down starting with the neckline ribbing. The front and back panels are made separately. The sleeves are also crocheted separately and sewn on.*

## Sizes

1 (2, 3, 4, 5) (6, 7, 8, 9)

**To fit bust:** 33 (36, 39, 42, 44.5) (47, 50, 53, 56)" / 84 (91, 99, 106, 114) (120, 128, 135, 143) cm

**Finished bust:** 36.5 (39.5, 42.5, 45.5, 48) (51, 54, 57, 60)" / 93 (100, 108, 115, 123) (130, 138, 145, 153) cm

## Gauge

12 sts x 12 rows = 4" / 10 cm in tks with 7 mm Tunisian hook

16 sts x 16 rows = 4" / 10 cm over widest part main stitch pattern

**A Note on Gauge:** The gauge/width will vary depending on which part of the stitch pattern is being measured. Work your gauge swatch in Tunisian knit stitch. Measurements given for the finished bust and finished half-bust are taken from the widest points in the stitch pattern.

## Yarn

Fingering weight, Rowan Mohair Haze (70% Mohair, 30% Merino Wool), 112 yds / 102 m per 25-g skein

## Yardage/Meterage

1245 (1340, 1405, 1520, 1585) (1695, 1805, 1875, 1965) yds / 1140 (1225, 1285, 1390, 1450) (1550, 1650, 1715, 1795) m

### Shown in

Colorway Embrace (526)

## Hooks

7 mm Tunisian hook for Body and Sleeves, or size needed to obtain gauge

7 mm regular crochet hook without a handle

I/9 / 5.5 mm Tunisian hook for Ribbing

## Notions

Tapestry needle

3 stitch markers

## Skills

Experience with Tunisian crochet cables

Experience with making and sewing crocheted sweaters

## Special stitches

**Tks:** Insert hook between front to back vertical bars of next st (from front to back of work), yo, pull up a loop. Leave loop on hook.

**Tps:** Bring yarn in front of work, insert hook from right to left under front vertical bar of next st, yo from back to front, draw through vertical bar. Leave loop on hook.

**TC12B:** Skip next 6 stitches and leave at back of work (mark first and sixth stitch). Tks 6, mark next st (for easier pass to the next repeat), then take your regular hook and tks 6 starting and ending with first and sixth marked stitches, slip the 6 sts just made through the other side of your regular hook onto your Tunisian hook, continue to work according to the instructions starting with your next marked st. Remove all markers.

**TC12F:** Skip next 6 stitches and leave at front of work (mark first and sixth stitch). Tks 6, mark next st (for easier pass to the next repeat), then take your regular hook and tks 6 starting and ending with first and sixth marked stitches, slip the 6 sts just made through the other side of your regular hook onto your Tunisian hook, continue to work according to the instructions starting with your next marked st. Remove all markers.

**Tks inc:** Insert hook in next space between sts from front to back of work, yo, pull up a loop.

## Abbreviations (US terms)

Ch = chain
FwP = forward pass
Inc = increase
St(s) = stitch(es)
Tks = tunisian knit stitch
Tps = tunisian purl stitch
Yo = yarn over

| Size | A—finished bust | B—finished half-bust | C—length | D—sleeve length | E—upper arm |
|---|---|---|---|---|---|
| 1 | 36.5" / 93 cm | 18.25" / 46.5 cm | 20" / 51 cm | 20" / 51 cm | 15" / 38 cm |
| 2 | 39.5" / 100 cm | 19.75" / 50 cm | 20" / 51 cm | 19.75" / 50 cm | 15.75" / 40 cm |
| 3 | 42.5" / 108 cm | 21.25" / 54 cm | 20" / 51 cm | 19.25" / 49 cm | 16.5" / 42 cm |
| 4 | 45.5" / 115 cm | 22.75" / 57.5 cm | 20.5" / 53 cm | 19" / 48 cm | 17" / 43 cm |
| 5 | 48" / 123 cm | 24" / 61.5 cm | 20.5" / 53 cm | 18.5" / 47 cm | 17.75" / 45 cm |
| 6 | 51" / 130 cm | 25.5" / 65 cm | 21" / 54 cm | 18" / 46 cm | 18.5" / 47 cm |
| 7 | 54" / 138 cm | 27" / 69 cm | 21" / 54 cm | 17.75" / 45 cm | 19" / 48 cm |
| 8 | 57" / 145 cm | 28.5" / 72.5 cm | 21.5" / 55 cm | 17.25" / 44 cm | 19.75" / 50 cm |
| 9 | 60" / 153 cm | 30" / 76.5 cm | 21.5" / 55 cm | 17" / 43 cm | 20.5" / 52 cm |

*Hem ribbing measures 2" / 5 cm. Neck ribbing measures 1" / 2.5 cm. The sweater is designed to be worn with 3.5 (3.5, 3.5, 3.5, 3.5) (4, 4, 4, 4)" / 9 (9, 9, 9, 9) (10, 10, 10, 10) cm of positive ease. Size 2 is modeled on 33" / 83-cm bust model.*

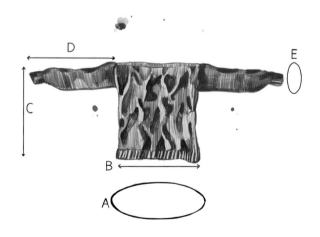

# Nakts Night Tunisian Sweater Pattern

The sweater is worked in the Tunisian crochet technique. Both Front and Back panels are started at the neck ribbing and worked down using Tunisian cables and ending with the Hem Ribbing. The sleeves are crocheted and sewn on separately.

**Throughout, work return pass as follows:** Yo, draw yarn through first loop, [yo, draw yarn through first two loops on hook] across until one loop is left on the hook.

## Front/Back

### Ribbing

**Foundation row:** With your smaller Tunisian hook ch 74 (80, 86, 92, 98) (104, 110, 116, 122), insert hook into the second chain from the hook, yo and pull up a loop leaving the loop on your Tunisian hook, [insert hook in next chain, yo and pull up a loop leaving it on the hook] across; return pass. 74 (80, 86, 92, 98) (104, 110, 116, 122) sts

**FwP 1–3:** Tks in next st, [tps in next st, tks in next st] across; return pass.

## Body

Change to your larger Tunisian hook.

**FwP 1–4:** Tks across; return pass.

**Repeat:**

**\*\*Next FwP:** Tks 0 (3, 6, 9, 0) (3, 6, 9, 0). [Tks 12, TC12F] 3 (3, 3, 3, 4) (4, 4, 4, 5) times. Tks 1 (4, 7, 10, 1) (4, 7, 10, 1); return pass.

**Next 12 rows:** Tks across; return pass.

**Next FwP:** Tks 0 (3, 6, 9, 0) (3, 6, 9, 0). [TC12B, tks 12] 3 (3, 3, 3, 4) (4, 4, 4, 5) times. Tks 1 (4, 7, 10, 1) (4, 7, 10, 1), return pass.

**Next 12 rows:** Tks across; return pass.\*\*

Rep \*\* to \*\* one more time.

**Next FwP:** Tks 0 (3, 6, 9, 0) (3, 6, 9, 0). [Tks 12, TC12F] 3 (3, 3, 3, 4) (4, 4, 4, 5) times. Tks 1 (4, 7, 10, 1) (4, 7, 10, 1); return pass.

**Next 9 (9, 9, 11, 11) (13, 13, 15, 15) rows:** Tks across; return pass.

### Hem Ribbing

Change to your smaller Tunisian hook.

**FwP 1–6:** Tks in next st, [tps in next st, tks in next st] across; return pass.

Fasten off.

## Sleeve

### Make 2

Choose a size that is closest to your wrist measurement: 5 (5.5, 6, 6.25, 6.75) (7, 7.5, 7.75, 8.25)" / 13 (14, 15, 16, 17) (18, 19, 20, 21) cm; you will be able to adjust the sleeve circumference later as you work (adding or removing increases as desired).

### Ribbing

**Foundation row:** With your smaller Tunisian hook, ch 24 (26, 28, 30, 32) (34, 36, 38, 40), insert hook into the second chain from the hook, yo and pull up a loop leaving the loop on your Tunisian hook, [insert hook in next chain, yo and pull up a loop leaving it on the hook] across; return pass.

**FwP 1–6:** Tks in next st, [tps in next st, tks in next st] across; return pass. 24 (26, 28, 30, 32) (34, 36, 38, 40) sts

Rep FwP 2 increasing by 2 sts every row until you reach 46 (48, 50, 52, 54) (56, 58, 60, 62) sts.

**\*\*Next FwP:** Tks 16 (17, 18, 19, 20) (21, 22, 23, 24), TC12F, tks 17 (18, 19, 20, 21) (22, 23, 24, 25); return pass.

**Next 12 rows:** Tks across; return pass.

**Next FwP:** Tks 16 (17, 18, 19, 20) (21, 22, 23, 24), TC12B, tks 17 (18, 19, 20, 21) (22, 23, 24, 25); return pass.\*\*

**Next 12 rows:** Tks across; return pass.

Rep from \*\* to \*\* of Sleeve one more time.

**Next 15 (14, 13, 12, 11) (10, 9, 8, 7) rows:** Tks across; return pass. Fasten off.

Continue to work tks until your Sleeve (including ribbing) measures 20 (19.75, 19.25, 19, 18.5) (18, 17.75, 17.25, 17)" / 51 (50, 49, 48, 47) (46, 45, 44, 43) cm, or until your desired sleeve length is reached. Fasten off.

Make the second sleeve following the instructions above, except work TC12B instead of TC12F and vice versa.

## Finishing

Block all parts according to fiber type. Sew shoulder seams leaving a 10.25 (10.25, 10.25, 10.75, 10.75) (10.75, 11, 11, 11)" / 26 (26, 26, 27, 27) (27, 28, 28, 28) cm opening for the neckline. Sew both Sleeves to Body, matching the center top of sleeve to the shoulder seam, then sew the side seam and sleeve seam. Weave in all ends.

## Sleeve

Change to your larger Tunisian hook.

**FwP 1:** Tks 1, tks inc, tks across to last 2 sts, tks inc, tks 2; return pass. 26 (28, 30, 32, 34) (36, 38, 40, 42) sts

**FwP 2:** Tks 1, tks inc, tks across to last 2 sts, tks inc, tks 2; return pass. 28 (30, 32, 34, 36) (38, 40, 42, 44) sts

# Blocking

The importance of blocking is something I cannot stress enough. Blocking is a final stage of making a sweater that will adjust the shape of your finished piece. Although it might seem like an irrelevant step, blocking is one of the most transformative processes in crochet. Watch as your stitches become even more beautiful in front of your eyes as you block your sweater. The fibers and stitches will relax and your sweater will form the desired shape.

There are several methods to block your sweater. To make sure you are using the one best suited for your sweater, check your yarn label to see what fibers are in your yarn and what are the washing and ironing recommendations.

### Dry Blocking

My all-time favorite method is dry blocking or steaming: Pin your garment to the blocking board using rust-proof pins, then steam all over with a steam iron. Leave the sweater to dry completely and remove the pins.

### Wet Blocking

Wet blocking is also known as washing. To wash your sweater, see Caring for Your Sweaters (page 210). Pin your sweater to the blocking board using rust-proof pins and leave to dry completely.

### Spray Blocking

Spray blocking is similar to dry blocking: After pinning the sweater to the blocking board, lightly spritz each piece with a spray bottle and then gently smooth each piece out with your hands. Spray a little more if you feel the pieces aren't relaxing into shape.

# Yarn Substitutions

The yarns featured in this book work brilliantly for their respective patterns, but they are not the only options. I frequently substitute yarns when making patterns for myself and encourage you to try other options, especially yarns that are already in your stash.

You will find substitution information in the yarn section of every pattern.

There can be lots of reasons for using a different yarn than the one listed in the pattern: Some yarns aren't easy to obtain because they are produced in small batches, or are not local to you, or they might be discontinued while the publication of this book takes place. Budget considerations are also important, as many yarns are not financially accessible to every crocheter who wants to make a pattern.

Substituting yarn can be tricky, but if you keep these two things in mind, you'll be on the right track:

- **Length-to-weight ratio.** This means the number of yards/meters to ounces/grams. Check your yarn label info and see how many yards/meters there are and how many ounces/grams. If your yarn's ratio is similar to what's listed in the pattern, your yarn should be good to get the gauge right.

- **Yarn characteristics and fiber type.** Choose an alternative with similar features to the yarn listed in the pattern. Try sticking to the original fiber type, like wool, alpaca, silk, cotton, etc. (which and how many fibers are represented) and make sure to check how the yarn is made—is it fuzzy, twisted, stiff, etc.? This will ensure that your finished piece has similar drape, structure and fabric characteristics to the one the designer had in mind when designing the piece.

# Translating Yardage/Meterage into Skeins

A question that I receive quite often is how many skeins of yarn are needed for the pattern. Yarn skeins come in various weights, like 25/50/85/100/150/200 grams. Keep this in mind when calculating the number of skeins needed to make a finished piece.

There is no one right answer to this question, but let me share an easy formula that will help you calculate the number of skeins needed.

First, you need to look at your pattern's total yardage/meterage section to find out how many yards/meters are required for your size. The yardage can vary from fiber content to fiber content, but overall the number will be close to that indicated in the pattern. This total yardage/meterage is referred to below as A.

Next, you need to take the total amount of yarn needed in yards/meters (A), and divide it by the yards/meters in your skein (B).

$$A / B = C$$

**A—total yardage**
**B—yards/meters in one skein**
**C—number of balls needed**

For example, if you need 2,000 yds (1,830 m) for your project and there are 200 yds (183 m) in your 3.5 oz (100 g) yarn skein. 2,000 / 200 = 10 skeins that each weigh 3.5 oz (100 g). (In metric form, this would be 1,830 / 183 = 10 skeins.)

Usually you will not get a round number, but 5.4 or 7.8 skeins. That means you need to take one extra skein—5.4 will round up to 6, and 7.8 will round up to 8 skeins, and so on and so forth.

In most cases, the supplemental round ups are already included in the pattern, so you don't need to worry if you'll have enough. Remember that if you change something in a pattern—like adding length to the body or sleeves—you will end up needing extra yarn to account for that.

Multiply one skein's weight with the number of balls (= 35 oz [1 kg]), and you'll get how much your entire project will weigh.

# Using Different Yarn Weights

As this book is geared toward intermediate/advanced crocheters, I'm sure the topic of this chapter has crossed your mind several times.

Let's say the pattern is written for worsted weight yarn, but you accidentally bought DK weight yarn or you already have a bunch of DK weight yarn in your stash. You'd like to use it for the pattern in place of the called-for worsted weight yarn. But how?

First, do some swatching to see which size hook to use. Do you want your garment to have some drape? Are you afraid it will be too loose? If it's a larger item (or size)—keep in mind that shoulder parts might weigh down from the weight of the garment.

When you have chosen a hook, you'll have to make the actual gauge swatch and see how many stitches there are in 4" (10 cm). Let's say you have 15 stitches in your DK weight swatch.

Next you'll have to decide how much ease you want your garment to have and add that measurement to your bust size. Let's say 34" (86 cm) bust + 6" (15 cm) ease = 40" (101 cm).

Now do some math—calculate how many stitches you'll have in your 40" (101 cm). 40" x 15 sts/4" = 150 sts [101 cm x 15 sts/10 cm = ~150 sts].

Next, you have to look at the pattern and see which size falls the closest to your 150 stitches in the finished bust. Be careful with this when you are trying to find the bust section in your pattern. Depending on the construction of the sweater, the bust measurement might be right after the split for the body and sleeves (for top downs), or it may be a half-bust measurement if the sweater is worked bottom up with seperate front and back pieces.

When you've found the place in the pattern where the total stitch count for the bust is, mark the size that is the closest to your 150 stitches and follow the pattern for that size.

This is a rough estimate for how the conversion should be done and cases may differ per different constructions—however, I hope this comes in handy.

# Caring for Your Sweaters

Did you know that crochet sweaters shouldn't be washed too frequently to ensure their longevity? It is advised to wash your crocheted pieces only once or twice per season.

There are a few other options for how you can take care of your crochet garments. First, and my favorite, is to air it out. Just hang your piece near an open window or outside (avoiding direct sunlight) and let the fresh air do its thing. Yarn basically acts like a sponge—picking up various smells (like smoke, smells from foods, etc.). Airing your piece out will ensure the bad odors are gone and you don't have to wash your sweater too frequently so it can last longer.

Another way to freshen up your crochet pieces is by steaming. What I usually do is turn the piece inside out, put it on a mannequin, and steam all over with a steam iron (or steamer, if you have one). I usually do this twice, paying attention to places that are worn out or need a bit of shaping, then I let it dry completely.

Another option instead of washing is to fold your sweater neatly and place it in a zip-lock bag, seal the bag and insert it in a freezer for 48 hours. After that, the sweater will feel as good as new. Some sources say the low temperatures will kill the germs, but others do not confirm this. Still, this trick is good for preventing the fiber from shedding and pilling—it is especially easy to shave the lint off of pure wool after it's been in the freezer.

We all know those little nasty balls of fluff that occur on the sides of a sweater. Pilling typically happens when a harder material rubs against a smoother one. Or when your arms rub against the sides of a sweater when you move. Pilling will most often happen with fluffier yarns and the ones that are spun from shorter lengths of fiber. If you have a wool sweater, there are a few ways to de-pill it: 1) freezing, 2) brush it with a sweater brush, 3) use a lint remover/fabric shaver. I have also noticed that wool de-pills nicely, while synthetics (like polyester or acrylic) are much harder to de-pill, if not impossible.

As mentioned before—there's no need to wash your crocheted pieces more than once or twice per season. Here are a few tips to know before washing your sweater:

- There are special detergents available for knitwear in most big supermarkets. Or use mild detergent or soap for washing knitwear.
- Follow the manufacturer's recommendations for the yarn used.
- The basin should be big enough to rinse or swirl the garment easily.
- You will need two big towels for drying.

And here's the safest way to wash a crocheted sweater:

1. Fill the basin or sink with lukewarm water. Make sure it is not too hot as you don't want your sweater to shrink. Add the wool detergent.
2. Squeeze and soak the piece gently.
3. Take your garment out, lay it flat onto a towel, then roll it up to press out the water. Be gentle.
4. Lay the sweater flat onto a new fresh towel, giving it the necessary shape. Leave it to dry completely.

Another important thing to keep in mind is properly storing your sweaters. Hangers are not a very good option to store your sweater because of possible misshaping in the shoulder area. If a garment is heavy, hanging will also stretch it. (Please be sure not to hang your sweater right after washing as the weight of the water will stretch it down and the damage can be irreversible). The best way to store sweaters is by folding them and placing them on a shelf or in a drawer. Make sure your sweater is completely dry before folding. If you want to store your sweaters away for a longer period of time, it is advised to use cotton or linen storage bags so they can breathe. Use cedar blocks or lavender sachets for moth prevention.

# Resources

Below you will find a list of resources that will help you as you work your way through this book, as well as links to more of my patterns and designs.

**Craft Yarn Council:** https://www.craftyarncouncil.com/

**Ysolda Sizing Chart:** https://ysolda.com/blogs/journal/ysolda-s-sizing-chart-for-knitwear-designers

**Digits and Threads Sizing Chart:** https://www.digitsandthreads.ca/new-representative-sizing-standards-for-garments-that-fit/

**Linda's Web Page and Shop:** https://www.lindaskuja.com/

**More of Linda's Patterns on Ravelry:** https://www.ravelry.com/designers/linda-skuja

**More of Linda's Patterns on Etsy:** https://www.etsy.com/shop/LindaSkujaDesign/

**Supplementary Video Content:** https://www.youtube.com/user/ElevenHandmade/videos

# About the Author

Linda Skuja is an independent textile designer from Riga, Latvia.

Texture, along with her signature short row and three-dimensional stitches, is Linda's trademark. Since she began designing crochet patterns in 2010, her designs have been published in many of the industry's major magazines, such as *Vogue Knitting Crochet*, *Moorit* magazine, *Interweave Crochet* and *Inside Crochet*, among others. Linda has also worked for fashion designers worldwide—making samples for the runway of New York Fashion Week was one of the most exciting freelance jobs she's ever taken on.

Nowadays, Linda happily designs for her own brand, collaborating with yarn companies and working on publications for magazines. Linda is a lover of nature, architecture, art, fashion and mid-century modern interiors, and strives to curate her authentic aesthetics into her everyday life.

# Acknowledgments

Every person and every situation that has ever crossed my path has led to me writing this book. Without knowing it, they've played a role that has created this book to be exactly like it is. I'm grateful to every one of them.

However, there are some special people without whom this book would be impossible.

The Page Street Publishing team—thank you for trusting in me and giving me full creative freedom. Special thanks goes to my dear editor Emily Archbold, who has made this process extremely smooth and enjoyable. A heartfelt thank you goes out to both of the technical editors, Amy Curtin and Emily Reiter—your attention to detail is what adds to the excellence of this book.

All my admiration goes toward Inga Bitere—the soul photographer who has captured the innermost spirit of every sweater and has translated it into a visual work of art. Thank you, dear, for being a significant part of this journey.

Photo shoots have been an extremely important part of this book. Thank you to the talented set designers who surrounded the room with mood and sense, Baiba Prindule-Rence and Lelde Fraktniece. Thank you to the style, hair and makeup magicians, Līva Hausmane, Lolita Graudiņa and Violeta Jakubāne. All the models have been wonderful muses and have captured the essence of the sweaters perfectly: Diāna, Olīvija, Nadege and Anna. You were all a joy to work with; thank you so much for bringing this book to life.

Thank you to the talented artist Zane Veldre, who has transformed the ever-so-boring schematics into little pieces of art.

Thank you, Jānis, for bearing with me and for your inexhaustible support. Thank you, Ādam, for being the little bundle of joy that you are.

# Index

## A

Ainava Landscape Sweater, 74–87
    about, 52, 75
    construction notes, 78–80
    pattern, 81–86
    photographs of, 74–77, 79, 82, 85–87
airing out, of sweaters, 210

## B

blocking, of sweaters, 206
body measurement, 7
bottom-up worked projects
    Ainava Landscape Sweater, 74–87
    Jūra Sea Sweater, 102–111
    Mēness Moon Sweater, 158–169
    Sniegs Snow Sweater, 44–51
    Zvaigznes Stars Wrap Sweater, 128–145
broomstick loop, instructions for, 175

## C

crocheting
    basics of, 6–9, 206–211
    resources for, 212

## D

de-pilling, of sweaters, 210
directional sweaters
    about, 52
    Ainava Landscape Sweater, 74–87
    Jūra Sea Sweater, 102–111
    Liedags Seashore Sweater, 54–73

    Zeme Earth Sweater, 88–101
dry blocking, 206

## E

easing, of sweaters
    modifications, 7
    using different weights of yarn and, 209
Ēna Shadow Sweater, 34–43
    about, 10, 35
    construction notes, 38–39
    pattern, 40–43
    photographs of, 34–37, 41

## F

fit, of sweaters, 7
freezing, of sweaters, 210

## G

gauge
    defined, 8
    importance of getting right, 7, 8
gauge swatch, making and blocking of, 8

## H

hooks
    size and gauge swatch, 8
    using different weights of yarn and, 209

## J

Jūra Sea Sweater, 102–111
    about, 52, 103
    construction notes, 104–105
    pattern, 106–110
    photographs of, 102–103, 107-108, 111

## K

knitting, yarn twist and, 8

## L

left-handed crocheting, yarn twist and, 8

length-to-weight ratio, yarn substitutions and, 207

Liedags Seashore Sweater, 54–73
  about, 52, 55
  construction notes, 58–59
  pattern, 60–73
  photographs of, 54–57, 62, 66, 71

linear sweaters
  about, 10
  Ēna Shadow Sweater, 34–43
  Māls Clay Sweater, 12–23
  Piens Milk Sweater, 24–33
  Sniegs Snow Sweater, 44–51

## M

Māls Clay Sweater, 12–23
  about, 10, 13
  construction notes, 16–17
  pattern, 18–22
  photographs of, 12–15, 21, 23

Malduguns Fen Fire Sweater, 184–195
  about, 185
  construction notes, 188–189
  pattern, 190–195
  photographs of, 157, 184–187, 192, 195

Mēness Moon Sweater, 158–169
  about, 159
  construction notes, 162–165
  pattern, 165–169
  photographs of, 158–161, 166, 169

moth prevention, 211

## N

Nakts Night Tunisian Sweater, 196–205
  about, 197
  construction notes, 200–202
  pattern, 203–204
  photographs of, 196–199, 201, 204–205

negative ease, 7

Nora Forest Meadow Sweater, 170–183
  about, 171
  construction notes, 174–176
  pattern, 177–183
  photographs of, 170–173, 175, 179–180

## P

Piens Milk Sweater, 24–33
  about, 10, 25
  construction notes, 28–29
  pattern, 30–33
  photographs of, 11, 24–27, 31–33

positive ease, 7

## R

Rasa Dew Sweater, 114–127
  about, 112, 115
  construction notes, 116–118
  pattern, 119–126
  photographs of, 114–115, 119–120, 125, 127

right-handed crocheting, yarn twist and, 8

## S

Saule Sun Sweater, 146–155
  about, 112, 147
  construction notes, 149–150
  pattern, 151–155
  photographs of, 146–148, 152–153

short rows, about, 52

sideways worked project, Liedags Seashore Sweater, 54–73

size of sweaters, modifying of, 7

slanted drop stitch, 175

Sniegs Snow Sweater, 44–51
  about, 10, 45
  construction notes, 46–47
  pattern, 48–51
  photographs of, 44–45, 49–50

special stitches, instructions for
  broomstick loop, 175
  dc-sc-tog, 93
  long loop stitch (ll), 38
  p4 puff stitch, 93
  p5 puff stitch, 93
  puff stitch, 29, 105, 189
  sc-hdc-tog, 46, 79, 93, 105, 163
  slanted drop stitch, 175
  TC12B, 201
  TC12F, 201
  tks, 201
  tks inc., 201
  tps, 201
  V-puff, 29, 189

spray blocking, 206
steaming (dry blocking), 206, 210
S-twist yarns, 8–9
sweaters, caring for
    airing out, 210
    de-pilling, 210
    freezing, 210
    steaming, 210
    storing, 211
    washing infrequently, 210
    washing tips and safety, 211

T

"thoughtful" sweaters
    about, 156
    Malduguns Fen Fire
        Sweater, 184–195
    Mēness Moon Sweater, 158–169
    Nakts Night Tunisian
        Sweater, 196–205
    Nora Forest Meadow
        Sweater, 170–183
top-down worked projects
    Ēna Shadow Sweater, 34–43
    Māls Clay Sweater, 12–23

Malduguns Fen Fire
    Sweater, 184–195
Nakts Night Tunisian
    Sweater, 196–205
Nora Forest Meadow
    Sweater, 170–183
Piens Milk Sweater, 24–33
Rasa Dew Sweater, 114–127
Saule Sun Sweater, 146–155
Zeme Earth Sweater, 88–101

U

"unexpected" sweaters
    about, 112
    Rasa Dew Sweater, 114–127
    Saule Sun Sweater, 146–155
    Zvaigznes Stars Wrap
        Sweater, 128–145

W

washing, of sweaters
    tips for sweater care and, 210, 211
    wet blocking and, 206

Y

yarns
    ball-winders and, 9
    length, weight, and fiber
        characteristics, 207
    skeins and weights of, 208
    translating meterage into
        skeins, 208
    using different weights of, 209
    Z-twist and S-twist, 8–9

Z

Zeme Earth Sweater, 88–101
    about, 52, 89
    construction notes, 92–94
    pattern, 94–101
    photographs of, 53, 88–91, 93, 96, 99–100
Z-twist yarns, 8–9
Zvaigznes Stars Wrap
    Sweater, 128–145
    about, 112, 129
    construction notes, 132–133
    pattern, 134–145
    photographs of, 113, 128–131, 137, 142